T0065650

OTHER BOOKS BY WILFRID SHEED

NOVELS
Middle Class Education
The Hack
Square's Progress
Office Politics
*The Blacking Factory and Pennsylvania Gothic:
    A Short Novel and a Long Story*
Max Jamison
People Will Always Be Kind
Transatlantic Blues

ESSAYS
The Morning After
Three Mobs: Labor, Church and Mafia
The Good Word and Other Words

NONFICTION
Muhammed Ali
Clare Boothe Luce

A Memoir
with Parents

A TOUCHSTONE BOOK

FRANK
and MAISIE

WILFRID SHEED

Published by SIMON & SCHUSTER, Inc.
NEW YORK

Published by Simon & Schuster, Inc.
Simon & Schuster Building
Rockefeller Center
1230 Avenue of the Americas
New York, New York 10020

TOUCHSTONE and colophon are registered trademarks of Simon & Schuster, Inc.

Designed by Edith Fowler

Manufactured in the United States of America

10 9 8 7 6 5 4 3 2 1
10 9 8 7 6 5 4 3 2 1 Pbk.

Library of Congress Cataloging in Publication Data

Sheed, Wilfrid.
   Frank and Maisie: a memoir with parents.

   1. Sheed, Wilfrid——Biography. 2. Sheed, Wilfrid——
Biography——Family. 3. Ward, Maisie, 1889–1975
4. Sheed, F. J. (Francis Joseph), 1897–1982. 5. Sheed
and Ward (Firm) 6. Authors, English——20th century——
Biography. 7. Publishers and publishing——England——
Biography. 8. Catholics——England——Biography. 9. Parents
—England—Biography. I. Title.
PR6069.H396Z467 1985   823.'.914 {B}   85-18356

ISBN: 0-671-4490-7
ISBN: 0-671-62813-5 Pbk.

FOR ROSEMARY

Author's Preface

I N 1972, I WROTE AN ESSAY ABOUT MY PARENTS, FRANK SHEED AND Maisie Ward, for *The New York Times Book Review,* and I awaited their response with gloomy apprehension. Frank's turned out to be straightforward enough—a simple "Attaboy," or words to that effect—but Maisie said, "You should have mentioned Uncle Henry" or somebody.

Well, I'm afraid I've gone and done it again to Uncle Henry, and scores of others. What follows is a highly selective and impressionistic version—one of many possible ones—of Frank and Maisie, but first I'd like to salute the missing. Before me as I write pass the reproachful-looking names of countless Sheed & Ward authors and employees and of Catholic Evidence Guild speakers, and other activists (and pacifists), and of at least one sister, several cousins and myriad aunts. My parents' lives were in fact so full of names that if I wrote them all out, this book would begin to look like a directory, or a Marx Brothers stateroom. And for everyone I do mention, a dozen more suggest themselves as equally worthy. Because most of these people were not extras, but central players, and I apologize to all of them. It's just that the focus here is close up, and the background tends to blur at times.

Fortunately, both Frank and Maisie wrote books about themselves—Frank's *The Church and I,* and Maisie's *Unfinished Business*—which cover much of the absent ground. I haven't read either book recently, because I was afraid I would end up simply rephrasing their versions, which are highly contagious. Nor have I asked for any out-

side opinions of them. Instead I have blocked my ears and tried to remember. And that's my acknowledgment: memory, and the construc-
tions put on memory.

A couple of last points: Maisie also wrote two fascinating books
of Ward family history called *Resurrection and Insurrection* and *The
Wilfrid Wards & The Transition,* so I have felt free not to repeat her on
that either. But Maisie's mother and that side of the family in particular deserve much fuller treatment than they get here.

The second concerns point of view again. A child's history of his
parents is largely a history of himself, and how they look to him. As
he and they grow older he can begin to fade away, and I have tried to
do so, omitting every part of my adult life that does not bear somehow on them or their affairs. A memoir without parents would contain a rather different cast of characters and episodes, and obviously
much more detail about the superb family I collaborated in starting
myself. But this is their book, appearances sometimes notwithstand-
ing, and I have tried to figure in it primarily as simply as an aspect of
them and as a vantage point, for looking at two outstanding people.

The World of Sheed/Ward

T HEY WERE VERY HARD PARENTS TO EXPLAIN. TO TAKE JUST ONE
thing: whenever they were in England, Frank Sheed and Maisie Ward
trudged off every single Sunday afternoon—my father moaning to
beat the band and praying for rain—to preach the Faith from soap-
boxes; and not just in glamor spots like Hyde Park, but in backwaters
like Clapham and Pimlico and other places that properly belong in
English comic monologues.

At first, the only thing that really struck me as strange was the
sound of a man praying for rain in England: then again perhaps he was
the cause of it all, and was doing a bang-up job. What does one know
at five? Only slowly did I begin to realize that other people thought
my parents were a little crazy. Soapbox oratory is by definition crazy.
And when I attended my first meetings I saw little to shake the definition.

A group of city strays would gather in front of a rickety platform
and hurl tipsy taunts or village-atheist challenges at my parents, who
would answer with a gravity worthy of a lecture hall. My first thought
was that they were going to get killed up there by some loudmouthed
bully, and to this day I myself suffer from incurable stage fright. But
on the way home, they might well complain about the blandness of
the meeting. "If only a good drunk had come along," my father
would sigh—surely as strange a wish as for rain on Sunday.

As the reader will discover, my parents were very far from being
fanatics with that telltale gleam in their eyes. My father believes that

he would not have been a religious man at all if he hadn't found himself a Catholic. Of my mother, I am not so sure. She would certainly have been a causist of some sort, and probably an orator as well, because she was so good at it and because, unlike Frank, she burned to speak out. But her mind was down-to-earth, in a high-minded sort of way, and I'm not sure she would have gone looking for a religion if she hadn't been drenched in one from baptism on.

Anyway as I slopped around at the edge of the crowd in my gum boots and little school cap, I cared little about what got them up there. All I knew was that no amount of respectability in other sectors could make up for this one eccentricity; we were gypsies, oddities. "My parents are publishers," I would emphasize. But their Catholic publishing seemed almost as bizarre as their Catholic tub-thumping in the starchy secularity of England. So I resigned myself to the delicate pleasures of outsideness at an early age.

This was the world I found myself in from December 27, 1930, on; and if I had woken up in any other house, I doubt even more strongly than my father that I would ever have gone to church at all. By temperament and intellect, religion as such strikes me as a desperate attempt on the part of mankind to bore itself to death in expiation of some forgotten excitement. But what we had was never quite religion. It was a whole life and a merry one, and it never occurred to me not to live it. It was simply the thing we did.

In this atmosphere to be a Catholic was to be an ardent Catholic. It had nothing to do with sanctity or native spirituality: it was more a matter of correct technique. Certain games have to be played hard, if they're to be played at all. So if you were supposed to make humble confessions, that's what you made: it was just as easy as the other kind. And if Communion was the bread of life naturally you wanted all you could get of it.

Above all, you might as well enjoy yourself. If you yawned your way through Mass, for instance, you were only making things duller and worse. Contrariwise, if you prayed, pondered, paid attention in the right proportions, the time would fairly whiz by. Thus by simple habit and custom, my sister Rosemary and I and who knows how many thousands of others became what would now be considered freakishly devout Catholics. That it was not altogether dissimilar from being a Dodger fan does not trivialize it. A child's intensity doesn't come in different strengths according to the object. My love of the Dodgers was in its day quite a noble thing; and in fact it actually helped me to make a necessary distinction.

One must begin one's story somewhere, and perhaps here is as good a place as any to show what it was like to be a little Sheed/Ward. Although I hung pictures of ballplayers where a better boy might have hung saints and Sacred Hearts, and although my heart welled with sorrow over Mickey Owens' dropped third strike as I could never quite get it to well on Good Friday afternoon, I did figure out (with maybe a little help from Frank) that it was right to pray in church but wrong to pray in ballparks. The point of sporting contests was to see who was better at that particular activity, not to test one's spiritual clout. Otherwise Catholics would never lose and the other guys would simply cease showing up.

As I write this, I am transported back to a football halftime prayer-huddle, where I, age eleven or twelve, am explaining all this to our coach, a patient Benedictine monk. I say patient gratefully, because if he hadn't been he would have *really* exploded. As it was, he tersely told me to pipe down and get on with my Hail Marys; and then bowed his head so that he wouldn't see whether I was doing it or not.

Next day this good man talked to me more calmly of the residue of luck in all sports, and why shouldn't one pray for that? Well, why *should* one? I asked. (To forestall the suspicion that I was *just* a precocious creep, I should add quickly that this priest and one or two others encouraged this kind of talk: Catholics were and are fascinated by moral questions beyond anything I've met outside. Besides which, a son of Sheed/Ward had special powers in this area—was practically a Dalai Lama, though thank God I didn't know it.) Suddenly I realized that Father Frederick's heart wasn't really in this argument. The real dirty little reason for the prayer was to make the team feel good; and this blasphemous use of divine intercession my man was simply too bright to defend.

Anyway that's the kind of thing that happened when the world of my parents hit the outside world, with me in the middle. That world began for me—not literally, but rather in the sense that Amerigo Vespucci discovered America—in a Quonset hut my parents had had built in our backyard and which served as the Catholic parish church in the town of Horley, Surrey. I have memories from before that, churchy and otherwise, but I lacked one thing at the time: I didn't know what the hell was going on.

The religious component of our little caravan swam into focus in that Quonset hut as quickly as my learning to read the same year, age seven. Just as I seemed to go overnight from near-dyslexia to something like fluency, so at roughly that speed I glimpsed what the big people I lived with were up to. But before I get on with my tingling discoveries, which were probably much like yours, I should say a word about the genetic components of Sheed/Ward, which had obviously happened earlier and taken a little longer.

Frank (for Francis Joseph) Sheed was born in Sydney, Australia, on March 20, 1897, about as far from England or, for that matter, Rome, as a man can get. Maisie (for Mary Josephine) Ward was born on the Isle of Wight, England, on January 4, 1889, in a family so suffocatingly Catholic that a strong-minded woman like herself might have been expected to make a break for it. So for Frank and Maisie to collide exactly where they did, he had to make a pilgrimage while she stayed in the same place: not easy for either of them.

Frank Sheed, Pilgrim

WHEN I SAY THAT MY FATHER HAPPENED TO FIND HIMSELF A Catholic, I don't mean he did it the easy way, with genial priests rubbing their pink hands in the parlor and jubilant celebrations at Christmas and Easter to make Church and home seem like one to the polymorphous mind of a child.

Frank's father's people were wintery Scotch-Irish Presbyterians with a particular antipathy to Rome. Years on the sea as whalers and merchant seamen had lined their faces with negative convictions. In fact, just in case little Frank might be leaning toward the hated Rome, an aunt once left a copy of the notorious *Maria Monk* in his path. *Maria* was all about the salacious doings in convents, full of underground tunnels and such, and it served the same kind of purpose as the *Protocols of Zion* for a certain school of bigot. But my father reacted the wrong way. He decided that only a very bad person would give such a foul book to a child, for any purpose whatever; he did not, he later insisted, even enjoy the damn book.

In a sense he backed his way into the Church while warding off less savory possibilities. His father was a premature Marxist (premature for Australia anyway) who, in a routine fit of perverseness, sent my father to Methodist Sunday school, in order to madden his Presbyterian kin and his Catholic wife all in one go. Again it worked out wrong. Frank, without trying, learned a lot of Methodist hymns—in fact he still absentmindedly hums "Shall We Gather at the River" at odd moments, such as during dull sermons. Otherwise, he paid the services no mind at all—except in his last weeks (call him ten or twelve) when he helped out the instructor a bit—but just sat there reading the Bible through and through, something little Catholic boys seldom got to do, and began to gather the ammunition that would years later make him a match for the Bible-bashing hecklers of Hyde Park. He also formed a rather Protestant crush on the personality of Jesus, by not having his words filtered through a clergyman, and nothing could ever make this personality seem unreal to him, or made up, or a composite, as it did to some textual critics.

Methodism, of which he is still fond ("I knew they'd be saved, of course; I just didn't want to be saved with them"), did Frank another small favor. It drove his real religion underground, which is much more exciting for a kid than the up-and-up stuff. While he was officially going through his Methodist motions, Frank was secretly making his first confession and Communion and getting himself confirmed. This subterranean religious life made him in a small way one with the early Christians and with the Catholic recusants of the sixteenth and seventeenth centuries, who hid priests in the wainscot and held whispered Masses in makeshift chapels. This mood is hard for a child to capture if they march you through the front door at the age of six and *make* you do these things, as they make you brush your teeth. The Church always had a rare whiff of adventure about it for Frank, however artificially arrived at, which later gave an edge to his speaking and caused even young lovers to drop what they were doing in Hyde Park and wander over to listen. From a distance he could almost have been a revolutionary urging a crowd to action *right now*.

But what got him hooked in the first place? The frontier-style Protestantism he had seen lacked a certain charm: the Presbyterianism seemed harsh, the Methodism bland. This left the field clear, since his father's droning Marxism had made even rationalism a thankless chore. But of course it takes more than an absence of anything else to make one an ardent believer. The personal heat required for this came originally from Frank's feelings for his mother, Mary Maloney of County Limerick. Her own faith was probably intense enough to convert a son all by itself, as Saint Monica's converted Saint Augustine; but besides the faith there was, as the Irish say, the Situation.

Frank seldom talks about his father, and he has a stubborn sense of privacy about such matters. But I don't see how his lifelong religious mission can be understood without some reference to this spiritual and physical counterforce.

John Sheed was a brilliant draftsman, unfortunately in more senses than one. While stationed in the Outback for a lengthy spell, he developed an ungovernable thirst for beer, as indeed does everyone stationed in the Outback, where the weather is screeching hot and there's nothing else to do except gamble on the flies landing and taking off from the windowpanes. Unfortunately, John brought his thirst back to Sydney intact, though at first quite artfully concealed. Mary Maloney actually fell in love with his *dancing,* which was rated among the best in Sydney, and his all-night gaiety.

John retained these qualities all his life long, and years later when I met my Australian relatives they still marveled at his unfailing "street charm." John had a smile and a cheery word for everybody. So these same relatives were downright incredulous when Mary "Minny" Sheed and her two little boys, Frank and Jack, came to them looking for sanctuary from such a darling man. It seems that once his own door was shut, the street charm came off like greasepaint, to be replaced, if John had been drinking, by murderous rage. Domesticity must have clawed at him, strangled him. Still warm from a laugh at the bar, he would find himself locked in for the night with a pious, possibly prudish wife and two brats who needed feeding out of his good beer money. Worse, like the other barflies, he came home to failure.

I was to note when I visited Australia in the 1950s a frequent sense of sourness among the middle-aged men, even ones who had done quite well for themselves. Australia is a wonderful country to be young in, with its year-round beaches and endless playing fields, but one can pay for this later in middle-aged envy and regret. Besides that, there was a sense with these sardonic fellows of an adventure flunked. Australians seem biologically geared for adventure, as anyone who has fought alongside them in war will testify. So if one doesn't even go to England or America but settles down instead to a middle-class life in Sydney, there is, or was, a gnawing dissatisfaction that could take itself out in some ugly drinking.

John Sheed, descendant of ships' captains and whaling men, compounded this tendency by becoming an out-and-out failure by any country's standards. He lost job after job for the usual drinker's reasons and was never more than a yard or so ahead of his creditors. My father remembers at least thirty-three Sydney addresses by the time he was thirteen. These moves can hardly have seemed like escapes to Frank, since Bluebeard (I realize that Bluebeard is not a precise metaphor for the monogamous John Sheed, but years later, whenever Frank let us children watch him shave, he called himself "Whitebeard the Pirate." The two images of fatherhood stuck in my mind) always turned up alongside him in the new residence, so his relief at getting away completely for a breather at the age of six and staying with the Maloney cousins must have verged on ecstasy.

In my imaginary rounds, where one poses in all the ancestor pictures, I used to ask myself if John Sheed could really have been as bad as all that. Having been in a bar or two myself, I was anxious to sympathize with and greet a fellow spirit on the family tree. Since this was perhaps the only subject my father wouldn't talk to me about, I was free to indulge myself—until I met those Maloney relatives in Sydney and discovered how bad things really were. It seems John Sheed was a hitter, and it didn't much matter with what: a belt, a razor strop, a chair—whatever came to hand. And a generous share of this weaponry landed on Frank.

So it is not surprising that he formed a fast alliance with his mother, and everything she stood for. If you loved Mary Maloney you had to love her religion. It was central to her. Her father had been a "hedge teacher" in Ireland, which meant bootlegging education to unreconstructed Catholics as the priests bootlegged Mass. Priest and teacher were brothers in crime. The Church was also Mary's rod and her staff in a strange land (she had emigrated at fourteen) and a strange marriage. So just as her beloved Ireland grouped itself around

Catholicism in the face of persistent bullying, so did she and her little garrison within a garrison, herself and her two small sons.

Going to stay with his Catholic cousins while on the run from John may well have sealed the deal. The Maloney side was and is as kind and happy-go-lucky as the Sheeds were frequently not. (Frank's grandfather Sheed had been known in his prime as the stingiest man in Sydney.) Frank proceeded to pass the pleasantest two years or so of his life: the Good Time by which one measures everything else. He had two slightly older girl cousins called Bernie and Diddy who became his real family, as they would become mine when I went out there later. Frank has always had an unusual number of women friends (and I mean friends, not the other stuff) but it all began with those two. Bernie Carrick and Diddy Reid are the kind of people you meet at the end of a Dickens novel, the impossibly happy part, so that moving in with them must have seemed like dying and going to heaven. Just to top it off, the Maloneys, who except for my grandmother, had never cracked a book, thought that my father was a genius, which does wonders for a boy.

Who knows, Frank might have been an incurable optimist whatever happened. He had already had one peculiar advantage—so peculiar that many people wouldn't call it an advantage at all—in that his cantankerous father refused to let him go to school until he was at least eight. This pretty much gave him the run of Sydney during the daylight hours, and he proceeded to fall in love with it, as few people can have ever loved a city, with its English architecture and its tropical setting, where one ate passion fruit in a waistcoat. His description of it carried such an afterglow that for a time I wanted to be an Australian myself, and even pretended to be one once or twice (readers of *Transatlantic Blues* may note that this, not America, was my *alter ego*, or *altera patria:* I thought I had half a right to it and God knows it had rarity value). Frank's only complaint about his country seemed to be that the skies were somewhat tediously blue, and that the sun hung around rather stupidly all day.

Otherwise Sydney in the 1900s sounds ideal: bustling, eccentric, as packed with "characters" as Joyce's Dublin. My father remembers

standing on the hill (or bleachers) at Randwick racecourse with a
group of like-minded small fry, squintily watching their last-second
bookie, who was likely to make off with their mini-bets the moment
things looked bad; if he did they would do their best to tackle him
and crawl through his pockets like termites. Frank later learned that
one of his Catholic aunts used to pray that his horses would lose, so
that he wouldn't form a taste for gambling, which might have told
him right there something about the power of prayer, because his
horses miraculously did lose when he bet on them, but did quite well
when he didn't.

Having myself seen horseplayers hanging on to horseplayers who
were themselves hanging on to horseplayers, all bulging and swaying
from the sides of trolleys headed for this same racetrack in 1955, I
could imagine the bowler-hatted hilarity of my father's day. The trolleys had just arrived from San Francisco back then and must have set
young Australia on a roar.

And when it wasn't that, it was the Sydney cricket ground, which
came equipped with a similar hill, where even in my culturally evolved
day one received an orange sharply between the shoulder blades if one
stood up at the wrong moment, in front of the wrong party. "Get a
peach basket," they yelled, if a fielder dropped the ball. "Get a bloody
move on, me watch has stopped," was what a slow batsman might
hear. (I'm sorry I've forgotten the really inspired stuff.) It was all a far
cry from Lords Cricket Ground, the Westminster Abbey and mausoleum of the game, which hallowed ground was once actually owned
by my mother's great-grandfather, William Ward. Anyway, there was
Frank already getting the steamy feel of crowds while Maisie was still
miserably trying to decide which dress to wear for breakfast and which
for tennis.

Sydney was, above all, relaxed, a quality Frank came to treasure
and possibly even to simulate from memory. It was a city of sunshine
and water, with beautiful beaches tucked snugly into every crevice of
the Harbor and heartier ones outside, brazening on the Pacific and its
surf: and everywhere, lush passion fruit and kiwis and mangoes and
melons dripping into your mouth.

Since Australia is the oldest continent geologically, I see no reason why the human race didn't start in Sydney, Garden of Eden and all. But, mind you, there was no bloody Outback about it. It was also urban through and through, and curiously disciplined. The kids wore uniforms to school right through their teens, and my father, who did finally get to school, remembers the following illuminating exchange between parent and teacher: *Mother:* "My son is very sensitive. He has to be led, not driven." *Teacher:* "I shall lead him, madam—by the nose." Frank's own teacher whapped you with a ruler every time you made a mistake in arithmetic, producing, Frank swears, a classful of terrified mathematical prodigies. "Knowledge maketh a bloody entry," my father would intone: but he could not, if an Einstein himself were in the balance, hit anybody himself.

This was the dream Australia that dug itself into the beaches at Gallipoli, a magical mix of irreverence and duty, jauntiness and stern sportsmanship, ripe for slaughter. But it wasn't quite blown away in 1915. I found many traces of it in the fifties, especially when I saw three Turkish veterans leading the Anzac Day parade, as they had every year. They were "beaut" fighters and you had to give them their due.

This sense of honor does something to explain my father's curious career. "The money does not exist," I can remember him standing up to emphasize, the first time he saw a famous person doing a TV commercial, "it does not *exist*, that would get me to say those things in public." (I have lived in unwarranted dread of commercial invitations ever since.)

This somewhat alarming personal integrity was wound up in a paradox that puzzled me for years. Although Frank was an Irish Nationalist from the day he first heard the facts, he was also beguiled, like many Australians, by the Imperial ideal, which burned more purely Down Under than it ever did along the seedy, deal-stained corridors of Whitehall, where Australians were probably considered provincial jokes who had to be humored in the light of post-Boer War morality.

The Federation Act of 1900 which made Australia one nation for the first time was akin to Vatican Council II in the political sphere: it put everyone on his honor to do the correct thing without coercion. Britannia has given you her laws, and her literature, her civilization:

go thou and try not to make a total ass of thyself. From now on, Britannia will be a friend, not a parent. The outcome was, among other things, a Gallipoli for the Anzacs and (after the even more persuasive Commonwealth Act of 1926) a Dieppe for Canada. No parent would have dared ask so much.

Stuck out at the arse-end of nowhere, as they're the first to tell you, Australians were especially susceptible to the new arrangement. Cherishing their independence but craving *some* international connection, they suddenly had both. And by george, they would live up to it. Frank not only got a more English education than you can now find anywhere in England, but he became more fussy (as I learned to my cost) about English usage than any Englishman. Suffice it to say that the London *Times* crossword seemed specifically designed for him. Whatever impelled his countrymen to die for the Crown drove him to read Browne, Peacock, Macaulay and become, intellectually at least, the perfect eighteenth- and nineteenth-century Englishman.

In this same Federation Act glow, Frank and his Irish mother became the most unlikely pair of monarchists you have ever seen. They agreed, as one must, that the English ruling class was unspeakable. But the monarchy was something else. For one thing, the royal family, like the pope, can be anybody or nobody: the scepter is sturdier than the holder thereof, and can survive any amount of stupidity and depravity. In an international arrangement this is very good to know.

In the 1913 elections my father became an ardent fan of the Australian Labour party. Unfortunately, it won and set some sort of record for breaking its promises. Frank decided then and there to put not his faith in politicians. So the negative factors were all in place for a Commonwealth-Catholic vocation. One longed for an international brotherhood which did not break its promises, which by covenant could not let you down, a spiritual British Empire. And across the table one had John Sheed once again, still proposing such a thing in the form of the Communist party. Although Sheed Sr.'s personal brutality* made nonsense of his ideals—even the unlettered Maloneys

* When Mary and the family rejoined John after two years of peace, he picked up briskly where he had left off, handing Frank, age ten, such a hiding that nowadays the boy would have been hospitalized. But already Frank had seen daylight, and

must be onto something better than this—it would be a mistake to think that John and his ideals were not a major factor in Frank's intellectual formation.

"I'll say this for him, he was intelligent," concedes my father; and although Frank himself suffers fools, not so much gladly as willfully, blindly, like Lord Nelson, he truly worships intelligence, almost as though it were a physical perfection. Thus Katharine Hepburn was the actress for him and Maisie the wife. So although he had set his heart against his father, and attributes his sanity to that,† it's a cinch he didn't close his ears. And what he heard was the wondrous logic-chopping of Marxism so easily transferred back and forth, to and from, Catholic scholastic philosophy. Few young Jesuits can have received such training, such table talk so early, and all the more compelling accompanied by slight terror.

When Frank did get to school he whistled right through it, winning scholarships as fast as they could hand them out, and he credits this to the fact that his mind was left blank for the first eight years, so he had nothing to unlearn. Ingenious at least, but I think he also learned from two very bright parents, on separate time (when John spoke, that was the meeting). Anyway, Frank later wrote a book about communism, as if to kiss all that goodbye, and a very good kiss-off it made. After a typically lucid and fair summary of Marx, the book went on to accuse him of being too mathematical—of thinking that two boys working together would do a job twice as quickly as one, and so on. Whether this is the last word on Karl Marx, it very likely wraps up old John Sheed, who first brought the news home.

---

from then on he haunted the Maloney household where he could lick his wounds and try to forget them. Also, in the interests of fairness, it should be mentioned here that there were some nice, though less demonstrative, cousins named Stafford on the Sheed side and he spent time with them too. Slowly, John Sheed's black shadow recedes, dwindles: but *slowly*. That last beating seems to have frightened even him, and he pretty much laid off the physical stuff after that. But the memory lingered on.

† Frank's brother Jack, a hauntingly handsome young man in a photo that always hung in our hall, did not. And it was his mother's fixed belief that Jack's death at sixteen of a freak heart attack was partly caused by unrequited love for his father. I think this legend speaks, in a very Irish way, for her own heartbreak and Frank's.

My father continues to have a deep respect for Karl Marx ("He was *necessary*"), and a total respect for his diagnosis if not his medicine. What is perhaps interesting is that Frank himself turned out to be a natural mathematician, who still has to fight the mathematician in his own thinking. There may even be some among his bruised hecklers who could say that he learned his dialectic too well. Certainly he has never heard anything on a street corner that his father's table hadn't prepared him for.

Anyway, the scholarships were proof enough even for John Sheed that he had an intelligent son on his hands, and having done his best to block the whole business, he proceeded somewhat touchingly to try to get something out of it. Like many drinkers, he had amassed a portfolio of ailments and he thought that a doctor in the family would be a wonderful economy. So he strewed medical books around the house, as his sister had once strewn *Maria Monk,* and with even less effect.

Frank had reluctantly decided at sixteen that, since he could never write like Shakespeare, he would never write at all. But he did turn out some nice light verse and he formed an abiding interest in metrics, such that he still can't take a poet seriously who doesn't know his way around his trochees and anapests. This is certainly the long way round to medical school, and it is a measure of John Sheed's distance from his family that he could have been so spectacularly wrong. If Mary had wanted him to be a priest, which she surprisingly didn't (she did want me to become one, but for Frank it was famous lawyer all the way), she'd have been at least in the right ballpark. Frank has been at least a sort of para-priest all his life.

As John Sheed's terror pulls out, so does his value as a teacher. There was nothing more to learn from him anyway; Frank at sixteen and lying about his age had entered Sydney University, where more grown-up minds than his father's could be found.

In totting up John Sheed's legacy, one finds a weird bag. For instance, Frank became a mean dancer in his own right, capable of waltzing across sofas like Groucho while his partner remained floorbound. This foot-tapping tendency passed through him to me, along with a lamentable capacity for remembering popular songs. The latest receptacle of this gene is my son Frank, who, among other things, plays passable jazz piano and clarinet and who at seventeen hitchhiked down the Mississippi in quest of jazz.

We can call this one a biological draw perhaps. Mary Maloney was also musical, and practically her last words to me were "Play some more Fats," referring to the great Fats Waller, who was her ruling passion and "main man." This taste may finally be the only rational explanation for her marriage. "When I think of John Sheed I think of music," says a cousin. So picture if you will a handsome couple dancing their brains out to the strains of Strauss and Stephen Foster. If only they could have danced forever.

Charm would have to be called another draw. Mention of John's "street charm" reminds one of an Irish politician, and so at times does Frank's, whose blarney conceals, as blarney must, his inner self as successfully as his father's had. I was astonished when I saw a picture of John in his fifties to find that he looked exactly like his son. So much for deserving your own face after forty. By whatever dark route, he had arrived at even the same expression as the later Frank, which meant an expression born to please.

But Mary Maloney could also light up a room, though more with laughter than with calculated charm. When she was merry, *everybody* was merry. I have never seen anyone so infectiously rollicking. Nor, on the other hand, have I ever seen anything darker than her dark moods. At those times she seemed quite out of reach and hard as stone, and the only cure was to make her laugh, if you possibly could. It may well be that any success my father and I have had in amusing people goes back to our desperate attempts to loosen up "Auntie Min," as she came to be called.

John's contribution here was more saturnine. He was witty all right, but with that overlay of sarcasm that Sheeds tend to put on everything,* like those pitchers who can't help throwing curves. My father was as busy rejecting this as he was absorbing it, and this was to

---

* My favorite cousin on that side, one Alan Stafford, overheard himself being blackballed. "I could never vote for that sarcastic bastard Stafford," explained the deciding vote. My Slovak critics have accused me of English arrogance, but there's nothing English about it. The English were much gentler than the Sheeds.

be a lifetime struggle for him. At law school, he made one of those resolutions of his, akin to his leaving literature to Shakespeare. A fellow grind had just said to him that he found the law an "ungrateful mistress," to which my father retorted, "In your case, I can't see that a mistress would have much to be grateful for."

This may seem harmless enough to a nonaddict—we hit harder than that in my crowd—but for a Sheed, it was the fatal glass of beer. You either practice custody of the tongue at all times, or it is down the slippery path for you, making wisecracks and enemies till there is nobody left. I cannot express my gratitude for my father's decision that day. His tongue could be rough enough as it was, and it was best to handle him with care in certain moods. (Since he worked hard at his equanimity, he might be surprised to hear that at times he reminded me of a hard-nosed Irish monsignor.) Unbridled, his tongue would have been a deadly weapon, equipped with nuclear capacity— and he would never have made a single convert from his soapbox. (In fact, he was so alert to this problem that he counseled *all* his fellow speakers not to score off hecklers: which was good for the Faith, but bad for entertainment.)

John's final legacy was an abhorrence of drunkenness and adultery worthy of Saint Paul. As to the latter, Frank does not seem to believe that his father played around—though perhaps he just doesn't want to believe it—but that is not his angle on adultery anyway. According to Saint Thomas Aquinas, if I understood him aright, this sin is primarily one of injustice, not sex. (The sex would be the good part, but the absence of good in the bad part overwhelms it, or so I imagine. Any trained Catholic can run you up a batch of these half-baked Thomisms at a moment's notice.) My father's focus is always on the wronged woman, and this his mother undoubtedly was, whatever the details. Curiously, Auntie Min herself thought that all the trouble in the world was caused by scheming women—"bold hussies," as she called them—and that men, left to themselves, were practically perfect.

How she arrived at this in her particular situation is a mystery beyond me or probably beyond even her in her day. It did give her another excuse to adore her sons, which, according to Freud, is useful all around. But it was one message she couldn't get through to Frank. To him, the man was almost always guilty. No sooner had a marriage busted up than the husband became for him "a bounder"—and the wife frequently became a family friend. It goes without saying that he was never irrational about this: if the evidence ran overwhelmingly the other way, and if he knew the couple well enough to *feel* the situation, he could always make a troubled exception. But the bias was constant—he is one of nature's feminists—and it was to cause him some grief later in my own life, when bias briefly rubbed against bias.

For booze, his feeling is more one of unshakeable contempt. He has helped a great many people with their problems, and some of them have been drinkers, and he has done his best about it. But if I were a drinker, I would not go to him. His underlying disgust puts complete sympathy just out of reach. Alcoholism to him is infantile greed: it may become a disease later on—we'll leave that to the medical chaps to squabble over—but it starts as pure slobbering greed. I have seen with dismay drunks crowding him physically, thinking that Frank is the one little old buddy in the whole wide world who understands them, and I have felt sorry for both parties.

It's probably more a nervous reflex than a deep point of principle. Although he personally thinks that wine tastes like iron filings, he quite enjoys watching other people drink the stuff, and has never given a temperance lecture in his life, even to his thirsty children. It's just that people must be held accountable for any evil they do in a state of drink. Deep down he didn't want to, or perhaps simply couldn't, think of his father as weak or diseased. Better an act of will, however vile.

Not so strangely, perhaps, he once told me that the reason he'd never taken a drop was that he feared that he'd have made a pretty fair alcoholic himself. His teetotalism at least gives him a handy guide to new doctors. If they tell him to quit drinking, as they often do, the jig is up with them. Frank has a nose best conveyed by a line spoken to him in awe by a female elevator operator. "If W. C. Fields wasn't dead, I'd swear you was his brother." So doctors, when in doubt, latch onto the proboscis.

This distinctive physiognomy was positively the last gift of John, although it may have been delayed somewhat. No one's face ever changed more drastically from youth to middle age than Frank's, despite his claim to have felt no inner change at all. The Frank who entered Sydney University at sixteen was a bag of bones back then, skinnier than the young Sinatra, with a long, somber face dominated by forehead. When one of my English aunts said on first meeting him a few years later, "Who is that divinely good-looking man with the atrocious manners?" I reckon she limned the wraithlike Aussie for fair.

Running through the list again, one sees that most of Frank's religious predispositions were simply the healthiest responses to his life and the world around him. Anthony Burgess has more recently described how his own feeling for the British Empire, with its teeming variety, dovetailed with his Catholic upbringing, and I'm convinced the same went for my father: the one institution confirming the other. He also loved goodness for its own sake, having seen the alternative. He had learned from his mother how to pray and how to take the supernatural for granted as a plain fact of everyday life (without which peasant foundations, all the intellectual superstructure in the world will buckle sooner or later). He loved the Blessed Virgin, an emotion that I frankly still can't fathom, and which he had unusual trouble explaining lucidly: it just went with the set.* And finally, he knew how to argue. Oh, my, how he knew how to argue.

It was just as well his equipment was so deeply dug in because there was little at Sydney University to encourage the spiritual life. It was a ribald, electric place, perhaps feeling an extra tingle from the distant war. One pictures the students standing eternally around an upright piano, beer-pots in hand, belting out funny songs they'd just that minute written. "Perhaps they didn't teach as much but they taught us all they knew" was how they serenaded the help. "Some day the profs will all pass away," goes a song about the grading practices, "not 50 percent but all . . . we wonder if on that day of days there'll be a terrible wail/when Saint Peter opens his mouth and says/that '50

---

* Mary the Perfect Human, God's own choice and our champion, didn't seem to have enough "who" about her to love. Yet the brightest Catholics have invariably worshiped her.

percent must fail.'" The Sydney University songbook is abnormally dominated by that generation; and although it's not exactly Rupert Brooke, it reads wistfully today.

Because of my father's relative youth and un-Australian sobriety, I had assumed that he watched all this from the sidelines. If you want to act older than you are, it's best to limit your appearances. Also, as one of the first full-scholarship boys in Sydney history, he was a marked man who couldn't afford to goof off for a minute. Frank knew all the songs of course, but that went for any song anywhere that he'd happened to hear more than once. Otherwise I couldn't picture him as a rampaging student. To this day he is *slightly* less at ease with men than with women, because he had always been the youngest kid on the block. So I was surprised years later while strolling with him through Sydney to be accosted by a middle-aged citizen with the words "*You're* Frank Sheed. You're the one who stole the organ from the town hall!"

My father blushed prettily and said that, hmmm yes, he dimly remembered hearing of such an episode. "No, it was you—you and another fella. You *are* Frank Sheed, aren't you?" That seemed the only matter in doubt. Since Frank had raised me to deplore practical jokes as he did (with, it now seemed, much the same results), he was fairly pinioned. So he allowed himself a small smile and murmured, "Perhaps . . . something of the sort," and we slipped softly away. I'll never know what he stole the organ for, but one imagines quite a lamentable civic uproar over the incident if this stranger could remember it so vividly thirty-five years later.

On that same trip, I heard from across a crowded bar (actually they were all crowded) an ex-student of Frank's intoning a song my father had himself written for the Sydney Law School. Frank was older by then, of course, and more confident—but that doesn't explain the missing organ. My guess is that he left the sidelines just often enough to keep his hand in. His early life had had its jolly moments, enough for him, incredibly, to call it happy, but it lacked one thing: the company of intellectual equals, both men and women.

With these he could now unleash one of his most endearing qualities: the capacity to have as much fun as the drunks are having, in fact the same kind of fun they are having. "Maisie drinks and I get noisy," as he explained it in later life. The one thing that made him uncomfortable was profanity, without which Aussie discourse would be a series of puzzling gaps: but again, the varsity was a refuge from tyranny. "Swearing indicates a small vocabulary," said John Sheed, of all people, and it may have been a mark of education in Australia not to do it. At any rate, my father was puzzled years later to hear that the actor Cyril Ritchard swore, not because Ritchard was a Catholic, but because he had gone to Sydney University.

Somehow Frank contrived to wrest quite an education out of the bacchanalia. He had had from early on an abiding interest in words and where they came from, so he proceeded now to fashion for himself, in that free and easy atmosphere, a course all his own, made up of Latin, French and English with a special view to following words from one language to another, until one saw dimly how language worked and how purposefully it drifted (permissivists who talk about the inevitable growth of language conjure a vision of weeds; my father's pleasure was to find the inner logic that made English in particular so improbably lovely. Just as he liked the argument from design in explaining creation, so too with the miracle of language).

Among his souvenirs from all this were a love of Horace's *Odes*, which he always packed before his pajamas wherever he went; a facility in French quite unmatched by his ears (so that in France Maisie would listen to the phone and he would speak, an awkward but cozy arrangement); and of course, more and more of his beloved English.

By the time he went on to Sydney Law School, coins were being dangled before his eyes. The talent in Australia had to go a long way in those days, and all sides of the family disagreed only as to which kind of star Frank would be. He lost the Sydney Rhodes Scholarship by a dubious eyelash to Bert Evatt, who inevitably went on to be prime minister in a thin field. When an Oxford Union debating team visited Australia, it was only natural that my father was assigned to it in a mixed team debate: he understood their language.

So what was it to be: politics, diplomacy, perhaps even the first Catholic chief justice? The only career the relatives never considered was the one he finally took. And it is worth emphasizing this because he knew from the start that it would be so, that even his near and dear, his Bernies and his Diddys, even his mother at times, would consider his final choice a puzzling disappointment. From a Sydney point of view, he had simply balked at the first jump and trotted off the course.

His own view was, as usual, very different. As a fan of Thoreau, he knew all about different drums. He was at an age, and in a position, where a man commonly starts to ease away from the religion that got him this far. And Frank embarked on law school with an open mind about the future, along with the kind of aptitude that often makes up your mind for you. To be paid for arguing?—it was like paying Willie Mays to play baseball.

Yet almost at once, the question of what am I arguing for? began to nag him: certainly whatever it was was nothing he believed in or cared about. Proving that black is white, however one dilutes the phrase, was a wrong use of intelligence (he'd heard enough of red is white to know that). So the better he got at the game, the worse he felt. One of his favorite bits of doggerel (by a remittance-man type named William Goudge) concerned two chaps named "Brown and Jones of Simpkinville who owned adjoining land." After they go to law over their boundary—a matter of inches—their worries are magically over, because within five stanzas "the lawyers owned the land."

In between law classes, Frank was doing something much closer to his vocation, though it wasn't quite it yet: he was teaching at the Sydney Grammar (High) School. Faced with his first incipient riot— Australians were not *that* disciplined—the skinny young schoolmaster hit on the inspired notion of making the whole class stand on its chairs until it calmed down. (How often he must have wished for such powers later.) He also became intrigued by his fellow teachers, who sound like rejects from the French Foreign Legion; brilliant misfits, bitter and despairingly witty men. One in particular used to go on a bender for two weeks every year in some country town or other, to return with the explanation "I was bitten on the groin by a scorpion." He spoke for all of them.

This was not, as I say, quite Frank's calling: but it was closer to his calling than law school. He was, as I was to learn to my advantage, a great natural teacher. The only question was, what was worth teaching? Just as it had been, what is worth arguing about? Or to put it less world-wearily, what's the one thing I can do better than anyone else?

To take a breather from his conscience, Frank lit out for Home, Great Britain. This was a great escape hatch for Australians, as I was to use Australia in reverse when I came down from Oxford. Simply making the trip was creditable enough, and it allowed one to disappear from sight for a while. It's a special antipodean privilege to be able to escape thirteen thousand miles from your relatives, and Frank must have needed all of that. Every family yearns to boast its first Great Man, and Frank was the only decent prospect in memory. And since on the frontier the lawyer is the biggest man in town, he had made a promising start in everyone's eyes. Although his scruples about the law were basically spiritual, the Church was no help either, because the Australian wing of that wanted a great man too. And the Irish, in their usual role of upstarts, were about ready for their first John Kennedy, or at least Al Smith. What probably nobody felt they needed right then was a street-corner speaker and small-scale religious publisher.

The only thing to do with pressures like that is to shrink them. Viewed from the other side of the world, it all added up to the same thing: a big fish in a little pond—a phrase he used often. In Australia he would be free to choose his brand of fish, but that was all; he couldn't enlarge the pond any which way. Better, perhaps, to serve in England than rule in Australia. But then again . . .

Frank did not make the decision on that first trip for at least two reasons. He had gone over with a fuzzy notion of doing a little something about the Irish situation, only to find that the Irish were already fighting each other. What he could have done anyway is hard to conjure. Since childhood, he had been subject to chronic nosebleeds (more of John's legacy? One tap in the nose too many? Frank never said so) which, if unchecked at once, assumed hemophiliac proportions. This knocked him out of sports and military service at one blow—both blessings as it turned out. (He was time-wastingly obsessed by sports.) I still remember Frank having his nose cauterized every few months, which is a much less pleasant route to a prize strawberry than the one W. C. Fields chose, and I also remember us all watching in trepidation every time he sneezed—always fourteen times in a row (I can only do eleven). So outside of writing a few songs— the only thing the IRA already had enough of—I can't imagine his role in the Troubles, except as a potential handicap.

However, he was thinking about Ireland when he got to England, and this made him see the place in a rather different light. As he traveled through the industrial North with its grimy row houses and belching chimneys and tiny, ancient-looking children (five inches shorter per head than the Top People in those days), it dawned on him that the English treated their own natives every bit as badly as they treated the Irish.

Thus to "succeed" in this country was to join a conspiracy against the rest of the population. The pond would be big enough now, but he would have to become a shark, if only by association. I am guessing at his thoughts here. But I don't see how anyone raised a Marxist Christian, with an earful of Dickens, could fail to have some such thoughts. After all, Marx had had them himself when he lived in England. So success as such was tainted; and if here, probably everywhere else. Frank used to quote a line to me of Hilaire Belloc's to the effect that monarchy was the only form of government where you didn't get your hands dirty reaching for power (your nose might be another story).

Worldly success had to be reexamined very closely—and so did England. His first months there my father described as the loneliest he had ever spent. To a talkative Australian (I know of no other kind) an English railway carriage seems like a morbid nightmare. The passengers used somehow to contrive in those days to look as if the place was empty except for themselves. Later Frank realized that this was really just a respect for each other's privacy, and he came rather to like the idea, although it seems like thin consolation to me.

Anyway with nothing better to occupy him he just took to watching these people like specimens under glass, until in a very few years he was able to pass as a perfect English gentleman. As noted, he already had the education: all he needed was the manner. So, without precisely setting out to do it, he had Henry Higginsed himself up a social class or two. I don't know whether he had ever had a dinkum-Aussie accent (his mother didn't), and he swears he made no effort to change whatever it was he had. But either way, the main lesson he learned was that first one: leave them alone—they'll be frightfully grateful—and don't *worry* about them. The secret of the English gentleman is bottomless indifference, and my father proved quite a hand at it.*

But all this was in the future. If his first months were the loneliest, the subsequent ones were the coldest, as all that boring, stored-up sunshine was finally spent. He had a job pushing rather simple-minded Catholic pamphlets—a job that led in no direction whatsoever. So there didn't seem to be a hell of a lot to detain him here. Law school still called, and probably would have kept him for good if it hadn't been for a chance encounter—so "chance" in fact that I don't even like to think about it, since my very existence hung on it.

Frank had taken to filling in the cracks in his spare time with his first outdoor speaking. Something called the Catholic Evidence Guild† had just come into being (which is chance right there) and my father used it to unlimber his tonsils and learn a little theology, of which he knew none at all, except for some old Methodist stuff. To pay its tiny expenses, the Guild held an occasional junk sale, and it was at one of these that Frank found himself addressed by a somewhat officious young woman with the words "Are these good scissors?" (I don't think she called him "young man," but she didn't have to.) "Madam," said Frank, looking at the merchandise for the first time, "these are the very *best* scissors."

This is one version of Genesis. The deuteroversion has the young

---

* When he married Maisie, a viperous Australian aunt accused him of social climbing and marrying for money. Thus speaketh, now and forever, the voice from the small pond.

† The CEG was founded in 1919 by a bluff New Zealander called Vernon Redwood. Redwood had no particular interest in theology, but wanted to use his platforms to stump for various political causes, chief among them keeping Prohibition out of England: now that was his idea of *real* Catholic evidence. Unfortunately his movement was swiftly subverted by young theologians, including some people called Ward of whom more later. But Redwood kept coming to Guild parties right to the befuddled end, happy perhaps that *something* he'd founded had lasted so long.

woman talking to a huge crowd which Frank promptly lost the moment he stepped on the platform. So the young woman had to come
back and draw another crowd for him, and so through the long afternoon.

These and all other legends are true. Anyway Frank met Maisie.

What precisely he was meeting I'll try to describe in the next
chapter. Enough for now to say that the encounter led Frank to the
vision he was looking for, the solution to the great fish and pond
question and the only type of success he could live with. But not immediately: he had to go back to law school first. On the way home, he
breezed through the United States on a lecture tour—anyone could
give a lecture tour in the U.S. back then. You only had to ask. Henceforth, his life would somewhat resemble a pool hustler's, as he paid his
way from coast to coast playing the speaking game, but there was always something 1920s about his view of America: a very lawless country, an alcoholic country, he would say. Also poorly educated,
unmodulated voices. Beautiful young people but no real faces among
the middle aged. Fat. For a future apostle to this country, Frank took
his sweet time about liking it, and even longer about respecting it.
But then, as he might say, who knows what Saint Patrick really
thought of the Irish? And there was something else. I occasionally
sensed a certain colonial envy as he ticked off America's defects against
an invisible list of dinkum perfections. If only the War of Independence had gone the other way—why America might have been just
like Australia!

Being abroad always makes him twice as Australian anyway. And
this particular tour, his first, must have played hob with his nostalgia.
In fact his lover's vision of Sydney may even have crystallized once and
for all in Prohibition New York. By the time he sailed back into the
Harbor, he can't have felt much like going anywhere else for a long,
long time. As for Sydney, he now shone all the more brightly there, as
a man of the world. By the end of the twenties, the Labour party
would go on to win the first Depression election and would be looking around frantically for Catholic judges for the High Court. A genial classmate of Frank's named Eddie McTiernan got on the court at
a ridiculously early age, and I mean no disrespect to Eddie, whom I

later worked for with great pleasure, to say that, if he could get there, my father certainly could have.

Frank has described the torture he put himself through to get this thing over with one way or the other. He compressed the law course into the shortest possible time and then flogged himself methodically through it. The final exams coincided with a heat wave, which in Sydney means 110 degrees or so and wet, and the last nights were feverish.

He was still racked between the law and England. Being a man of the world cuts both ways. Australia still seemed small from up close but size wasn't so important now. More to the point: his difficulties with adversary law had crystallized from vague distaste to a real fear for his soul. "As soon as I realized that some lawyers were paid more than others, I knew there was no justice"—another Marxist thought. You get only the amount of justice you can afford, no more, no less. As for the High Court—if he thought about it at all—it was still only a tugboat sailing alongside His Majesty's Privy Council, the real court of last resort in the Commonwealth. When I worked there years later our chief concern was interstate commerce and the legal status of Doberman pinschers riding shotgun on trucks.

Then there was England: a cold place where there was nothing for him to do. Outdoor speaking was not a career, and a Sydney law degree was a worthless appendage in any walk of life. On the other hand there was Maisie. And not just Maisie in herself, though that was certainly enough, but Maisie in her setting. He could always at a pinch hope to transport Maisie to Australia, but he couldn't transport the living Catholic culture in which she breathed: a culture that was literary and English, both excellent things, but also hooked into the international family of Rome. It was everything a man could desire, even including cricket.

Maisie and her world proved not only the tie-breaker, but under inspection, the tie itself, because there really wasn't that much else on the English side of the argument. While this matrimonial case was still being tried in his own head, he took his exams and the law proved a grateful mistress: he did brilliantly. But no sooner was he called to the bar than he cabled Maisie. Her favorable answer came on the same day that he had a big winner at the track.* The omens were set fair, and he shipped out for England with his dream Sydney intact forever. The reverse colonial boy was not to see his golden city again for over twenty years. But it didn't matter whether he did or didn't. To the day he died, which happens to be the day I am writing this—November 20, 1981—he swore it hadn't changed a hair.

* A second memory persists of that day, in which Frank's horse actually stops in its tracks and trots over to nuzzle the telegram. This would be an even deeper omen. But, sadly, I can't check it with anyone now.

Maisie Ward, Stay-at-Home

THE DISPARITY IN THEIR AGES MADE NO DIFFERENCE TO FRANK OR anyone else, because Maisie always looked young and retained till the very end the enthusiasm of a teenager. But I find it makes a difference to me now as I set out to describe her. It's not just that she seemed to belong to an earlier generation than Frank, but that the generation she belonged to seemed itself to belong to an earlier generation, and so on, back at least to Jane Austen. The English gentry resisted change with ease, because, snug behind their hedges and stone walls, they barely knew it was going on. As late as the 1930s some aunts of mine drove me all over Liverpool in search of a two-piece "bathing slip" to cover my seven-year-old chest. Finding none, they probably presumed that there had been a great run on the things.

If by chance you were Catholic gentry, you had one more buffer against change. Change had caused quite enough trouble in the past. Any more of it, and your lot might go out of existence altogether. For a few weeks a year, my sister and I were slipped into this strange old fortress of class on visits to cousins, but we never stayed long enough for it to take. Most of the time was spent with nannies in back rooms known as nurseries, and you didn't get to learn much from that.

Otherwise we lived more or less in the twentieth century, but with a nineteenth-century mother. Maisie still talked of "rum goes" (for odd doings), of "dropping bricks" and "making appalling bloomers." She even tried to get me to say "goff" instead of "golf," although I explained that this might not go down well with the hobbledehoys at school. And she stuck to "gairl" for grim life, even in America.

So her upbringing remains a slight mystery to me which all the Edwardian TV specials in the world cannot clear up. The decor and the patter are easy enough to reproduce, but not the mind-set that was fixed so firm and steady that neither my adventurous mother nor her sister and brothers, nor indeed anyone I've met from that class ever saw fit to change an accent or an attitude or a belief. Two earth-trembling wars made no material difference: a world cataclysm was no excuse for flightiness.

But besides (and this is the creepy part), most of them couldn't have changed if they'd wanted to. My mother lived in the United States for years, falling with gusto on such not-quite-right regionalisms as "Philly" and "Frisco," as her parents might once have toyed with the latest small talk from London; but in so doing she only demonstrated how sunderingly alien the phrases were. Even "okay" was said in quotation marks by survivors of that era. When I heard P. G. Wodehouse on television shortly before his death, I realized how this heritage could be turned to account by genius. Wodehouse had lived over here for maybe half his life, and he owned perhaps the century's greatest ear for dialogue, but he still spoke in the fluty tones of a Victorian great-aunt. No wonder he could write of a timeless world: no outside event could budge the inner clock of his generation.

So this may begin to explain why my fiercely intelligent mother never even questioned her beliefs (so far as I know), let alone changed them. For one thing, there were no alternative ideas in the air: if you wanted some in order to rebel a bit, you had to go looking for them. They weren't in the school library. And of course if you *did* rebel, it was immediately put down to perversity or some defect of character, and your position in the family was at risk until you came to your senses. If change was to be rejected on a universal scale, its individual agents must be quarantined at once. So you had to want to do it awfully badly: rebellion was not considered amusingly roguish, except perhaps on the French stage.

For Catholics, the constraints went even deeper. Faith was a virtue and not just an intellectual feat, so losing it was in the area of Sin.

By hardening your heart in Pride, you were keeping God's greatest gift out, which made you at best an object of pity and sorrow. Your family might even pray for you, a galling prospect. So rebels in Catholic families tended to shut their eyes and charge: out of town, out of the country, out of everything they had ever been. In this state they might very well go on to become the fallen men and women the family already thought they were, and feel quite Satanic about it too, or so one imagined. (In real life I suspect many younger relatives being surprised to come upon old Uncle Blacksheep living out his days respectably and serenely in Florence or Antibes.)

Anyway, rebellion was somewhat overdefended against, which might have made it attractive to someone like Maisie, if it had occurred to her at all. But she didn't have a Situation like Frank: on the contrary, she loved her parents distractedly and uncritically. And if they didn't want her to enter that vast territory known as the Unthinkable it was fine with her. The thinkable was quite pleasant enough.

The Wards had entered the Roman Church on a wave of ardor just two decades before and the wave was still rolling in when Maisie was born. Her father wrote Catholic biographies, and her mother wrote novels with a Catholic accent. More tellingly still, her little brothers Herbert and Leo used to play games of Mass on cardboard boxes, and later wrote funny songs on purely ecclesiastical themes of which the following is a fair sample: "The pope who is infallible/and seldom goes far wrong/has always taught/that time is short/eternity is long . . ." The next two verses dispose of the Eastern Orthodox and the timid Church of England which "thinks there is a *sense*/in which tis not *too* strong/to say that time to *us* seems short/eternity seems long." And finally in comes the march of modern thought to prove the complete opposite of the above. Now I ask you—how many teenagers do you know with minds remotely like that? (Actually they were slightly older when they wrote the above, but it could have happened anytime.)

This was the particular greenhouse in which Maisie grew. It was churchy through and through. Bear in mind that for a long time there had been no place else for Catholics to go: not Oxford or Cambridge or the many corners of the Establishment which required the Oath of Supremacy,* so they got to know their chapels tolerably well. Maisie's first and strongest link with the Church was liturgical. During Holy Week, she became a dervish whirling from church to church as others whirl to theaters and casinos. What happened in church was (as Genet of all people once said about the moment of consecration) the central drama of life, and she couldn't get enough of it. In fact, it would be fair to call her a liturgical junkie: virtue had nothing to do with it, as far as she was concerned. She once told me, in answer to an impudent question of mine, that in her case, going to Mass was indeed no better than going to the theater. It was too much fun. So Maisie certainly wasn't trying anxiously to pile up merit points as some church-haunters do. Virtue would have to reside for her in outside activity: Mass and Communion were purely rest and relaxation.

Mea patria mea ecclesia est (My church is my nation). That's not Maisie speaking but her brother Leo. It was the family given; religion was simply what Wards did, as it later became what Sheeds did. The intellectual armor would arrive in due course, but it was not strictly necessary. Maisie did not have to strain herself to find proofs for the sacramental reality. Maisie knew what she knew.†

The religious history of the Wards has been thoroughly written about already, by Maisie among others, so I should confess right away that it not only didn't interest me for years, but that it struck me as a dusty old bore, a Victorian monstrosity that ought to have a cover thrown over it. It had nothing to do with my own pip-squeak religious impulses: if anything it warred with them, striking me as fetishistic and narrow, a stale family joke. Being a Catholic was fine: being a Ward, Oxford Movement, ultramontane Catholic repelled me as much as it attracted my father. The reason is simple enough. Frank came from the outdoors, his city of light and water where a man could actually grow tired of the sun, and was happy to bend down and enter the haunted house of Ward; I was trying to bust my way out.

* This requirement, that you have to replace the pope with the king as your spiritual leader, was actually lifted in 1868, but styles had hardened by then, and there was still no such thing as, say, a Catholic Oxford don in the 1920s.
† The phrase comes inevitably; the Henry James title *What Maisie Knew* was part of the family baggage.

My favorite Ward ancestor was actually the only one who might have made it as an Australian. This was my great-great-grandfather William, whom I first read about in a history of English cricket (none of the other Wards seemed to know anything about him). As the family's last genuine businessman in a hundred and fifty years or so, William was in a position to tear off a check saving Lords Cricket Ground from urban development; and as a cricketer, he managed to make a record score on that ground which also stood for over a hundred years. A jingle of the day memorialized him as a "well-employed man and a city MP."

What happened after that is something of a genetic puzzle. The game of cricket disappeared completely from the family heritage to be replaced by that of religious controversy. In fact, something of the sportsman did linger in Maisie's grandfather William George, "the buffoon of the Oxford Movement," as he was sometimes called. W.G. was a math prodigy who became a tireless and ferocious battler in the fields of the Lord, or of the pope anyway, with an unflappably sweet disposition: one played hard but there was nothing personal about it. What most alarmed people about him was his annihilating candor. Whatever was on his mind got said loudly and instantly: you couldn't pussyfoot around old Ward any more than you could pussyfoot around his granddaughter Maisie.

The Oxford Movement has been exhaustively sifted through by now, but a small child's even smaller history of it might boil the Ward contribution down to something like the following. In an effort to contain its Left and Right, or rather its high and low, the Church of England had all its life been forced to compromise. The Reform Act of 1832 caused Anglicans to reconsider these compromises, which had been codified back in the sixteenth century under the title of the Thirty-Nine Articles. Many on both sides now found these crafty old Articles intellectually and spiritually shoddy beyond endurance: good politics perhaps, but terrible religion.*

The Oxford Movement was a loose coalition of those who felt

* The Thirty-Nine Articles became a rather comic piece of old furniture in the Ward collection. When the Anglicans held a conclave in a certain hotel, the joke went, "Imagine—forty bedrooms and only thirty-nine articles [chamber pots]."

that an Anglo-Catholic Church could not much longer endure half-Catholic and half-Protestant. The only question was, how Catholic could one be and still be Anglo? Ward, as was his wont, went the furthest, all the way to Rome itself. If you're going to be a Catholic, *be* one, don't fiddle about. So he gave up his Anglican orders, got married, and while he was about it, demanded that Oxford make a public act of contrition to Rome for its sins against the True Church. Oxford, then a hotbed of parsons, responded stiffly by stripping him of his degrees, which he took as cheerfully as everything else, signing his future correspondence "W. G. Ward, undergraduate."

His friend the Hamletlike Newman (Maisie's phrase for him was invariably "madly sensitive") tended to agree, but he was not the man for such bold, headlong gestures. Still Ward wore away at him with the remorselessness of a good theorem, and in the event he did follow Ward to Rome—and in a sense follow him home as well, because Cardinal Newman remained a spectral presence in the Ward household for the next three generations. "He's just a fellow who lives at our place," I once described him to a young friend.

Unfortunately, the alliance between Ward and Newman was not altogether made in heaven. Grandfather William George, as a Catholic convert, wasted no time flinging himself to the far right corner of his new lodgings, demanding even more papal authority than he was getting. His ideal, he said famously, was a papal bull with his breakfast every morning, along with his *Times*. The term "ultramontane" referred to this wish of his for orders from "beyond the mountain," from the vicar of Christ himself and not from some fly-by-night earthly power. "Madam, you will find me strong and narrow," he once said. "*Very* strong and *very* narrow."

It would be unjust to call Newman the exact opposite of these: he had a kind of willowy nervous strength that you challenged at your peril. But as a religious genius, he had no inclination to bow his neck to Rome one inch more than he had to, whatever Ward might say on the subject. When Vatican Council I was convened in 1869 (not to be confused by young readers with its frisky descendant Vatican Council II a hundred years later), the burning issue was the proposed declaration of papal infallibility. At some point, while the debates were at their very hottest, Cardinal Newman is said to have proposed a toast to the pope, "but to conscience first." So inevitably he and Ward had to fall out eventually—quite far out as it happened—which did not prevent son Wilfrid from writing a loving biography of the cardinal, and another of his father, to be on the safe side. Later, Maisie would write a biography of *her* father and mother—and another of Cardinal Newman. Whether in opposition or alliance, the Wards orbited about this last English religious virtuoso, as it might a pop star. One sometimes felt that the family style was not so much dictated by strong idiosyncratic parents, though it had plenty of these, as handed down like a tradition of which they were caretakers: doing things the Newman way, as they understood it.

It was all very much "religion in the head." Wilfrid edited a quarterly called the *Dublin Review* where the Left and the Right of the Church slugged it out far above the heads of the masses, who went on about their increasingly irreligious business as World War I approached. It was hard for me to picture a Ward in action of any kind, unless firing off theological broadsides could be called action.

To gauge how wrong I was about the family, there is no better place to begin than with Maisie's brother Leo—although to get to one Ward you have to keep passing through the others. Leo grew up in the same sealed room as the rest and inherited the same "Ward nerves." His brother Herbert had come back from boarding school in muted shock, having, so Maisie believed, encountered sex in some repulsive form, with no preparation whatever, not even such rudimentary defenses as the dirty ruck of mankind intuitively runs up for itself.

The Wards were so ethereal that they barely knew they had bodies at all; so sex must have seemed totally foreign to them, designed for some lower order of creation. I remember thinking, as Maisie (who was a rabid gardener) carried on endlessly about "the miracle of growth," that to the Victorian mind, furniture and houses were real, but things that grew were extraordinary. If we add to this the further remove of the Wards, we are practically floating. "How remarkable of you to know so much about the *minutiae* of botany," said my grandfather, to someone who had just named a couple of the commoner trees in his garden.

Leo had his own kind of breakdown somewhat later, and it illumines two other aspects of that curious household. After Oxford, Leo enrolled in a Jesuit seminary, and found himself virtually the only postulant who followed the stern *Exercises* of Saint Ignatius to the letter. Since the *Exercises* taken straight might prove almost too much for Bunyan's Pilgrim, Leo not unnaturally buckled. (Maisie, for this and other reasons, most notably their smugness, never forgave the Jesuits.) But the point is that it was inconceivable for a Ward to do less than he was supposed to. I don't know which caused which, but the Ward conscience and the Ward nerves jangled as one and were equally imperious and tormenting.

Still shaken, Leo entered an ordinary seminary, where he bobbed along adequately until he got to his exams and found that he was still too nervous to take them. The priest in charge wisely took young Ward for a walk and a chat, at the end of which he told Leo, "That *was* your exam and you passed brilliantly." But the incident illustrates the difficulty *all* the Wards would have when they left their cozy, loving bombshelter to face the competitive world. Years later, in a very different crisis, Maisie would say to me, "I find myself at such a *disadvantage* when confronted with reality."

Anyway, one would have supposed that from now on, Leo should take things quietly, settle down with his books in some rural parish full of peaceful old people, and perhaps write a three-volume biography of his father or somebody else in the family.

But not a bit of it. The jittery Leo promptly set sail for Japan to become a regular parish priest in a strange land. He did not, by intent, have a missionary order to buttress him out there or even a smattering of seminary Japanese. He was determined to wing it alone.

And so he did, triumphantly. Outside of an unfortunate sermon in which he confused the words for charity and diarrhea, causing some tittering behind fans, he never put a foot wrong with his hosts. And Maisie found, long after the war, that Father Leo was still something of a legend in his parish, while the out-and-out missionaries were forgotten.

Unfortunately, the Second World War interrupted Leo's work and although he had already gone native to the point where he could have fooled *me*, at least, as Japanese, he was clapped into jail as an enemy alien. His few letters from there, as well as at least one he wrote when he was on the high seas and free to speak his mind, stressed the gentleness of his captors. "Do not blame the Japanese," he repeated. But their gentleness seems more an ardent wish than a fact. Other witnesses report that Leo was beaten savagely and was also nearly starved, and there is no question at all that he died on the ship home of acute internal hemorrhaging.

So Wards could be heroic if called upon (and I think this went for all of them). Unfortunately, they were not much called upon. Leo's career indicated what a difficult fate it was to be a Ward. All four children were raised to have a stern sense of duty, but the only thing they were actually taught to *do* was be Catholic, and there are only so many ways of doing that as a career, outside of writing biographies of each other. Leo chose the one logical way to do it, but Herbert and Theresa ("Tetta"), lacking clerical vocations, never really did solve the problem. They lived good lives but always with a slight sense of missing the boat. So Maisie more or less *had* to have a unique career, if she was to have a career at all.

The young Wards did not even learn the things that the useless classes learned. My mother never knew the right dress to wear on country weekends, and I still picture her striding grimly in to dinner in her tennis outfit, though it may not have come to that. Tetta, who married a squire, was to find in her turn that she could not run a house full of servants, out of very terror. Faced with the horrors of laying out the day's agenda, she would ask the housekeeper for advice, which turns out to be the worst possible thing to do with housekeepers. The contempt in the kitchen must have been almost palpable— and none the less so for being partly imaginary. It goes without saying that Tetta eventually had *her* breakdown too, though it wasn't just caused by domestic unease: she also lost through illness her husband and youngest son within months of each other. (I intentionally use the word "breakdown" in the vague sense of the period, which could cover everything from madness to the common or garden "life crisis." The Wards' troubles were perched variously along this scale.)

As for Herbert and Leo, the very thought of either of them skeetshooting or fly-casting or practicing other gentryish pursuits would bring a smile to anyone who knew them. The one time Leo was improbably seen with a billiard cue, and even more improbably sinking a ball, he made a typically ecclesiastical joke of it, to wit: "accidents can happen in the best regulated substances." This Thomistic pun virtually defies translation, as does Leo. The Wards were simply not of this world. Although they were conventionally well educated in languages and literature, they were not even precisely intellectuals. Leo came closest and was a good friend of Aldous Huxley's at Oxford; but pure intellectualism was too self-indulgent for him,* and there remained a feeling that the Wards were designed for *something else*, if they could only find it.

Whatever it was, it could not in Maisie's case "require new clothes," as Thoreau puts it. It could not require worldly small talk either, of which she had none, or a university education. This last deprivation made her bitter when she thought about it, which was luckily not too often. Catholics had only just begun going to Oxford again, after a short lapse of three hundred years or so, and both her brothers took gleeful advantage of this. But very few women of any stripe had so far cracked this glorified smoking room of a university. And those who did were still considered rather rum bluestockings, too brainy by half, the kind of woman who had to shave twice a day and, in my father's phrase, buttoned their cardigans on the wrong button.

Although the Wards were too brainy themselves not to know better, they were worldly enough to be aware of the consensus. I have so far emphasized their incorporeal side, but they were also English gentry. Wilfrid Ward had married slightly above himself in the kingdom of this world (in the other one, Wards soared alone) and Maisie says he was always slightly aware of it. Through his wife he was now connected to such tony folk as the Duke of Norfolk and—I won't bore you with the list, because I don't know it. By the time I came along, it was all quite meaningless except for collectors. But back then titles packed a wallop, and Wilfrid may have overcompensated a bit

* Maisie also had a lifelong contempt for egghead priests who did not shoulder parish work along with the life of the mind. Her one abiding prejudice, although riddled with exceptions, was, as noted, against Jesuits.

by swarming over those country-house weekends that spooked my mother so, perhaps more than a religious intellectual strictly should.

For some reason that remains a family mystery he preferred to take "wrong-clothes" Maisie along on these junkets rather than her sister Tetta, who was the "worldly one"* and would have handled them splendidly. Tetta adored her father, while Maisie fondly found him just a tiny bit silly: a harmless flirt, a benign snob. Yet it was Maisie he chose (family affections are seldom symmetrical), and not just as his traveling companion but as his secretary. Such as he was, he became her university.

At the time she did not complain. She considered her father a prodigiously hard worker, because he always wrote for four hours a day before playing golf. Since it was quite possible in her set to go through life without ever seeing anybody work at all, except for the chambermaid, Wilfrid must have seemed quite the iron man, though Maisie herself was seldom to work such short hours again.

For a woman of Maisie's brilliance, this career amounted to a grounding, though she characteristically made the most of it by later writing the definitive work on her parents and their world. If the only Ward vocation was to be writing about each other, she would at least be the best at that.

Naturally, while she was alive I asked all the wrong questions, so my chief image of her secretarial stint is of Wilfrid teaching her, much against her inclination, to smoke cigarettes so that he would have someone to smoke with. After coughing her way to mastery, she was some years later asked by my father to quit, because he couldn't stand smoking women.

What I didn't take in, because I simply heard too much of it and was immunized early, was what Wilfrid Ward was actually doing in his study. Besides smoking, and after writing two books about his own father's world, he embarked on his majestic life of Newman, which characteristically made him nervous (Newman was still a hot

* "I was the worldly one and Maisie was the brainy one," Tetta used to recall acidly. The pigeonholes cramped both of them as cruelly as bound feet.

potato, if one can attach such a phrase to such a personage: considered either a saint or a heretic or both), and found himself embroiled in something called the Modernist crisis, which *truly* made him nervous.

The heresy of Modernism is hard to describe, because it was defined and denounced in one of the most incoherent encyclicals ever to issue from Rome (Pius X's *Pascendi,* 1907), which was, to boot, never all the way properly translated into English; but it seemed to range from a condemnation of root-and-branch attempts to desupernaturalize the Gospels to the smallest openness to scientific inquiry: there is no theologian of moment today who is not a Modernist of some sort.

Such a document practically begs for a witch-hunt, and a modest one ensued in England (which was only on the fringe of the controversy). As editor of the *Dublin Review,* Ward was in something of a pickle. Father George Tyrrell and Baron Friedrich von Hügel,* the two leading names on the English fringe—and I grew mighty tired of both of them before I knew who they were—were family friends as well as contributors, and Ward agonized for them along with others caught in the crossfire. In fact he felt himself becoming an old man, so he said, between the ages of fifty-four and fifty-five, which covers the worst of it.

So Maisie saw some action in her father's study, though of a slightly cramped, parochial sort. Most of England neither knew nor cared about the crisis—it wasn't the least homegrown—and only a few sensitive intellectuals who wanted so much to do the right thing got in the way of it and were trampled. It was a sad reward for their unparalleled loyalty to Rome, but perhaps it taught them to take encyclicals just a little less seriously. At any rate, and without taking lightly the genuine pain of those concerned, I can only say that from this distance, the *Dublin Review* seems to have been at the exact center of the teacup in which the storm raged. The real tempest was in Europe,

* Tyrrell went all the way with the heresy and was excommunicated; von Hügel, helped by deafness, remained serenely loyal and as inquiring as he felt like, and is rightly remembered as a religious master.

where over the next fifty years it would proceed to tear down much of the rigging of the jolly ship Saint Peter. But in 1907, nit-picking biblical scholarship still struck most Englishmen as dry and German and probably half-mad.

If Maisie's university possibilities ever came up again, they were shoved hastily under a rickety family myth that women were better off without it: as all-rounders, as amateurs "in the very *best* sense of the word, my dear," they learned better from life itself. The notion that my mother was learning "life itself" in that household seems quaint, or that she could possibly have learned less of it at Oxford. Yet the myth survived all the way to my generation, so that my sister Rosemary cheerfully passed up Oxford too, while I, far less equipped, was force-marched in.

Maisie often wondered what a university would have done for her, and so do I. It may help to define her if I jot down some of my guesses. Maisie was obviously the real heir to the Ward intellectual heritage, brothers or no brothers. I can never read *Alice in Wonderland* without thinking of my mother: the solemn child asking literal but fiercely alert questions all day long. Since she was considered plain (I can't see how from the photos), her brain shone all the more brightly. And the family sent her to a crackerjack convent in Cambridge where she got a fine if lopsided education, better than a college one of today in some ways, less than a high school in others. Religious instruction, whatever its merits, takes up an awful lot of time.

On the emotional development which gives to ideas their specific feel and thickness, the convent offered if anything slightly less than home had. The nuns were French, which means nuances of prudery beyond the stodgy imagination of the English. For instance, one must somehow manage to wash all over without removing one's chemise—something I've tried to picture. Going to the bathroom was described by one of the senior sisters as *"cette triste nécessité."*

As for sex, the only advice I can remember, and it may have come from another convent, was the dark hint to girls going abroad that "they [Latins] can't help it. It's the climate, you know." Maisie at least found the whole place funny, and she picked up one of her lifelong favorite phrases, for which one must unfortunately imagine a French accent: "Can ze tee-ger chahnge ees streep, or ze leopar ees spo'?"

Maisie had a naturally earthy mind, and years later would chortle over a similar convent which ordered the nuns "to refrain from intercourse with the public," but she had made an awfully late start, and never really got the hang of it. At the age of eighty, the phrase "take a pee" was used in her presence and she said, "I've never heard the expression," an astounding admission from a street-corner speaker. Anyway, she learned a lot of good, clean French.

What would Oxford have made of this material? It would not have made her less formally Catholic, if my own case is anything to go by: the mild friction of skepticism at such places quickens one's beliefs. And Maisie's beliefs were as rocks to my pebbles. As for Anglicanism there was no way a Ward was going to go back to that.

But a university might have widened Maisie's world and given her other subjects. I was intermittently amazed at how much vintage secular thought she simply hadn't heard about. Street-corner speaking can delude one in this regard. Maisie thought she was meeting the modern mind out there and not just a gruesome parody of it. Only toward the end did she wonder whether she'd spent a bit too much time jousting with the second best.

This delayed second-guess serves to introduce the Maisie I knew, the master of the afterthought. Maisie could never even decide whether she'd ordered the right meal in a restaurant until she'd gone home and slept on it. So her later doubts about her street-corner work are not definitive. I believe that a more scholarly Maisie would have reached fewer people and lived, by chance, a duller life. She might even have become a don, which would have been curtains for little me. Anyway, her tilts with the street crowds may not have done so much for her brain cells but they shaped her as a woman of action, which was what she preeminently was.

Leo Ward once remarked that, from all the various accounts of it, he and Maisie seemed to have grown up in a different family from the other two—a happy one in their case, with a brilliant mother and a so-so father (Tetta's version reversed this completely). And whatever the truth of it,* Maisie and Leo came out blazing, the others did not.

But Maisie had too much mental energy even for an activist, and she did write a lot of biographies and such between adventures, and here I think a university might have helped. Oxford could not have made her a better scholar—her capacity for original research was prodigious and rapacious. The specialists, whose pleasure it is to lie in the long grass waiting for amateurs to blunder along, were trampled into the ground by Maisie's brute information, sometimes more recent than theirs. And if she didn't know it today, she would by tomorrow. That afterthinking mind, which could make her a scourge in restaurants, so that we kept swapping plates with her till she gave up and ate, was more rationally employed in constant revision of her work to the point of starting over if necessary. Because of her old-fashioned premises concerning character and the need for heroes, readers assumed that her research was equally old-fashioned, and she received her share of condescending reviews. But I pitied the reviewers when they got to their mailboxes the next day.

If she had a weakness in this respect, it was that her research was somewhat unselective—everything interested her, so she bunged it all in, as she would say—and Oxford might at least have taught her to be less profligately interested. But my father covered for this weakness by editing her to the bone, a terrible test of love, and we were spared that dismal anomaly, an uninterested Maisie.

Her biographies might also have profited from a slightly more skeptical mind. She herself came to see that her magnificent life of G. K. Chesterton was a little too innocent in the ways of men—not too serious a flaw in a book that doubles as a celebration ("a great plum-pudding of a book," *The New Yorker* called it). But I think a university might profitably have loosened the exclusive hold of Chesterton on her *mind*, thus improving the book and other books. Conservatives and Catholics alike are always delighted to find some brilliant journal-

---

* Of course no two siblings are born into *quite* the same family. Tetta and Herbert were the youngest and suffered the shock waves of an elder brother's death: Wilfrid II, or "Boy," died at twelve, leaving their mother in emotional ruins for a while. "If ever I'd become an alcoholic, it would have been then."

ist chappy who agrees with them, and the Wards fairly lionized the young Chesterton. *They* might not keep up with the modern world but *he* did, and he confirmed that they weren't missing a thing.

Thus, even before she hit the street corners, Maisie was having secular thought filtered for her through somebody else—in this case, an adversary journalist of genius, whose chief mission was to show what was *wrong* with secular thought. In cases like H. G. Wells and other pop sages, this was quite good enough; but with, say, Nietzsche and other real thinkers, it was embarrassingly clear that GK's reading had stopped at his first good debating point. In an essay on Tolstoy, Chesterton treats that great man purely as an addled old pacifist; it was only later that I learned that Tolstoy also wrote novels. As for Freud, Chesterton's prudishness would have bridled at the very idea; and as for Marx—well, that would have been right up his alley, but alas, as a journalist he frittered away the time on Fabians and other minor spin-offs who were passing through the public eye just then.

So while Chesterton was never less than illuminating, even on people he hadn't read, he shouldn't have been one's *only* guide and interpreter; yet through Maisie's formative years he came perilously close to being that. And I don't suppose we ever had a serious discussion in which she didn't drag him in by the ears, often to quote some quite commonplace remark that didn't require a Chesterton.

This addiction went along with a battery of middlebrow tastes presumably picked up at home and never discarded. The Wards would take turns reading a Walter Scott for the boys, a Jane Austen for the girls, and a Dickens for everybody; nothing wrong with that, Maisie later did the same for us, but the needle seemed to get stuck there. "Of course, all the Russians are quite mad," she would say brightly, if any one of the great ones was mentioned. Far better to have a good talk about Jane Austen. My mother would glow with a kind of eager relief upon meeting a fellow Jane-ite; but the "good talk" usually consisted of listing one's favorites, with much hesitation and backtracking. "You know, *Emma*'s awfully good." "Yes, but *Persuasion!* My dear!" And so on, a feast of afterthoughts.

Maisie's mild philistinism would have been lost in the crowd, based as it was on any Victorian schoolgirl's reading list, if she hadn't attempted literary biography. Her fine life of Robert Browning does show her innate, tragically undeveloped passion for literature to fullest effect. She worshiped Browning's work, and got everything out of it that one could possibly hope for from a highly intelligent, slightly prosy fan. But she lacked the surrounding knowledge of poetry to write a critical biography per se.

Maisie had no ear whatever for style: she could not even see what was wrong with Agatha Christie's, to take a worst case. What she did have, and what saved the book, was a gift for linking a man's work to the events that shaped his mind. Her *Browning* counterpoints the subject's verse with his life until the book positively pulsates. This is not the usual way to write about a poet, but surely it's one way. The Oxford argument bogs down here. Would she have been better off adding one more volume of criticism to the Browning canon, or did her method of wading in, all elbows, knees and enthusiasm give us something unique and worth having? I will admit that I'd have liked to see the straight criticism. But one couldn't possibly have both. And I found it curiously thrilling to see her clamber over her shortcomings and make the most of what she had.

But why were the shortcomings there at all? Here I draw a blank. Her mother was quite a good if conventional novelist, and her father wrote in and around literature. Yet no one seems to have had much interest in literary form. Grandfather W.G. had a beautiful voice, and father Wilfrid would have sung in opera if the family had permitted. As it was he settled for singing round the piano to the unbridled delight of his children, who memorized Gilbert and Sullivan to a man, even tuneless Maisie. Leo might conceivably have been a professional musician too if it wasn't for the mysterious Ward imperative.

So music seems to be the closest the family came to pure art, and Maisie missed it a mile. It is not in nature to be as unmusical as she was—which meant, according to Oscar Levant, that she had to love Gilbert and Sullivan, so even that didn't help much. Otherwise, one must face the possibility that the Wards were simply more mutton-pudding English than they cared to realize. Descended from businessmen, culminating in W.G., who was an Anglican divine before he "Romed" it and must have run *his* household like a spirited personage, the Wards had only this tropical bird, the Church of Rome, to separate them from their stodgy Class-mates.

Religion *was* the art and color in Maisie's life, reason enough to hang onto it tight. But, with her as with Leo, one couldn't just sit around stroking it, one had to do something. So young Maisie took up the kind of circumscribed charity work in the East End of London that was available to young ladies of her class. She saw it later as a charade, which probably did the young ladies more good than it did the poor and which fooled her at least into thinking that English poverty was housebroken, containable and even curable if enough young ladies pitched in. But it was a start, and the only one open to her.

If she made it all sound a bit like a scene from *My Fair Lady*, with the deserving poor getting their soup and dancing off gratefully, she had for once a reason to make mock of herself. She never considered herself observant, because her mind was always off someplace else, so perhaps she missed some clue even in these orderly scenes. But what she couldn't get over was how long, at least until sometime after World War II, she continued to underrate the sheer scale of English poverty. She was apolitical from way back, perhaps from meeting the Ruling Class romping together on those weekends (if you believed in something, you didn't play croquet with the enemy). So she had a temperamental stake in believing that private effort could cure all problems. When she first encountered bureaucracy in its full density in 1946, she couldn't imagine *any* problem that these people wouldn't make worse, and for a while she sounded almost Tory about it. But that's further along the line. The point here is that she flung herself into good works and stayed there for years, while retaining a blinkered Victorian view of the total situation.

Idealism was, she knew, her strength and her weakness. She worked in a military hospital in World War I, where her nose was rubbed in the detritus of combat, the broken, wasted men, some of whose nervous systems were smashed beyond repair, others who were lucky enough to live out their lives in wheelchairs; but she never questioned the noble version of the war. Nobody else did to speak of, at least on the home front, but I doubt whether Maisie in particular could have lived with the idea that the whole thing might be a mistake. When I brought it up in the 1950s, she told me she still believed that the war was caused by the Germans invading Belgium, where they raped nuns. By then, she was quite willing to consider other causes, but at the time, Maisie couldn't have fought a war she didn't believe in. Maisie couldn't do *anything* she didn't believe in, which, as with Frank around the same time, rather narrowed the openings, which were for women needle-sized anyway.

The Wards all came tumbling out of the war higgledy-piggledy, as they would say: Tetta, the worldly one, with the immortal (in the family) phrase, "Girls who say 'cawfee' and 'awficer' seldom drink coffee with officers," Herbert with diabetes which, when it hit wrong, made him unseasonably thirsty and inclined him toward the quiet life. The Vera Brittain generation, I suppose. Tetta worked in troop canteens, Herbert served in Mesopotamia, which was the equivalent of John Sheed's Outback. Few people came away from that mess intact. But Tetta married a nice, sobering squire called Francis Blundell, a Tory MP, with a social conscience, and Herbert went on to become a magistrate on the Isle of Wight, where he exercised the Ward scrupulosity punctiliously. He told me that a lorry or taxi driver who bent the law always got a break in his court, because driving was the man's living—that kind of thing. Leo went capering off on his own fandango, the ultimate (from the shreds I remember of his style) Gilbert and Sullivan Koko, with a serious purpose. Which left Maisie.

By 1919 Maisie was really at loose ends. Her father had died in 1915, and nobody had given a thought to another career for her. Why should *she* be different? Even men in her class didn't have to do much of anything, though they were encouraged to keep occupied. Good works could expand indefinitely to fill a woman's time. And perhaps a little writing? This had become practically a family twitch by now, something that passed the morning—for which reason I swore I would never get into it.

If the Catholic Evidence Guild was a good chance for Frank, it was a blooming miracle for Maisie. Otherwise she would have been like all those great violinists who died before the violin was invented. She was, it turned out, a great outdoor speaker, whose greatest asset was perhaps her stage fright. Even after fifty years of it, she never gave a talk without feeling nervous in advance. But she alone possessed the secret of turning the Ward nerves into pure, natural energy which grabbed passers-by by the hair on their necks.

Nervousness also put a slight throb in her voice, as felicitous in its way as Bing Crosby's glottal stop or whatever. When Maisie got fully worked up, with all sails flying, she seemed about to cry, and people leaned forward with concern: if it means so very much to her, the least we can do is listen. If Frank sounded like a revolutionary calling one to the barricades, Maisie was more like a mother pleading with her children to come home. And because her style did so much, she did not have to make emotional speeches. In fact she might be giving the exact same speech as my father. It made no difference. The impact was all her own, and it could be positively Churchillian, striking deeper chords and sympathies than Frank could ever reach; or want to reach.

"Will she boss him or will they fight?" Frank overheard a Guild member say of his engagement to Maisie. My mother must have seemed mighty imperious in this largely middle to lower class group. But never was a class misunderstanding wider of its mark than this one. Maisie never bossed anybody, although she could boil up at lazy waiters and bored shop assistants. As for fighting, not only did Maisie not fight with Frank, nobody fought with, or even around, Frank. There was something indefinable in his manner that made it seem childish and unworthy of one. The bloodiest family quarrels fizzled at his feet. "I'll believe that a man has an uncontrollable temper when he tries to punch Joe Louis," he used to say: and one would stop in mid-tantrum.

Frank remembered (I must sadly switch to the past tense for him) the first time he met the Wards. They were all clustered round the dining room table, talking to beat the band. His entrance made not the slightest difference to their torrent of jabber, and as my father quietly found a seat, he noticed that they didn't even listen to each other. So Frank took a deep breath and simply began talking himself, and the Wards loved him on the spot: he was one of them.

That was the easy part. There was also a wall of Wodehouse aunts for him to wade through, and no fraternity hazing ever sounded more blood-curdling than this gamut of befuddled bluebloods. Unfortunately, the only fragment I remember concerns an especially mad aunt who stared at Frank wildly and said in a loud voice, "Am I in hell?" Assured that she hadn't made it yet, she said craftily, "Then who is *he?*"

High time to call in the New World to restore the (mental) balance of the Old. Frank became a champion of mixed blood, the more mixed the better, citing as his ace Don Juan of Austria, the famous nonmoronic Hapsburg, but I think, just for once, reflecting on himself. He was pleased when I said to him once that the Sheeds were so outbred that we didn't bleed at all.

Frank's best pal in the family was probably his mother-in-law Josephine, by an eyelash. Josephine Ward, by now in her sixties, actually had the gumption to mount a platform herself to help make the Guild more theological and less political.* Now that must have been a grand sight. But I don't suppose she thought talking to a London street crowd was anything special. Naturally one preached the Gospel whenever one had the chance. She was much too aristocratic to feel self-conscious about it, or to see any incongruity in the setting.

This I think tips the family debate in her favor. Her child-rearing methods still puzzle me: she doesn't seem to have prepared her young for anything at all. But I'm not sure how much of this a mother was expected to delegate to others in those days. Certainly shrewdness in selecting nannies was the crowning virtue of motherhood; all the love in the world couldn't make up for a dud nanny. Whoever was responsible, it transpires that Maisie, by then in her midthirties, had to have the facts of life explained to her the night before her wedding (she took to them delightedly, she told my sister once), but this seems to have happened even to certain males in that buttoned-up era. Perhaps more serious was Frank's charge that Maisie, when he met her, had the emotional development of a twelve-year-old. The English upper rungs probably teemed with great big twelve-year-olds, but Josephine Ward was a novelist and should have known better.

---

* Since Maisie, Leo and Josephine all spoke for the outfit, it's impossible to tell who had the idea first, but probably they were all talking at once and they all had it together.

"My mother understood evil all right, although she didn't write about it," Maisie once said to me, and I thought that was sad. Her mother could surely have shared her little bit of knowledge of evil with the kids, if only to help them over the bumps of kindergarten. But an iron curtain of prudery still hangs undented between that era and this. Josephine used to maintain that she was quite sure that the cad Thackeray would have taken advantage of the modern license to write about sex (this was the license of 1910 or so, mind you) but that the sainted Dickens would surely not have. Maisie was surprised, though not by then shocked, to learn years later that Dickens had actually envied Balzac's license to write about sex in the 1850s; by that time Maisie had moved far beyond her mother's ghost-stories-in-the-dark "intuition of evil," and thought that dirty books were merely rather silly. "It all seems to hinge on whether the gairl is wearing underwear or not," she said of one such. "Honestly!"

But Maisie's slow start is essential to her later job description. She would have had a slow start anywhere, even in a bordello, because nature had decreed for her a long leisurely parabola of a life. But the Ward world view retarded it still further, till her life threatened not to get off the ground at all. The one member of the family beckoning her upward, never mind where just yet, was, despite everything, her handsome mother standing small on the platform and fielding the same rotten fruit, in the form of questions that the mob dished up, as unflinchingly as the youngest, cockney speakers. All is possible, Josephine's manner suggested: we'll think of something. Maisie and Josephine and Leo, as the three upstarts who turned the Catholic Evidence Guild around in their restless search for something to do, had a magic thread running between them that I could sense even as a child. The other Wards slip away now and go about their own errands.

It was commonly understood in the Sheed household that Frank rescued Maisie. Certainly *she* so understood it and conveyed a life-long sense of gratitude to him, which sweetened their marriage, however cloying and childlike this might seem to modern feminists. In fact, there was gratitude on both sides, as Frank treasured his gift in endless amazement, and it gave a vibrant endurance to their love such as I have never seen, regardless of method. They were not just hanging on like marathon dancers for the sake of the record. But more of that later.

At least Josephine Ward knew a rescue when she saw one and must have practically yelped with delight; not over a husband, but over an opportunity. It was no routine case of a man saving a woman—the Wards were too proud to think they needed saving by anyone, and a lower-middle-class Aussie was a matchmaker's disaster; it was more like a stranger turning up with the other half of the code, just when one had despaired.

The code was to be the strange world of Sheed and Ward, a Siamese twin of a vocation which neither could have pursued solo. Josephine divined one element in it right away, when she said, "Frank would be in two places at the same time if there was a night train." The motionless Wards, who had trouble being fully present in *one* place at the same time, would now, in the person of Maisie, have to hit the road and stir things up a little.

It was what, without precisely knowing it, Maisie had been waiting for all her life.

The issue is joined. Sheed married Ward in 1926. "Will she boss him or will they fight?" Symbolically, Frank stands behind Maisie (right). Any fighting they do will not be with each other.

LEFT TOP: Maisie (right) and her brother Wilfrid, or "Boy," whose death aged eleven cast a deep shadow over the cheery Ward nursery and haunted the survivors forever.

LEFT BOTTOM: Maisie dressed entirely appropriately for once as the fairy godmother in Cinderella.

RIGHT: Frank at about fourteen (upper left), making it his business, as usual, to look older, and his brother Jack, about twelve. The woman to Jack's right is Min's sister and indispensable friend, Sarah (to us, Auntie Sar).

BELOW: The Sheeds didn't go in for dating pictures, but this looks as if Frank has about polished off Australia and is ready to take on England, and anything else that comes along.

OPPOSITE, TOP LEFT: All roads lead to Rome in our family, even if we (in this case Rosemary) have to be carried there kicking and screaming. Horley, about 1932.

OPPOSITE, TOP RIGHT: Taking in America for the first time. Rosemary is already counting the days till she goes home; Junior is trying to figure out how to look just a little bit less like Freddie Bartholomew. Those teeth are an awfully tempting target.

OPPOSITE, BOTTOM: The Sheeds in all their finery, a shot in a million. It took Rosemary's wedding in 1954 to do it.

ABOVE: Frank at play, jousting with the higher clergy: in this case, the foxy old Cardinal Daniel Mannix, still a cutting wit at ninety. Maisie and I (recently arrived in Australia, 1954) might be laughing at either one of them.

BELOW: Maisie in her late-blooming prime—the face she first had for me and hence will have forever.

PHOTO: MARIA DARLINGTON

ABOVE LEFT: Frank looking positively beatific. (If I referred to him, however, as "laid back," all that would change.) In general I do not trust this expression: somebody's going to get it in the next sentence.

ABOVE RIGHT: Frank and his mother Aunt Min in later years, herself looking particularly roguish in her best hat (actually, all her hats looked like that).

BELOW: Maisie in action: part Major Barbara, part scholastic theologian. The quintessential street-corner speaker.

Movement Brat

WHAT FOLLOWED WAS PERHAPS JUST AN APOCALYPSE IN A SMALL pond. The Catholic Revival, of which Frank and Maisie provided, in Churchill's phrase, "The Roar," and the megaphone too, lasted not much more than a generation, and scholars with pointed sticks are still picking among the aftermath. The least that can be said for it, in a sardonic sort of way, is that it enabled Anglo-American Catholics to follow the Second Vatican Council intelligently and other people to take these same Catholics seriously for the first time (when Frank died I was amazed at the number of people who wrote to say what an eye-opener Sheed & Ward had been); the most is a longer story.

But all movements are exciting in themselves, even if nothing comes of them. A child who grows up in a movement is equally marked by it whether it succeeds or fails or, as in the Catholic case, can't decide. Not that we ever thought of ourselves as a movement, just the old Church going about its business: but no Communist brat ever grew up more single-minded or dedicated. In our beautifully integrated world, God was our dialectic and our class struggle; he was, in Frank's simile, the hook behind the overcoat. My view in the next pages will be largely that of a movement brat for our side: the subject is not so much what my parents were doing as how it felt around the house.

Of course the mood in the kitchen was set long before I came along. Frank and Maisie had, for mature theologians, a very romantic courtship. They went to Venice, where the tune that year was something called "Ukelele Lady," and I must have heard Frank a thousand times singing about "the tricky wicky wackies" who feature in that song. Maisie for her part always went rubber-legged over Italy. No one has ever reacted more passionately to religious art—"erotically" would be slightly misleading, but the overall sensual glow was surely next door to erotic and she did confide to me once that she was positive that I was conceived in Florence. (Yes, I was mildly embarrassed, as many were, by Maisie's dazzling candor.) So a day spent visiting basilicas need not be supposed to have clashed with the usual spirit of a honeymoon: quite the reverse. Liturgy was fire and water to my mother.

Upon their return to England, with Frank still warbling about his wicky wackies, they were confronted with a situation (not quite a Situation) whose resolution probably affected my life more than anything else except that night in Florence. The question was, what do we do with Mary "Minny" Maloney? She had escaped, Australian-style, to the ends of the earth to get away from her nerve-racking husband, who was still flourishing in his own odd way (he was eventually to die from a fall downstairs at the age of seventy-nine, by then a rather shrunken figure who didn't get out much), and you couldn't send *anyone* back to John Sheed. Nor could one very well board her out in London, or send her on a permanent tour of relatives.

The tough decision here was Maisie's. She knew that nobody was going to be good enough for Minny Maloney's son, let alone herself. As an Englishwoman eight years older than her son, and with a toffy voice and manner, she was worse than Minny's worst dreams. Although Min was superficially cordial and once told me stiffly that "Maisie is a good Catholic girl," which was all she ever asked of anyone, or again, "Your mother is a very clever woman," nobody could emanate hostility like Min. You found yourself reaching for your hat and coat when Min put it to you. But Maisie gritted her teeth (literally: she was a fierce teeth-grinder) and said, we'll take her.

It is hard to imagine a less well-suited couple even in the bleak history of mothers-in-law: my grandmother who had sometimes scrubbed floors in Sydney to keep her boys fed, and my mother who couldn't fry an egg without danger pay. Min's life had been circumscribed by hardship, and her small talk was, perforce, back-fence gossip about people no one had ever heard of in London. So my mother's pipings of Newman and his circle crisscrossed endlessly with talk of Bernie and Diddy and Uncle Vin at the Railway Department. I felt, as I turned from the one to the other, as if I were visiting different pavilions at a world's fair. Only long years of this produced at last a common subject matter: us. And a sort of odd couple friendship.

Everybody suffered a little bit. Frank had to labor to keep Min's old world alive for her, and to find her congenial company in the rock quarry of English society. My mother was just plain uncomfortable. Any mother-in-law is bad news. But one who at least subconsciously despises you for not being able to cook or do laundry must be a particular torture. Min used to tell me with glee of how she first met me. Picture a small, viciously antisocial child crawling malignantly about. No one can do anything with him: his misanthropy runs deep in the bone. Then enter an Australian grandmother, fresh from a trip home, and the weasely little politician scampers straight over and sits on her lap, beaming.

This was Min's ace, her ascendancy; she was a real mother, by God, and perhaps that was more important than all your fancy intellectual doings. Maisie was more than willing to concede the point: in fact, she was completely in awe of Min, who could do the work of a whole staff of servants. If Maisie had ever intimately known another average housewife, her admiration might have been qualified. But thank God it wasn't. Because Maisie's unstinting and uncalculating praise of her mother-in-law was one of the few positives in the equation. Minny was queen in the kitchen and queen at the grate: she was also, on the shoe-tying level of life, my real mother.

None of this was ever quite enough for those sensitive Celtic nerve endings. Minny knew exactly where a queen of the kitchen fit into Debrett's peerage. She was, at base, all alone with no one to talk to except Frank, and you could only puff her up for short intervals to make her forget this. To compound the desolation, the Ward absent-mindedness could easily be construed as good old British coldness, and Minny could easily believe that a whole class had rejected her.

Frank's intense concentration on things of the heart, on the nuts and bolts of friendship, was never put to a sterner test. Fortunately, both women had funds of clumsy goodwill for Frank's diplomacy to play with, and somehow he made us all seem like a byword in happy families. And even though by that time my sister was locked in a death-struggle with Min, much grimmer than anything before, I think we were. Especially when Frank was around.

What is interesting about the deal is that in the end everyone came out slightly ahead. When the whole family got to America in the forties, all the attention Min had missed came pouring out of the closet. To American Catholics, Frank's mother was a heroine as such—and the more working class the better. Everything was magically stood on its head. This was the country where you lied upward about the number of floors you'd scrubbed, and where every old hardship was lovingly unwrapped and put in the window. Minny loved America.

But that was a small payoff compared with Maisie's. To put it briefly, Minny made my mother's career possible. In those preliberation days *somebody* had to be sacrificed—although for Min it was no sacrifice compared with the alternatives. So my grandmother took on the pots and pans and the endless baby-sitting—all the trappings of motherhood except the Jocasta complex—while Maisie wrote and lectured like a dervish and published a little.

The publishing seems to have been even more distinctly Josephine Ward's idea than the Guild had been: at any rate, she backed it enthusiastically and staked the new house to £2,000—a sum slightly harder to translate into modern currency than the Roman denarius. The original Ward of Sheed and Ward was to be Leo, but he veered off in his own direction, leaving Maisie to step rather vaguely onto the masthead. Publishing, as those who know can tell you, is what you do when you can't think of anything else to do. It is even more amorphous than starting a magazine or opening a restaurant, those other late-night brainstorms. A publisher simply puts up a soapbox of sorts and hopes that interesting performers will turn up.

Sheed and Ward had a little more on its mind than that. The Modernist crisis in the Church had blown over for the time being, leaving the reformers in shambles. The Vatican had thrown up a Berlin Wall between the Church and the secular world. There would be no further attempts to make doctrines more palatable or the Scriptures more scientific; there would be no flirting with intellectual fashion.

Considering the callow nature of the fashion just then, this taboo makes some sort of evolutionary sense. But meanwhile, it left the Catholic mind with no place to go. Non-Catholics became more than ever convinced that Catholics simply weren't allowed to think (in fact they thought furiously though sometimes in circles). But World War I had rather shaken faith in the March of Thought as well. And such famous postwar converts as Chesterton and Ronald Knox* valued the Church for its sheer steadiness. The doctrine of progress had been methodically blown apart in the trenches, while on the various home fronts, civilization seemed to be plunging into an era of unprecedented silliness ("What's going to happen to the children when there aren't any more grown-ups?" wrote Noel Coward) and ugliness. With Europe possibly on its last legs from its recent attempt to kill itself, Dada, Cubism, and the rest must have seemed like graffiti on a cathedral wall. It was an excellent time for Rome to stand still.

This was the world that young Sheed and Ward confronted in 1927. Speculative theology was down to cautious, house-to-house fighting. There was not much news breaking in that direction, although Ward's, as its impish U.S. employees used to call it, would cover what there was. But with forward progress momentarily blocked, it seemed like a good time to look around and see what we'd got. People had been blindly pushing the Church forward without always knowing quite what they were pushing. So one of Sheed and Ward's first revolutionary books bore the unrevolutionary title *The Spirit of Catholicism* by Karl Adam.

The Catholic literary Revival set out at first to be just that, a revival, and not a new departure. The immediate agenda was to ransack the Church for treasures: to rediscover Aquinas with Jacques Maritain, to collate Christian mysticism with the Oriental variety with E. I. Watkin, to place the Church in the history of culture, and to place

---

* *Always* described as brilliant, Monsignor Ronald Knox was the most famous Anglican clergyman to "Rome it" in this century, and a leading character throughout Sheed and Ward's history.

culture in the foreground of history with Christopher Dawson, and many other wild-eyed projects.* It was like looting the Vatican itself, but not for antiques; this was a live tradition, we were frequently reminded. The chain had held. This was Our Father's House, and we had the run of it. Our patron G. K. Chesterton wrote a book about a man who circles the globe, clawing through jungles and what not, to discover his own home; that was our movement in a nutshell.

This might have been all the excitement my father needed, if he'd been on his own. To find that William of Occam had beaten Bertrand Russell to some punch, or that Duns Scotus or someone just like him had anticipated David Hume's difficulties with cause and effect: this was heady stuff for a boy book-bum from Sydney. "Do you realize that the age that built the cathedrals was prouder of its *philosophers?*" he would say, falling on John of Salisbury with happy cries.

But Maisie of course had to *do* something about all this. If she had been an archeologist, she would have done something Christian about that too: selling her diggings for the poor or mounting her art objects in the slums. The Church was not a living tradition for her unless it physically lived and brought forth life. This towering culture had been built on a gospel of charity, and without charity it was still nothing: the art she so worshipped was just a random collection of paint and stone unless the Spirit breathed through it.

I have never known Maisie closer to ecstasy than the day (Corpus Christi) we visited Assisi in 1947. Clouds of birds welcomed us, still waiting for Saint Francis to come back and feed them, the bus driver explained. (Maisie was probably the only English person on the bus to find this perfectly reasonable.) And then in the shrine itself, there was the living aura of Saint Francis, almost palpable to her, and the frescoes of Giotto: painted just there to honor just that, a gorgeous labor of love.

She wouldn't have felt that way about just any old saint. Francis was the one who had brought kindness back to the Church—a church so theocentric and God-crazed by then that it had forgotten its hum-

---

* The list of authors is endless and beyond the scope of this book. Never has so much talent been found lying about waiting for the right publisher.

bler duties. She certainly wasn't going to let Sheed and Ward make that mistake: to rebuild the glittering edifice and leave out kindness again.

So Sheed and Ward launched itself upon the social gospel. Frank the spoiled Marxist and lifelong Maisie-fan was wholeheartedly with her of course, but Frank the latent aesthete might not have gone in that direction. Two of his boyhood heroes were Belloc and Chesterton, and now he was getting not just to meet them, but to publish them!* So his first idea of publishing was simply more of that. Unlike Maisie, he had perfect literary pitch (especially for Catholics; he had trouble hearing, say, D. H. Lawrence). He wanted real writers, not just worthy people with something to say. The era of the nonbook was still some distance away. And he had a peculiar advantage. So much of his theological list was French or German that even though the books might be jawbreakers in the original, they could be rendered into passable prose by the right translators—Frank himself if necessary. It is a little-noted feature of the Catholic Revival that not only were English-speaking Catholics getting their first real dose of Europe, but they were frequently getting it better written than the Europeans were.

This I consider the English phase of the firm. Going to America in 1933 would alter Sheed and Ward's accent slightly, and give a much fuller rein to Maisie's activism. It would be too much to call the London branch Sheed and the American branch Ward. But in those first years on Pater Noster Row, in the lee of St. Paul's, Frank indulged every dream he might possibly have had about literary Catholic publishing. It was only when he ran out of Bellocs and Chestertons that he had to compromise with mediocrity like a regular publisher.

I don't think he got much more from meeting Chesterton than he already had. He admired the man so much to begin with that it was hard to go on from there and I felt he was too much a fan to be a

* Hilaire Belloc, poet, polemicist, politician and just about anything else that can be done with a mouth or a pencil, was the only one of the famous English Catholics to be born that way. His book on Danton, along with Chesterton's book *Heretics,* first awakened Frank to the notion that one could think and be a Catholic at the same time.

friend. But Belloc was an enormous influence. With his growl and his scowl, he was the most menacing of men, but if he gave you any thought at all, he engaged with you, grappled you close to him, poured his mind into you. Further there was something emblematic about his very face, so that you could practically put him on your crest if you published Catholic books. He embodied, to an almost suspicious extent, the myth of a Catholic Europe, which, in his view, slept fitfully under the sleazy skin of modernity, waiting for a wake-up call. True or not, it was something to be going on with. Just as a hypothesis, it inspired wonderful work which would stand even if the news turned out bad. Belloc's thundering affirmations gave Sheed and Ward something to march to.

But Belloc's personality had much more to it than brilliant bluster. He had at first offered to become a partner in Sheed and Ward, although all he had on hand to contribute was his name, which was a red rag to Protestant England and made Catholics uneasy too. (He believed in his noisy way that the Reformation had denatured England and was indirectly responsible for everything he detested—which was plenty.) But I think, from the amount Frank talked about him, that he was a sort of partner anyway. "Pay me twice as much and I'll do twice as much research," he once said airily, after some critics had savaged him; and this jaunty spirit reinforced and refreshed Frank. "She is a tart," said Belloc of Chesterton's sister-in-law, "and like all tarts she lacks perspective." (I have found this one of the most useful sayings I know, applicable to almost any situation—especially when reviewing the media.) And I imagine Belloc rolling out these quaint aperçus between bursts of Provençal song and Rabelaisian anecdote. This was the real stuff, what Frank had journeyed to find. His black cloak and slouch hat did not look like costume, as Chesterton's rig did, but organic, precisely what Catholic Europe should be wearing during its long winter.

"The Faith is Europe, Europe is the Faith." The odd disciple Evelyn Waugh swallowed this heresy of Belloc's whole and entire, and my father almost did, although Australia would have needed an asterisk. For the first years, Sheed and Ward could have been the house of Belloc, particularly in its emphasis on the French: Paul Claudel,

Henri Ghéon, the young François Mauriac, an original Sheed discovery. Frank's own university course of Latin, French and English might have been prescribed by Belloc himself, who believed that all that was best about England was really Roman. So Frank was more than willing to accept the old curmudgeon's hierarchy and express it through publishing.

Not so Maisie, who saw Belloc rather differently. She knew that young Hilaire had courted an upper-class relative of hers and had been cruelly snubbed, and that his lordly diatribes against the English rich might have something to do with things like that. Maisie was just enough of a snob to see Belloc partly through a class prism, where he looked much smaller and more manageable. Whatever she may have said or written publicly, her private tone about him was chilly. Although she admired his work, she was immune to his manner, and for years she lived in dread of being asked to write his biography. Anyway, in the early thirties she was just about to discover America where "Europe is the Faith" sounded like yesterday's newspaper: it might be true, but so what? It had nothing to do with Dorothy Day's soup kitchen, which began in New York the same year as Sheed and Ward did, or her other gritty new interests. Later, after World War II, Maisie wrote a book called *France Pagan?* which ruefully put paid to the sleeping giant, Catholic Europe, once and for all. So Frank got Belloc and Maisie got Chesterton, who appreciated women profoundly and probably gave them more. Belloc was just the right present for a boy.

It was during this early English phase that I somehow sneaked into the world. Maisie, who had helped Frank to publish on packing boxes, proved very fragile in the matter of childbirth. She was ill before my sister Rosemary was born, and then, after two miscarriages, she was violently ill before me. By mischance, she actually received the last sacraments twice on the same day, which as a glutton for sacraments she claimed not to mind a bit. I was certainly the last throw of the dice, and so I crept reluctantly into the world, like a grumpy old man, nineteen days late, just enough to ruin the Christmas of 1930 for everyone.

Among other trophies, Maisie had lost all her hair, had picked up a nasty scar on her lung and had developed phlebitis, an ailment which requires you to keep your feet up. These were just the afflictions that came to one's attention: I'm sure there were more and worse. Even Maisie, reeling under this load, couldn't have dreamed that the more active half of her life still lay ahead. My earliest memories include seeing Maisie crumple and faint—a tendency that stayed with her right through the thick of things. But otherwise she yielded no ground to any of this health business, and unless Rosemary and I were forcibly reminded of it, we tended to think of her as an exceptionally, almost boringly, healthy woman who yawned a lot.

I was promptly baptized a Catholic, so that was that: the full story of my conversion. Told here for the first time. G. K. Chesterton was my godfather and I allegedly disappeared into his lap and I guess that about ends my store of literary anecdotes too. GK dashed off a drawing on the spot, of a Dominican stealing me from my pram under the noses of a Jesuit and a Benedictine. Nothing the least bit like this has happened, unless I misunderstand something.

I don't remember any more of Chesterton, but I do dimly recall chasing Belloc around the yard with a large branch. "Maisie's boy is verry dangerrrous," he growled. I don't know what it was with me and branches. I had tried the same stunt when I was two on a flock of geese and had wound up with a huge white mother standing on my chest. And still I persisted.

"What's it like being the son of Sheed and Ward?" The question goes back almost as far as I do. It is asked, I think, in the same spirit as the one about Frank and Maisie fighting. It means, do they overpower you intellectually or with personality? Doesn't all that fame make you feel insignificant and hopeless?

If that's the question, I can only shrug. Nobody was overpowering anyone at our place any more than Frank and Maisie were fighting. I placidly assumed I was the house idiot, and I certainly was, compared with Rosemary, who was speed-reading *Lorna Doone* by about the age of four and no doubt finding it superficial. But it was no big deal. By the time I had digested the concept "smart" I had discovered Robin Hood, which seemed to me an infinitely higher calling. So I spent my days crouching and sprinting through the pathetic fringe of woods that rimmed our house, firing homemade arrows from my homemade bow. Everyone was so relieved to have me out of the house (I was a noisy chap) that they encouraged me in my delusions. Obviously Robin Hood was a very great man, and the perfect model for me—much better in my particular case than Cardinal Newman. Those trees of ours seemed like Sherwood Forest to a child's eyes, and I haven't been back to check. (I believe a high-rise apartment building now smothers my hapless hunting ground, my Eden.)

It wasn't exactly Frank's Sydney, but I remember a ballooning feeling of freedom as I strolled around our tumbledown village of Horley, Surrey. "There's such a thing as being too much of a father," Frank once said, in answer to a question about Saint Joseph. And he certainly believed it. Outside of a grim showdown concerning whether I had or had not taken a bath one day (I'd run the tub but neglected to wet the sponge and soap, as lawyer Sheed shrewdly pointed out), the domestic discipline was too mild to remember. "Wait till your father gets home" was usually quite enough. I don't know whether I was scared of him, but I was sure as hell scared of waiting, which could transform him or anyone into a monster. (Frank knew this better than anyone, and even used waitmanship to cow grown-ups at work. "Let's talk about this on Monday," was enough to quell any office malcontent.) The other threat, our little neutron bomb, was an object called the wooden spoon. This innocuous stirring utensil developed magical powers over the years: sparks, razor blades, who knew what it contained? As I fingered it gingerly in the kitchen drawer, it gave away nothing. But I didn't dare brave it. "I'll fetch the wooden spoon," Min would say, and the case was closed.

As for my parents' fame, it just never came up. By the time I knew they were supposed to be Somebody, I was used to them. Just old Mummy and Daddy. Nothing had changed. Certainly, for the first ten years or so, the son of Sheed and Ward could have been anyone, an intense little soccer player who was nearly driven into the ground like a tent stake every time he tried to head the ball; a lounger, a collector. Toys were toys in those days, perfect miniatures of Daimlers and Reos and London taxicabs; then as war approached, tanks, battleships (I owned all the British ones—and were there any others?) and war planes. A friend up the street called Norman Edmunds used to play total war with me, but most of our time was spent just deploying our arsenals. The guns didn't fire, and it seemed undignified just to push each other's stuff over, so we concentrated on occupying the heights and reinforcing the flanks all afternoon.

Edmunds also wanted to form a secret organization for blowing up railways. He'd found an abandoned bit of branch line in the woods, and he fancied he could make a bomb with a tin can and various items from the medicine chest that would blow it to smithereens. So we would go out and plant these objects by the track and dash for cover. Nothing ever seemed to happen at the time, but the next day Edmunds would turn up at school with a piece of twisted metal which he claimed came from last night's wreck.

The organization, which might someday have amounted to something under such inspired leadership, broke up over the admission of girls. Edmunds was for it, but I felt they would only weaken us. We couldn't take girls along on our bombing raids, for instance. Edmunds agreed to that, but thought that perhaps they could roll bandages for us or something. The whole thing degenerated surprisingly when he began to josh me rather heavily about being sweet on his little sister, which was quite possible. Although I disapproved of girls intellectually, I was forever being smitten by them and denying it hotly. Frank even used to accuse me of having fallen head over heels for Shirley Temple, which, since it must have happened before the age of reason, remained unarguable. I thought it a low blow.

The last time I heard from mad bomber Edmunds, who must have been all of ten by then, was after I got to the United States in 1940. He wrote with some of his cock-sparrow relish to tell me that if I'd been climbing (I was a fanatical tree climber) my favorite oak in his yard on the right day, I'd have been blown sky-high by a German air raid. So he'd seen his dream of gorgeous explosions come true. By his standards, it was a sober letter, and I hoped the war wouldn't proceed to knock all the lunacy out of him. (I also hope he is not in the War Ministry today.)

Other faces fade from the school photo. Oddly enough I remember the name *and* face of the class butt, the fat boy we made fun of when time hung heavy, but there's no point bringing it up now. Let's pray that wartime rationing worked its magic on him and his torpid personality. As suggested in *Transatlantic Blues* I felt bad about leaving my chums to their fates in 1940, while I high-tailed it for the Fatted Calf.

I also learned at that school—St. Hilary's in Horley—the value of charisma, which was then called animal magnetism, and which I hope someday settles down with the right name. I didn't learn it from myself, God knows, but from an affable lad called Walker. From the day he strolled in, everybody wanted to be liked by Walker, to be part of his set. I can't remember any of his accomplishments, if he *had* any accomplishments, but a salute from Walker in the village streets was like a royal blessing. I have met others such since—I suppose Jack Kennedy was the ultimate Walker—and the maddening invariable about them is that they seem to appeal to both sexes pretty nearly equally, so that it is bad form even to envy them. It is humbling, but I suppose useful, to know that one is not one of these Chosen, and will have to get by, as they say in baseball, with junk.

Though, as noted, I hated to leave, the cumulative effect of St. Hilary's was actually to drive me to America even more certainly than the war did. Because it bequeathed me a piercing cockney accent which carried for blocks like a dog whistle and which no amount of good example in the home could remedy. My mother, the sometime radical, was horrified. "You won't get anywhere in England with that accent," she groaned apologetically. Even an American one would be preferable, she told me—although she might have had second thoughts if she'd foreseen the strange overlay of New Jersey I was about to pour over my cockney. I am drawn to the demotic and simply pile it onto all the other demotics I've picked up, throwing out nothing.

The accent problem underlines a contradiction in the Sheeds which they passed on pretty much unresolved to me. They themselves spoke with cockneys and to cockneys all day long—it was their work—without defilement. And since neither of them could even *imitate* other accents, they were all at sea with a son who, like a sickly child, picked up everything that was going around, every bit of aural contamination, each debased vowel. Since their support of the local church and school was unstinting, and possibly crucial, they couldn't very well haul me out and ship me off to a posh school. But they couldn't have me talking like a guttersnipe either. Their solution, which I find touchingly characteristic, was to take me all the way to another continent, where the problem would simply disappear.

My unclean accent also testifies to the amount of time I had begun to log on the street, where I wasn't the son of Frank and Maisie in the least, but just a twerp named Sheed. The truth is, my sister and I got on each other's nerves to the point where no house was big enough for us. "Can't you take Wilfrid with you?" Maisie would say hopefully to Rosemary and her pals, and off we would trudge, me sniffing and babbling and Rosemary cursing the day she was born. "Couldn't you just disappear, Willy?" After all, she was three years older than me, with her own life to lead. "I suppose we can't simply arrange to lose him?"

Since I found her friends infinitely remote creatures, who wouldn't even play Robin Hood with a chap, I was as eager to get lost as anyone. But for a while, they were the only game in town, so I tagged along grimly. And there were some rough years before I got my freedom. Once Rosemary plugged me in the forehead with a hairbrush because I wouldn't leave her alone, and she received a scalding rebuke for it which scarred her a lot longer than the hairbrush scarred me (I overplayed my hand that day by saying, "I wish she was dead," thus forfeiting whatever goodwill I'd built up as a victim).

Our final showdown was a shoot-out on the kitchen floor. For an eternity it seemed we rolled over each other, pulling hair and banging heads dismally on the stone floor until it slowly dawned on me that I'd achieved parity, at least in willpower. I can still see someone sitting across the room (grandmother? a maid?) watching us, but I could be wrong. Either way, my phantom witness did nothing to stop us: might as well let them have it out once and for all, and be done with it, it reasoned correctly. After that, Rosemary took to criticizing my clothes—easy picking, then as now—and finally, we became fast friends and have been ever since. (I suspect her memory of the fight, if she has one, is of some brief skirmish; but that's how I feel about her and her damn hairbrush too.)

The age of reason couldn't come a minute too soon for me. Up to then, and a little after, I was given to howling tantrums, which could only be cured by a fat, occasional cook of ours called Lizzy, who would shake gelatinously with mirth until I was done. I was also fast to start fights and even faster to get out of them. From those murky years, I understand vandalism perfectly.

The same spastic energy, which nowadays flings itself into concocting the odd paragraph—the great editor Bob Giroux says that "writing is energy"—took itself out just as easily on religion when I discovered it at age seven. Having a church in one's backyard is like owning your own theater. Maisie's readings from the Gospels and from a children's book called *Six o'Clock Saints,* by Joan Wyndham, provided the drama. Thus equipped, and feeling like a Dead End Kid masquerading as an altar boy, I would fairly throb to the stations of the cross: Jesus falls for the third time, Jesus is nailed to the cross, ouch!—my kneeling on hard wood for three hours on Good Friday till both knees burned brightly was hardly enough to make up for all that.

My actual work around the altar was rather less sure of itself. The first time out, at the noble rite of Benediction, I got tangled up with the censer, a tiny tub of incense suspended by three wires which have to be pulled up and down in unison, like the cables on an old French elevator, or all hell breaks loose. I discovered in myself that day a grain of incompetence that would again and again render all the energy in the world superfluous: first one wire came up, then another until the tub tilted like a dying ship and the hot cake of incense flew to the altar carpet.

A priest is not supposed to swear, and I wouldn't have known what the words meant anyway, but I had the distinct sensation of being sworn at as Father Healy swept at the damage with his vestments while not letting the show collapse completely. My serving retained this cliff-hanging quality throughout its career: where would the boy strike next? My father topped me once by carrying the Communion plate to the wrong end of the altar rail (it's hard to explain the grandeur of this mistake if you haven't been there), but it's cold comfort to know that these mental lapses are in the blood, and that no earthly glory can disguise the Mass Book removed at the wrong moment, like pulling out someone's chair from under him, or the wine poured over the priest's shoes.

Maisie, bless her, thought that these were all signs of genius: she had come from a long line of such geniuses. Frank thought mistakes were very funny, and told stories about himself which made him sound like the village idiot. In this light my own blunders seemed merely to add to the family treasury, but in other lights, I wasn't so sure. Other people just didn't seem to relish clumsiness as much as we did. And I hesitated to tell my schoolmates about how my father had put both socks on the same foot and gone looking for the other one, like W. C. Fields, because I wasn't dead sure that they would laugh, and if they didn't, it would be awful. Like all of them, I wanted to have absolutely average parents with no characteristics whatever.

One characteristic that my father in particular did have, which helped in this respect I suppose, was chronic invisibility. Because it was during these years that Frank was somehow starting his American branch, and throwing in a lecture tour per trip to help finance it. This, of course, was real energy, as opposed to my lip-frothing variety, and I still don't know how he did it. Although he was a whiz at delegating authority, this creates its own kind of work: cleaning up other people's messes, or arriving to find mini-mutinies in swing, usually led by small fry whose brief authority had gone straight to their heads.

Frank was forever shuttling from one Sheed and Ward to the other, where he was greeted, like a father, with either tearful welcome ("Thank God you got here in time") or unspoken resentment ("We were doing fine without you"). I believe it was a dim memory of one of these latter visits that led me years later to write a novel called *Office Politics*, set in a magazine which has since been identified for me authoritatively as *The New Republic*, the *Reporter* and *Time*, among others.

I was barely aware of Frank's opening to the West in the thirties—hell, I didn't even know what he did in London. All I knew was that he brought back rather unusual presents: a Charlie McCarthy dummy which had the whole village trying to throw its voice, and the score of something called *The Hot Mikado* illustrated with manic black faces of a kind I didn't know existed. But these seemed more to be aspects of my father than of another country. There was a Sindbad the

Sailor—or as he preferred, Whitebeard the Pirate—aura about Frank's travels that suggested strange kingdoms. When I was three he wrote to me about an engine driver "dressed all in yellow" who asked, "Where's Wilfrid? I wanted to let him drive this engine." A year later, the subject was one Captain Thunderer ("If we find him, we'll run slap bang into him, and that will be the end of him. And a good thing too") and Red Eagle, another of my admirers. After one visit, he came back with a different shape—or perhaps he did it at home while I was out playing. How my father changed his shape was a mystery, but not a gripping one. He seemed about the same to me fat or thin, black-haired or gray; within five minutes, it was the way he'd always looked.

What had happened in fact was this. Frank had been driving himself at such a breakneck pace, in his lifelong quest to be in two places at once, that a kindly woman doctor friend—possibly at Maisie's urging—concocted a heart murmur for him which called for complete, abandoned rest. Frank's respect for authority caused him to buy the murmur, although he couldn't feel a thing, and his awesome capacity for resting completed the damage.

When Frank took a day off, it was really off—all cricket and crosswords and a little something for the inner man. This made him a treat to go out with, but it also blew him up within weeks to what he liked to call "gentleman's portly," an advertising felicity that pleased him. Becoming overweight would have been a funny way to treat a heart problem, and indeed, it may have helped cause one many years later. But the only effect for now was that a skinny, dashing Australian became overnight a fat man running for a bus. But in those days all parents were fat, so he just melted into the crowd, to my, I suppose, approval.

As the decade wore on, Maisie began to join Frank on his American trips, taking on these foreign aspects too (i.e. peculiar presents for us), along with the prized invisibility. But where Frank always seemed to drum up fascinating shipboard encounters (Little girl: "Are you Alistair Sim?" F: "Well, he says I am, but I say I'm not"), all that happened to Maisie was that she almost invariably got seasick, and Frank would go below every night to read her the menu with lip-licking gusto.

Of course, we only wanted them to be invisible when our friends were around. Although we loved to have them both around the house, they rather cramped our style socially. Maisie was convinced she was bad with children and this conviction just about paralyzed her. Alone with one or two of my friends, she would make desperate little stabs at small talk, leaning forward with a tensely warm smile to ask, "How do you like your school?" which just startled them and led nowhere.

My father, on the other hand (and this shows how you can't win with kids), was wonderful with children, playing the clown at birthday parties and such till they were sick with laughter, and I *still* wasn't satisfied for reasons I didn't dare name. I think I felt, "These are my friends, not yours. Don't you dare take them from me," but at the same time, "He's my father, not yours; he should be doing this for me, not you." (I have no trouble with the doctrine of Original Sin.) At one party, I remember a strange feeling of horror at adult berserkness, as such. This big, red face was darting and swooping among the balloons, and the little guests seemed to be screeching with fear, not laughter. That was my father? I imagine the children of comedians undergo this sensation often.

This was strictly Frank's party style, I never saw it any other time, and I now wonder whether he thought that "being good with children" might be good enough for other people's children, but not quite for his own. Because, although he was ceaselessly funny with us, the broad slapstick was strictly for the crowd just as the theology-made-simple was for the crowd. He and Maisie had an a priori faith in the excellence of their own children which might have put a strain on us to live up to—except that they assumed we were living up to it whatever we did. Or perhaps it was just that a crowd was a crowd, a different kind of creature altogether which required simpler methods. (His humor with us c. 1937 took the form of endless puns, which he dropped completely when we came to America—either because they had done their educational work or because he no longer had the London *Times* crossword to spur him on.)

Maisie's stiffness also disappeared in private, where she was, in my book, wonderful with children. I don't know where she got this thing about children anyway—probably from a malicious sibling who shall be nameless. The fact is that she was awkward with strangers of *all* ages, but that this was not necessarily unattractive. Self-assurance can sometimes put people off just as much as shyness can: especially when, as with Maisie, the shyness so obviously *is* shyness, and not some mask of superiority. Maisie made many friends in the uncomfortable silences of her life. And her diffidence worked like a coiled spring in her public speaking. That quavering passion of hers could almost be the sound of a spring vibrating upon release.

Privately, I remember best her reading aloud to us in a lovely, tireless voice, not just the religious stuff, but secular books proper to our ages (I'd heard all of Dickens between nine and twelve, and more of Walter Scott than I cared for—I always voted against another Scott). Certain passages she read with a syrupy enthusiasm that seemed a little faked—but this, like her shyness, was so manifestly charged with goodwill that I never minded it till adolescence, when one minds everything.

Her reading of Saint Luke's Christmas Gospel, followed by a nap and then a trudge in the snow to Midnight Mass did more to make me *feel* Catholic than anything so far. I think being waked up for it had something to do with this, and the bright snow (or was there really snow that year? There is now) and the hot soup afterward. One had entered a brotherhood, no doubt about it. The Church was not just a family secret after all.

This came just in time. The year one gives up Santa Claus is a year of stern decision. Although I claimed to have Voltaired the whole Saint Nick question out for myself by measuring the chimney, and so on, in fact I got it from Rosemary and her fast set. No Santa Claus, eh? So what else has to go around here? I wasn't going to play the straight man ever again. Three Wise Men following a star? Tell it to the Marines.

I recovered from this shattering blow to faith partly because of the aforementioned Father Healy, who impressed me by saying Mass with such matter-of-fact simplicity that he might indeed have been preparing a meal. Healy was a robust, well-set-up man, in the manner of the actor Jack Hawkins, and he certainly would never have fobbed me off with a contemptible pagan fable like Santa Claus. On the same principle, I believed that if a big strapping fellow like this felt that Christ was worth giving up marriage for—I assumed that this was tough, people said so—then Christ was surely no fairy tale.

Father Healy was, in short, my good priest, without whom it is impossible to get a toehold on Peter's rock: a man of such archaic integrity that younger readers will just have to take my word for it. He taught Sunday school pretty much by the book, as he had to. He didn't weasel about hell or purgatory or the terrifying risks of mortal sin: if the Lord ordered up brimstone, brimstone it was. But his manner completely undercut this part of the message. He could deliver the most hair-raising information in such a kind, it's-going-to-be-all-right voice that it still seemed like a religion of love.

Of course, it was all geared for eight-year-olds, for whom eternal fire means, conceptually, no longer than five minutes; but I gather that it makes a difference whether your teacher rather likes the idea or not. Some kids who get their views about hell from priests who seem ready to light the first faggot themselves never recover from it. In an atmosphere of love, you can swallow anything. "Do you think there are many people in hell?" I asked Frank one day. "I go up and down on that," he said, "but at this particular moment I tend to think there are rather a lot."

I suppose now that he was talking about authors. Anyway, hellfire put a little pep into my own confessions. I was playing for big stakes now; I might not be able to imagine hell but I knew for sure that it was the biggest. Kings and emperors dropped in all the time—it was the *dernier cri* in its field.

These supposedly morbid doctrines, which are said to haunt Calvinists and others all their days, did little observable damage in my crowd. To get small boys to behave at all, no threat is too great. Just to keep us from giggling through Mass, hellfire was hardly enough. Because deep down we were smug little beggars who knew we were a million miles from mortal sin. Only when sex came along to wipe the smile off our faces did hell seem like a real possibility: then the picture-book place with the pitchforks and red-flannel devils suddenly became (for me at least) a cold, black hole just beyond the edge of the universe. The fact that we'd accepted the deal so lightly for so long made it all the harder to shake off later when it mattered.

In sum, the Church offered a pretty neat prepubescence, if you were lucky and naturally buoyant, but then it seemed to run out of suggestions. In the teens, we simply acted out the catechism years for real, grimly applying the childhood answers to the roaring blood and squirming flesh of adolescence—which, it hardly needs saying, had crept up on us with even less warning than on other people. The results could be tragicomic, with the priest solemnly holding up the Boy Scout manual to some masturbation-scarred veteran, worn out from last night's fiery struggle with the Tempter, and the night before's. What the hell, *they* were the ones who had told us we would burn forever: and if there's one thing an adolescent *can* imagine (unlike a child) it's burning forever.

Whether, under this intolerable pressure, one decided "it ain't necessarily so" and began edging toward the exit, or whether one thought there must be some rational explanation for all this from an otherwise sensible institution, depended a lot on the prepubescent underpinnings. If you were bored spitless at ten, you could be out by fifteen; if you were unnaturally good, you were probably out too.

No danger of the latter in my case. I don't know at what point Christ's personal taste for sinners impinged on me, but I liked it right away. I already identified with villains, especially Long John Silver and his worthless cronies. If Robin Hood had been a law-and-order man, I wouldn't have given him a tumble. Of course, these men set a very fast pace which it was hard for me to keep up with just then. But if I did feel like telling a small lie or not saying my prayers, by george, I went ahead with it—if only to fill my confessional quota: four lies and three disobedients (the numbers being reversible), loss of temper, disrespect for parents.

One would have felt like a ninny going in there with nothing, yet it would be a sin to make anything up. Besides, my sister had told me that the Just Man falls seven times a day and if I thought I was better than *that,* then I was guilty of the big one itself: Pride, baby, the sin that was too much for even the Holy Ghost. I racked my brain trying to think how I could manage to fall that often: it was like figuring out how to spend a million dollars in one evening. The Just Man must be quite a guy.

There is no way not to make childhood sound cute, unless it is plagued by illness or hardship (a big "unless"). It was cute in this case because it was so damn serious. I would hitch up my short pants and stroll nonchalantly into Father Healy's box to unload my tiny wares. He would hear me out with proper gravity—even a smile would have snapped the spell forever, though I couldn't see him too well through the muzzy screen. He may have turned his head away now and then. Communion the next day was even more serious, an absolute riot of seriousness. I was talking to Christ right in there, under the breastbone, which meant pulling out all the stops, furrowing the brow, smoldering the eyes, and looking, I imagine, slightly ill. Then out into the dirty old world to shoot arrows at the Sheriff of Nottingham for hours upon hours.

I could capture this strange *persona* slightly better if I could remember something called the "William books." These were my favorite reading for a while, but they were so perfect of their kind that they have left no trace at all. William was a scruffy, presumably resourceful boy much like myself, I fancied. My confessions were William's confessions, as I imagined them. But I'm sure that if I looked at the pages now, they would yield me nothing. Just bad writing by a canny old lady, which in fact they were.

The coming of war was filtered through this paradise, blighting it not one bit. The *Anschluss* with Austria is the first I heard of it. I was riding on the London underground, and I made out the headline letter by letter on somebody's newspaper. "Hitler invades Austria." Huh. Well, maybe England would have to do something about it, put the fellow back where he belonged.

By Munich, I felt what I thought was real concern but what feels from here suspiciously like exhilaration. We listened to the radio with grim expressions, none grimmer than mine. Of course we should fight, we'd given our word. And we had the Navy. But then, the crowds applauding the billboards (English papers plastered their headlines on these things, the gamier the better), which said "Peace in Our Time," communicated such relief that it too was sort of conta-

gious, and I thought, Well, we'll fight them some other time. I inten-
sified my collection of Players cigarette cards featuring the world's latest war planes. Sheed at least would be prepared.

It's hard to convey, or even to recall, the seeping arrival of the
sense of proportion. When in 1939 war could be kept waiting no
longer, the right feeling seemed again to be relief, although surrounded by question marks, and I certainly went along with that. The
nightmare of being pursued everywhere by a bully was over. Whatever
happened next could not be worse than that.

Yet the emotion I remember most strongly from those months
was a genuine uncalculating sadness when the Australian rugby tour
was cancelled. A cousin of mine named Desmond Carrick was on the
team, and this was probably the last chance this glamorous figure
would get to play for his country (in fact he came down with osteo-
myelitis a short while later, and that was that). I'd never guessed that
war meant things like that.*

Nor that it meant the small herd of London refugees who landed
on sleepy little Horley to escape the expected air raids. A loud, vulgar
lot, triumphantly out of place in a country town; if anybody had to be
bombed, they seemed to me a happy choice. I can still picture a bunch
of them persuading a girl to climb a tree and then hollering, "We can
see your knickers [underpants]." Life would never be the same.

I wasn't there to see the other changes. No doubt the war cancelled the annual London-to-Brighton walking race, featuring scores
of earnest men waddling to beat the band, right past our front gate,
while lesser men on bicycles tried to feed them. That cancellation
alone would probably have broken my heart.

Standing at that gate, I seem to see the whole of prewar England
puffing past. A Morris Minor rolls onto its head in a ditch: the owner
jumps out, flips it back onto its wheels and drives off. Our own suc-
cession of cars is so primitive that the back tires fall off one of them
one day and we don't even notice it as we tootle along: Rosemary and

* Desmond's brother Vincent would probably have made the next Australian
cricket team, but I believe *he* caught malaria in the jungle. For this and other reasons, I have trouble worrying about ex-athletes who cry over losing their fast balls
or whatever.

I, sitting in the dickey (or rumble seat), observe crowds forming to laugh and cheer. Well done! Frank drives cheerfully on.

Another fossil, which Frank had painted himself, came out of the experience with flies permanently embedded in the paint. This may or may not be the one that he finally drove into a handy haystack to get rid of. Or the one Belloc jumped out of in horror two blocks from the Atheneum Club: it was all this doughty republican's reputation was worth to be seen arriving in such a heap. Or it could have been the one Frank sold for one shilling and sixpence in stamps after he'd had a slight accident, which mercifully ended the whole farrago (in the public interest: he decided he was just too damn absentminded to drive).

Across the street from my gate is a hotel trimmed in businessman's neo-Tudor. The cars there are a very different affair: long, sleek things that you can actually start without leaving your seat; that is, you don't have to crank them and leap in wildly, as you do with our cars. Portly men of affairs in tweed and gray serge alight from these battleships to discuss the state of the pound over lunch. Just about fifty feet away, but they might as well be in another world from ours. I know even then that none of us will ever cross that street but I'll admit that at the age of eight, I thought that world looked rather super.

Horley, I suppose, was doomed anyway, war or no war. Twenty-five or so miles from London, its hash as a bedroom community was no doubt being settled then and there by the men in the posh hotel. I think now of an old cartoon of a couple doggedly basking in tropical decor on a roof garden, with a second panel showing the skyscrapers and factories looming above them. The first panel was my dream Horley in 1939. There were probably model industries going up all around, but all I can remember is a gasworks which entered my dreams: I would imagine it getting louder and louder (though it was not noisy in real life) as I approached, until we were both screaming our lungs out. That, I supposed, was the future, and I hated it.

All this while, Frank and Maisie were starting their little revolution in America and somewhat lesser one in London, while plodding into town for their street-corner chores, and training the other speakers into a crack arguing corps; so one imagines them just glancing busily off Horley. But they managed to do a few things there. Right off, they converted our smallish library into the local parish church, just big enough for the Catholic residents. When the crowds began to overflow, Frank and Maisie donated our backyard to the aforementioned Quonset hut, where my father appointed himself unofficial choirmaster. The parishioners had been of the sort who could be heard mumbling their beads around the world in those days, but Frank had them all bawling Gregorian chant quite expertly in no time. He absolutely refused to assume mediocrity in anyone; just let me at them, was his attitude.

I think that Frank and Maisie and even precocious Rosemary took some turns giving religious instruction in the library. They could hardly sit down without giving religious instruction to someone or other. But for the time being, they spared me. Frank told me about cricket, and Maisie opened another Dickens. Frank took me to the zoo where the monkeys scrambled eggs in their hats (I've still never seen anything funnier), and Maisie cracked another Walter Scott. The Church was the air we breathed, so there was no need to go on about it.

I did have a theological thought once, and it saved my bacon at a bad moment. I had hidden out in the Quonset hut to escape from a piano lesson, and Frank had tracked me there remorselessly. I felt like Pepe Le Moko trapped in the bell tower. It didn't occur to me, in this fix, to appeal for sanctuary, but I did the next best thing: I tried to fake a religious spasm.

"What are you doing in here? You know Miss Bird is waiting." All aflutter no doubt. I dug my face into my hands. "I wanted to be with God," I muttered from my spasm. "But God is everywhere," said Frank, "so you might as well go outside." "Oh, he's only *everywhere* there," I said. This struck my father as pretty profound and sufficiently funny (his weakness) and he sent Miss Bird packing, or so I like to think. (My getaway line now strikes me as pretty profound, too, considering I had never even heard of Gertrude Stein.)

The interesting thing about this reminiscence is that I don't strictly remember any of it. Frank told me the punch line years later, and the rest is constructed of scraps: pianos, Miss Bird indeed, spasms. Ah, the secrets of the novelist.

The most characteristic of my parents' little dips into Horley life concerned a group known to me simply as the Farmfield boys. These were certainly the warmest, friendliest grown-ups I'd met. The first and nicest to make himself felt was a fellow who looked exactly like Jack Dempsey, the boxer, and who pitched forward in a dead faint, straight as a tree, while we were singing the Credo side by side.

The Farmfield boys, it was explained, were unpredictable. In fact, it turned out that Farmfield was a home for the criminally retarded. Pitifully downscale, to judge from the ones who were allowed out: kleptomaniacs in a small way of businesses, maybe a becalmed flasher or two, nothing much worse than my own raciest confessions or Norman Edmunds' bomb plots. They came to our place for singsongs and we went to theirs and of all the people I've met who were supposed to be good with children, these were easily the best: children themselves, I suppose, and delighted to be back in a family. Frank would bang the piano erratically, until one of their members would tactfully replace him; we linked arms and sang "Roll Out the Barrel" and "Knees Up, Mother Brown."

How my parents got hooked up with them, I'll never know. Frank and Maisie simply took what was there, and these odd groups sprang up wherever we went. Maisie was particularly on guard against a Mrs. Jellyby* complex: saving the world, while your children get rickets. This village right here was always the place to start, and by 1940, Maisie was helping people with their victory gardens or whatever those self-help patches were called in England, as if she had nothing better to do anywhere.

Maisie's unrequited love of the land is an important strand in her life, because it explains her way of looking at things. I still think of her as not so much a fisher of souls, as the Bible recommends, but as a farmer of souls. Her postwar book *France Pagan?* has this agricultural ring to it. She was to find the French countryside spiritually desolate, with a lone priest tucking up his skirts and bicycling forlornly from

* A character in Dickens' *Bleak House.*

village to village, like a missionary in China, not a priest in proud France. A land without God was to her like a field full of weeds and broken bottles, and these were not just words from a wordsmith. She was always hanging around real farming and trying to get into it herself. She couldn't have picked a worse passion, because you can't combine farming with *anything* else, let alone transatlantic publishing.

She knew it, but she never gave up. In 1933 Maisie bought a farm near Horley (which incidentally is what got us out of London) and tried to work it herself. Maisie was edified the first night when the Irish boys she'd hired stayed up late saying the rosary; less edified the next morning when the cows tried to break into the house demanding a milking. It would be like that all the way. Finally, having christened the joint "Misery Farm" after a song of the period ("We're miserable, sooo mis-erable, down on Misery Farm"), Maisie reluctantly hired a manager called Mr. Rosier and pulled out for civilization.

But she kept looking back, and we continued to visit the old dump at regular intervals, wading through miles of mud while my mother grew starry-eyed over the latest reports of egg production, or whatever the hell they grew there (nothing but mud as far as the eye could see).

These long marches effectively cured Rosemary and me of any desire to make it a tradition. We used to twit Maisie in soggy desperation about her jolly old "miracle of growth," while our father, the city boy, smiled conspiratorially. But Maisie didn't care. She had her miracle and she hardly heard us. Her problem was not oafish kids, but how to practice her obsession. As frustrated as any artist deprived of his tools, she would suddenly wedge a chicken coop into our vegetable garden, or later, in America, would keep a cow in a neighbor's field— only to be puzzled when the milk tasted strangely of garlic. There were no easy solutions for Maisie.

The decision to move to the United States seemed to put an end to all that, though it didn't quite, as the cow indicates. In other respects, it was quite a sundering choice, much more so than I could have believed possible. I assumed, for instance, that I would still hear my favorite radio shows over there, "The Band Wagon," starring Arthur Askey, "Monday Night at Eight" with Jack Warner, and so on, and that I could still pop down to the sweetshop to pick up a copy of *Film Fun*, which ran comic strips of the more smashing comedians getting eternally caught in the wrong bathing huts. (I'd been to the seaside myself, where black-faced minstrels still did skits and Punch and Judy whapped each other round the clock, and like the rest of *lumpen* England, I couldn't get enough of bathing-hut jokes.) I took it for granted that I could still play soccer and my new love, cricket, and go home to bangers and mash.

I was going to leave the frightful denouement of these hopes to a later chapter, leaving the reader in the position of a Victorian subscriber waiting for Little Nell to die. But I find in listing the expectations, I've already done the trick, and no more needs to be said, except that it wasn't so bad.

Meanwhile, England itself seemed to be becoming another country. Soldiers rolling through on trucks, singing, "We're going to hang out the washing on the Siegfried Line," seemed to have replaced all the walkers and cyclists and ancient cars on the London-to-Brighton road, and even the posh businessmen went underground. At home we took turns pinning up the black crepe so that no chink of light would alert the enemy to the whereabouts of Horley or the Sheeds. I remember years later my small daughter zestfully taping the windows to ward off a hurricane: preparing for war was just like that at our place.

At school we dug an L-shaped trench and piled sandbags around it and used the whole conglomerate for our own eclectic warfare, involving cap guns for effect and slingshots and bows and arrows for business. Being the kind of mutt who collects the arrows in no-man's-land (a barely possible metaphor for book criticism), I came within a fraction of losing my right eye to a sluggish but metal-tipped arrow which drifted like an afterthought from the enemy line. I had filed this incident away, along with the BB I once took in the chest, from point-blank range, and the headfirst fall downstairs onto a stone floor, age six, under the heading of All in a Child's Day's Work until I read the life of James Thurber and realized what a lifetime of torment that fraction of an inch had spared me. Thurber's arrow, equally accidental, finally cost him his sight and his sanity.

We didn't think of the war as phony that first year, not in my crowd. This was all there was to war, so far as we knew, and we were merrily bang in the middle of it. The Nazis, exhausted by now from the loss of the battleship *Graf Spee* and of the odd U-boat, each of which pinpricks was headlined like the Great Turning Point, would soon have to make a despairing lunge at the Maginot Line where they would run smack-dab into those much-photographed tank traps in which their vaunted machines would flounder and burst into flames. I had recently seen a newsreel of our latest antitank guns, which produced a conflagration like unto the Fire of London within seconds, and which as quickly cancelled my dreams of becoming a tank commander; and *that*, I thought, was that as far as the war was concerned. The rest was mopping up.

This I left to our latest swaggering heroes, the RAF. A film called *The Lion Has Wings* was my authority on this. I had had to wait outside the cinema all afternoon to get an adult to take me in, because the second feature was X-rated (be twelve or begone), so my blood was already up in a general sort of way. And seeing the brave lads giving Jerry what-for was just what the doctor ordered. In their Wellington bombers (soon to be outmoded), the RAF would reduce the Reich to rubble in nothing flat, if that's the way the swine wanted it. An Australian cousin called Frank Leaney dropped by one day, a lanky, dashing man, well known for swimming through shark warnings off Sydney beaches, and he flew a Wellington. What chance did a poor Messerschmitt have? (Frank died over Germany a year or so later.)

As for the French *poilu*—well, M. Belloc was our expert on him, and on the advanced weaponry at the brave *poilu*'s disposal. If the enemy had any new weapons too, we didn't hear about it. We pictured them using pretty much the same stuff as we dug out of the picture books of World War I: horse-drawn cannon on rickety wheels, and canisters of poison gas—and we knew the answer to that one. Everyday as we strapped on our smelly little gas masks for drill, we felt invulnerable: Jerry wouldn't even harm a child this time. "Underneath the spreading chestnut tree," we warbled (having removed the masks), "Mr. Chamberlain said to me/If you want to get your gas masks free/Join the local ARP [air-raid protection]." The Germans would lose because they had no sense of humor—certainly nothing to match this rich stuff, or "Kiss me good night, Sergeant Major," either.

I even knew all about German humor, because some priests had come from there in '37 or so to study Frank's methods on the street corner, after which they grilled him as follows: "They laughed. Why?" And "More wit. What was it?" Such heavy fellows didn't have a Chinaman's chance against the laughing lads who rolled past our house on their way to Dunkirk and Tobruk and Arnhem and all the five bloody years ahead.

Still, for some reason, and with victory in the bag, we were definitely leaving for America. I suppose I consoled myself that we weren't missing much: it would have been cowardly to miss a really good war. But I can't remember, because before we left, the Germans had suddenly by-passed my beloved Maginot Line, tank traps and all, and were on their way. The impossible had happened, and I can only remember a sense of black terror, as if a horror movie had turned out to be real and the monsters had stalked into the audience. No loss of faith was ever more brutal. It seemed that there *was* such a thing as an unstoppable enemy and an unhappy ending and that there was no Robin Hood (he'd have gone over to the enemy right away).

And we learned it all so quickly. The Dunkirk miracle, as we called it, and then Mr. Churchill's fine words, which were so perfect for ten-year-olds, dispersed this sense of fate, or lightened it, but it burrowed deep, in me at least, and nothing since then in the way of world or personal disaster has ever shocked me in the same way. A disease *can* be incurable, you can't argue with it, and death may be permanent. Although I still believed in the afterlife and would continue to, part of me wouldn't have been surprised to hear it had been called off. Dead seemed awfully dead after 1940. And all because of the fall of France. So much for wartime propaganda.

We kissed Horley goodbye and lingered a few days in London as a sort of limbo, and I'm glad we did. Although we'd spent a year in Ealing when I was six (and seen George VI's coronation on premature television at the home of a scientist-friend), I had no very clear picture of the London essence, the thing people compare when they compare cities, as opposed to the featureless nine-tenths of a city that they throw away. In the twilight of the Phony War, London seemed mightily majestic, gray but strong, definitely worth saving.

But we would soon be back. My parents artfully fudged this issue, because I wanted to take all my various collections with us, which would have made me the most cumbersome traveler since Wallis Simpson or until Elizabeth Taylor. Regretfully, I abandoned my tiny ships and tanks, little guessing the fortune they would someday be worth, and I have never collected anything else from that day to this, except for a few ballplayers' autographs, which were never more than an excuse to bask in a great man's presence.

If you had told me that in just a few years I would not *want* to come back, that I was in fact sailing toward my eventual home, I would have told you to stick it in your hat. You just don't know your Sheed, I would have said. But as it turns out, neither did I.

The HouseThat Frank Built

WHAT *HAD* THE SHEEDS BEEN UP TO IN AMERICA? THE OCCA-
sional smiling visitor (American smiles always seemed to be bigger
than regular people's entire faces) and a nine-year-old's harum-scarum
image of Hollywood—of dwarfs and skyscrapers and talking mice—
wound up leaving no image at all of a place where people actually
lived. Since no country could possibly be like that, it was reasonable to
assume a normal country underneath, where Frank and Maisie did
more or less what they did over here: publishing books, they called it.
It was years before I got any further than that phrase in describing
their work to my set.

There was nothing about skyscrapers or Hollywood to prepare
anyone for the Catholic Church in America. And since I consider this
institution to be Frank and Maisie's most peculiar challenge, and its
conquest their most aesthetically satisfying, not to say lasting achieve-
ment, I'd like to circle it for a moment, in the temporary guise of a
middle-aged buzzard, to point out some of the oddities.

America's many freedoms have not always and everywhere included the freedom to think. For Catholics before Vatican II, the land
of the free was preeminently the land of Sister Says—except, of course,
for Sister, for whom it was the land of Father Says. For "Frank Sheed
says" to wedge itself into this prim hierarchy would require a more
sinuous effort even than getting the English to pay attention to a papist.

Nevertheless, the English years made the attempt possible: I honestly doubt whether a native American could have done it right then. To begin with, the English view of the clergy was rather more relaxed. Evelyn Waugh, putting it most starkly, claimed that it was the duty of the educated classes to keep the clergy in its place. Or to hear it from a less antic voice: "Authority is intolerable but indispensable," said Grandfather Wilfrid Ward. On those terms the stuff could be accepted and even embraced gingerly.

"Rome says" was tolerable to English Catholics, because *somebody* had to say: the alternative being chaos or the insipidity of Anglicanism. But "Sister" barely existed to them as an intellectual concept, capable of saying anything, and "Father" was primarily a liaison figure with the Mind of the Church, as good or bad at it as his talent allowed him to be. One might in a pinch bend one's will to a bishop, but if some lower clergyman began talking rot, one simply looked for another one. At least for company: any damn fool could dispense the sacraments.

There was, its being England, an element of class in all this which expressed itself strongly to a child in atmospherics. When a priest came calling in America, it was a very big deal. The best of everything was trotted out for him, although he usually didn't look as if he strictly needed it, and he was deferred to in everything: not only ecclesiastical matters, but in all things short of sports, where a layman was encouraged to have his own opinions. Households varied in their degrees of pliancy, but very few Americans ever told a priest that he didn't know beans about politics or constitutional law, or, as Frank remarked after a sermon on marriage, "I was edified, Father, that you seemed to know so little about it."

In America, Father was the teacher once and forever. In the quixotic parochial school system, which undertook to instruct every Catholic kid regardless of whether English was his first, second or forget-it language, the people in black were teachers before they were anything else. And although some of them were palpably denser than their immigrant charges—and physically savage in ratio—one assimilated that fact very early on and continued to accept their authority—because the alternative would be chaos and Unitarianism.

The threshold of chaos rises and falls from place to place. In a colonial situation, like the American, any questioning of the status quo is much more dangerous than at home, because with its fragile, partly make-believe roots a foreign entity like the Church can be swept away overnight by some other wandering craze. In England one felt so close to Rome that one could almost reach out and touch it. And Rome was what one worried about, not its flunkies and emissaries. Vatican Council I, with its definition of papal infallibility, was excruciatingly serious; but not some parochial twit denouncing the welfare state over your brandy. (Who does he think takes care of *him*, the poor dear?) Thus, the priest-caller in England, while not quite a stage vicar wringing his hands between his knees, was a far cry from the plump know-it-alls of America.

Frank Sheed hit the United States with a very useful collection of attitudes about all this: Irish enough to reverence the clergy as such— and Irish-Australian enough to be cynical about them; and now English (and monarchical) enough to respect the office totally and take the man as he found him. Having swallowed the royal family, he had no real difficulty with the American clergy. His running mental reservation* about them is preserved in a story he used to tell about one bishop kissing another one's ring. "Oh, you needn't do that," dimples the younger of the two. "It's not you I'm kissing," growls the veteran, "it's your bloody office."

With this firmly in mind, Frank could cope with Father Says like a matador. The Catholic school system had provided him all at once with a thousand lecture platforms, and this is where his campaign began. For although the country was crisscrossed by lecturers offering as many routines as vaudeville, no one had ever used the platform quite like Frank: that is, to be a lay preacher, to play the clergy at its own game under its own nose. Because, whether in drafty gymnasiums with the chairs scraped hastily over the basketball court or in overblown, overendowed arenas, the clerical nose was always there; the people in black patrolled the world of talk like Secret Service men. So Frank's footwork had to be impeccable.

Outwardly the platform Sheed was a model of almost Oriental

* Mental reservation is a sly theological concept whose outward sign, or sacramental, is keeping one's fingers crossed.

deference to "the bloody office," seeming to me much more like a spy than a revolutionary. He had one particular silky-smooth trick that I never wearied of. Toward the end of a fairly rigorous theological lecture, he would somehow manage to suggest complicity with the fuddled monsignor, or whatever he found next to him on the platform, as if they'd practically written the speech together. "Of course you've heard all this many times before from Father McGillicuddy," Frank would tell the audience. "But sometimes it takes a fresh voice to make people listen." Father McGillicuddy would then do his best to look intelligent. The beauty part of the trick (and Frank played a hundred variations on it) was that the priest was now effectively silenced. His wisdom had been established by this clever foreign fellow: one word from him would blow the whole thing.

Of course many of them blew it anyway, accepting the compliment and ploughing straight into their own theological gibberish. Frank had a polite, attentive look for this emergency, worthy of a politician's wife. His face never slipped over the line into approval, although when the nonsense got hot and heavy, his attention seemed to slip slightly as if it had left the room for a moment. (He once literally lowered himself beneath a tablecloth and made his getaway on hands and knees, but this was extreme.) Usually, enough of him remained behind to say, "That was *very* interesting, Father," which, like his other unguent, "I had a lot of fun with your book," could mean anything you liked: in the latter case, *I tossed your book in a blanket, tried to drown it,* and so on.

These are dangerous games, and it would be too much to suppose that Frank always won them. Some priests resented him, either because on a careless night he had seemed condescending (he was never *quite* that, but in his cocky Aussie youth it could be close enough), or because they just didn't like a smooth-talking layman stealing their thunder, teaching theology where theology had never been taught before. All the soft soap in the world couldn't convince them that he hadn't come there expressly to show them up in front of their flocks.

The wilder of them might even challenge him in the early days, which created quite a pickle for our reluctant gunfighter. But lawyer Sheed usually came to the rescue, convincing the overmatched challenger that the two of them were really on the same side, saying the same things, and that they were separated merely by a form of words. "I wouldn't have said it quite like that myself, but I think I see what you mean." In a fan's eye, I now see the challenger backing off gratefully: he has gone a full round with the Sydney Slugger. And Frank has carried him, made him look okay.

All that Evidence Guild work had made the unexpected manageable, and even the dull endurable, for there were many other evenings when nothing happened at all, with the chair-priest dozing fitfully while the foreign smarty-pants talked himself out. Such chair-priests knew that if *they* couldn't follow what he was saying, the congregation certainly couldn't. So the fellow could do no harm. Now back to the ninth tee.

Thus, piling up enemies, aphasiacs and woolly admirers, as well as some young followers who would change the face of American Catholicism, Frank lectured his stormy way from coast to coast across the Catholic ghetto, incidentally playing John the Baptist to his own publishing house. Because in 1931 or so, he could have published all the books he wanted and nobody would have come. He, and later Maisie, had to go out and create an audience, a mailing list—and some American authors too.

Except for certain political presses, few publishing ventures can ever have been so closely tied to a lecture platform. Americans might not like to read but they certainly liked to listen. Since the English *hated* to listen (let alone pay to listen: in that gabby country, it was like paying for water), Sheed and Ward, London, had relatively little to do with lecture platforms. In fact by an irony almost too pretty to contemplate, the very same lectures that bought Frank a publishing house in America, complete with readers and working capital, could still be had for nothing at Hyde Park Corner by any bystander with nothing better to do. A full-dress affair at Notre Dame or a rainy night at Fulham were all the same to our speaker.

Thus the theology that was to revolutionize the American Church turns out to be just the old street-corner stuff hammered out and refined off the skulls of random hecklers. Frank always attributed his galvanic technique, indoors and out, to those bystanders who decided they *had* something better to do than listen to him, such as buying a sticky bun or taking in a flick or feeding the pigeons. Chastened by hundreds of backs receding over the years, sharpened to a fine edge by loneliness (he once recited the alphabet solemnly to an empty square, only to find a man standing in back of him*), and kept forever on his toes by Protestant Alliance rowdies who literally tried to tie his shoelaces to the platform, he had developed the urgency of a man on a burning deck.

And even now that he had captive audiences who couldn't leave if they wanted to, he wasn't fooled for a minute. He could still see spiritual backs turning, and visions of sticky buns beating his time; he knew that there is no such thing as a captive audience. On even his best nights a door might open and a latecomer would tiptoe in. "Look at you!" my father would suddenly shout to the crowd. "Every one of you has turned round. Will he make it to his seat? Will it collapse under him when he gets there? *Anything* is more interesting than a lecture." He knew that "the soggy mass in the middle," as he delicately called the average citizen, had to be constantly rewooed and rewon. Eugene McCarthy, himself a spellbinder of sorts, once told me that he had learned much of his style from listening to Frank back at school.

Back at school, everybody listened to Frank. I have yet to meet a Catholic over what?—forty?—who didn't catch Frank, or Frank and Maisie, at least once—a record, I think, even among preaching priests, and an incalculable influence: godparents to a generation and more, sly strangers who sneaked past the school's puzzled infrastructure, its banana-republic officialdom, to talk to them, as you talk to a bloke on the corner. After the rococo of official sermons, and the false bonhomie of "Father Joe talks straight from the shoulder," these street-smart aristocrats had to sound good whatever they said. If they had done nothing else, Frank and Maisie would have helped change the whole style of Catholic intellectual discourse—which was an absolutely necessary first step.

Because style was the Defense Department of Sister and Father

* A moral fable for young writers working for the *Toonerville Trumpet* or such: Someone may always be listening.

Says. Official theology was made to sound so dry and abstract that you wouldn't want to mess with it: only a few highly dedicated men had been chosen by Almighty God to think about it at all. (Sister had simply been chosen to pass it along.) Thinking itself was not only dangerous but dull, a cute double-bind so that if by chance you found yourself enjoying thought, you were almost certainly doing it wrong and heading for the tar pits. Only those hard, dusty years in the seminary, under proper supervision, qualified you to deal with the mysteries.

And once you had them, you just sat on them; above all you kept them out of sermons, which were strictly for uplift—which also sounded dull. Liveliness even in the cause of morality might stir things up. So loud, dull sermons came to seem part of the strategy, distancing the laity from even its own thoughts. Many native strains of anti-intellectualism helped to nourish this Catholic aberration. Yet it was not official, it wasn't written anywhere: as they used to say (of anticommunism) at the CIA magazines, anti-intellectualism was "not a line, it was an orientation." So if Frank and Maisie chose to challenge it, they could not be rebuked or silenced, only frowned at mightily.

Still an orientation can put up quite a struggle, and Sheed/Ward would probably have wound up in the limbo of the smarties, if they/it hadn't abided by certain principles: (1) To challenge *anything* in the Church, one must be personally devout. If the audience decides to plunk itself down for fifteen decades of the rosary and a couple of litanies between listens, you'd better plunk along with it (though Frank was known to peer dreamily through his fingers). (2) One must not make fun of other people's devotions, however asinine; Frank's private religious order, "The Little Dumb Sisters of the Ass of Bethlehem," only went public when the field was won. But anyway, his mother's peasant Catholicism had rubbed off on him; if that wasn't right, none of it was right. (3) Next, one must have all the makings of a demagogue, but manifestly not be one; in fact, I believe this requirement made Frank even more orthodox than nature intended (later critics who faulted him for this had no idea what it takes to start a revolution). (4) One must not tackle authority head-on, but, where possible, proceed as if it wasn't there. And finally, (5) one must (and this is a counsel of perfection) be foreign.

Because if Americans in those days loved to listen, they dearly loved to listen to foreigners, and foreigners were still rare and strange enough to get away with murder, whether as psychoanalysts or English mystics or as just plain lecture bums. And this, I believe, was Frank and Maisie's decisive edge over native Catholic pioneers, such as *Commonweal* magazine, which was considered wildly subversive for printing the same kind of stuff, and sometimes even the same authors, as Sheed and Ward.

Foreigners had credentials as such and the papist Sheeds slipped in on the same visas as the Reichians and the Ouspenskyites. So while Frank might seem like a layman poaching on clerical preserves, he came from abroad where perhaps things were different. (In fact, some Americans came to think of him as a sort of priest, which put *me* in a peculiar spot. "What's it like being Frank Sheed's son?" they would ask with wide eyes, as if I were the offspring of the Greek patriarch or some such exotic concoction.)

When Maisie arrived, she all unconsciously played the foreign card even better than Frank had (she couldn't play a card consciously without giving it away). Being more English, and much more blunt, she was also more definite about the role of the clergy in the life of the mind. In basic Catholic teaching, a working distinction is made between the spheres of intellect and will, and if you had to dump one of them off the sinking ship, intellect would have to go—but not in an argument it wouldn't.

In that one limited field, intellect is king. And if you've got a better one than the other fellow, it doesn't matter a fig (as Maisie would say) whether he's been ordained or not. In fact, you should use your advantage like Billy-O (another of hers). So Maisie would light in merrily, to the alarm of the white collars, who had enough trouble with her tactful husband without having to fend off this ladylike dynamo.

Maisie was, in this one respect at least, a better model for Catholic feminists than even the great Dorothy Day. Because Dorothy was always likely to yield ground to Church authorities, if only in a jiujitsu (or feminine) manner, while Maisie yielded nothing except what the Church or reason absolutely insisted on.

The rock-ribbed confidence of her Edwardian generation seemed at once comical and awesome to Americans. The word "faith" had a resonance for English Catholics of her era, like a summons in the Old Bailey, racketing down corridors of time, and that was quite enough sword and shield for anyone. The Church couldn't be threatened by an argument, so one argued with abandon. "Absolute bosh," she would say to the Lord's anointed or anyone else. And since she always talked to the subject—the opponent being merely an incident tossed up by a tedious fate—she couldn't be accused of personalizing issues in the female tradition.

Nevertheless, her being a woman sometimes did help her victims to escape. "Your wife certainly is a remarkable woman." Yessir, a real hellion. Maisie could be more outspoken than Frank partly because it meant less. There was a license for fiery women in those days: they could attack politicians and businessmen and such to their faces in ways their husbands were better advised not to. "Isn't she something? Wow!" Perhaps it was considered good for breeding to match these wildcats up with assorted shrew-tamers, of whom, now that I think of it, my poor father must have been considered quite a champion.

It was all very exasperating for Maisie, who was cursed, in the quaint language of the day, with a masculine mind trapped in a female temperament, so that she would literally sob with vexation after a particularly dense set-to. All she wanted was a fair fight, while all Frank wanted was to avoid one, fair or otherwise. But Maisie's life was strewn with *nolo-contenderes:* it was safer to admire her than to run the risk of 'Father Says' being routed by a woman. Her passionate conviction at times made it seem almost bad taste to oppose her. "Do you really mean that," she once said to me, "or are you just arguing?" By her standards, I seldom meant anything at all.

Curiously enough, the fiery female convention was finally to prove a great ally for both of them. To put the matter backward, Frank and Maisie both believed stubbornly that American women were brighter than American men. This biological improbability was, I believe, invented and promoted by them at least partly as a token of gratitude. Because, if one had to boil the Sheed/Ward American mission down to one sentence, it would be that Frank and Maisie finally gave Catholics permission to think without benefit of clergy. And in this respect, impertinent women already had a significant headstart. Since intellect as such was not considered of first importance for laypeople, women easily became the brains of a Catholic family, if it made the little dears happier, and easier to live and sleep with. I remember not once but often being driven to lectures by bland, inarticulate men whose wives had arranged the lectures, *and* study groups, *and* paraphernalia. And then later, aflame with the parable of Martha and Mary, the wives would sit at the Master's feet asking questions against a background of silent husbands.

American clericalism had completely neutralized the men; not only couldn't they talk religion, they couldn't talk anything that you'd want to bring into the living room. "Listen to how soon the word 'dollar' comes up at the next table," Frank said to me once, and the answer that day was approximately thirty seconds. But at home, in the soft religious glow, they couldn't even say "dollar," but sat mute and indulgent as Frank shone. It was almost as if he had decided to play with the girls at the feminine sport of thinking—a thought that bothered me more than once as a little fellow.

Not all the girls were blue stockings. There was one earth mother from New Jersey who looked like a construction worker and who had hired a butler to do right by Frank. As the evening grew hot and stuffy, the butler asked if madam would like him to open a window. "Sure thing, Bobby," she crackled, "I'm sweating bricks." Yet even she outshone her husband by a goddamn mile.

So, who knows, perhaps Frank by example did as much in the long run for Catholic males as Maisie for females. But during those years when the cat had the men's tongues, women, I'm convinced, made Sheed and Ward. They had rushed into the vacuum between Catholic ears, and the "Sister who says," like a recorded announcement, was the first to be upgraded to something serious. Sheed and Ward published a record number of books by nuns, and they were a far cry from the pious guff of yore. Some were asexually literary, others might be about life in the convent, opening those dusty windows for inspection and giving away the cabala-like secret that nuns were human. If the end of this line was to be short skirts, Sheed and Ward must shoulder an ounce or two of the blame: revolutions have a way of getting out of hand, and the Catholic Revival eventually drifted away from its founders' dreams, and in far more serious matters than skirt lengths.

But one shouldn't confuse eras. Sheed and Ward's first American authors were still predominantly priests and nuns, in the old order. To look on the darker side a moment: the Church did not quake and roll over right away in the face of thinking lay people, but continued on its jolly way toward one of its more arrogant phases, the postwar boom. By that time, Sheed and Ward had begun to look awfully as-similated, somewhere on the edges of the Universal Church; it serviced the incurably brainy and kept them orthodox.

In this, its role was almost like the meliorism of the New Deal: Sheed and Ward led its public exactly as far out of the Dark Ages as the powers that be felt it was safe to go. Frank, too, began to seem like an institution. All those bishops he had tactfully wooed bore fruit in a body, and he knew a depressing number of them personally. His writ-ings became textbooks, which is the surest method of embalmment ever devised. And worst of all, he remained alone on those platforms: no other lay preachers sprang up around him. He was an anomaly, there would never be another Frank Sheed, so his very eccentricity could be savored. He had sown no apparent seed in the new land that the landscape couldn't handle. Or so it seemed in the fat fifties.

Frank and Maisie were also an institution, but in some subtle sense, Maisie by herself wasn't quite. She was a wild card. After a time, one knew what to expect of Frank. But as late as the 1970s, nobody could have charted Maisie's next move. Her lectures were not strictly theological (which is why I have treated Frank's mission separately) but literary, historical, social—and whatever she had just discovered.

When I talk of the American Church as dead from the neck up, I am not doing justice to the whole cadaver. There was plenty of social action brewing in the thirties, as clergy and laity, together at last, strove to fashion a specifically Catholic response to the Depression, and this Maisie was alive to at once. Here was where the talent was, and more important to her, the vitality of the American Church. The soup kitchens and generally beat-up quarters where the Catholic Workers and others talked all night were a long way from the cushiony settings and faces of the lecture circuit. And Maisie (she of the wrong tennis dress) was wonderfully at home in shabby, *serious* surroundings; at least, they eased the Ward conscience for a while.

So although she continued to play all the instruments in her one-man band, Social Justice became Maisie's apostolate.* While the Trotskyites and Stalinists were having it out across town, Maisie was visiting Dorothy Day's place on Mott Street, and later Chrystie, "a slum within a slum," and Day's farms, erratically manned by bums, and everyplace else one could find where the Gospel was down on its knees scrubbing the floors.

It didn't occur to young Maisie to move Left politically with the rest of the crowd: Christianity was quite enough for her, if anyone ever tried it. And if this seems naive she might have asked the heckler to compare Dorothy Day's apolitical efforts for the poor with the Communist party's in the thirties, forties or any other time. The Communist superstition (later to surface as the "burn, baby, burn" fallacy) that you had to let things hit bottom before you could rebuild society drove Maisie simply wild. Dilettantism in the face of suffering was more than she could bear. "Pie in the sky when you die" was bad enough when attributed to Christians. From Social Realists it was—her most withering condemnation—"sheer humbug." In her view, if you didn't do it this afternoon, you surely wouldn't do it ten years from now. If she walked into an office and found nobody working, she wouldn't linger to hear about its manifesto. Maisie even battled Dorothy Day about this when she found that the Catholic Worker farms were not producing. How condescending, how pointless.

Since Dorothy Day remains for many the towering Catholic figure of the period, not to mention a rival institution, perhaps I should add another word about her here. Sheed and Ward published her first

---

* A distinction is sometimes made between the "Catholic Revival," which was largely literary, and the "Lay Apostolate," or declaration of independence. It was all the same to Maisie.

book, and they loved her dearly, but they sometimes had mixed feelings about her—Sheed's being more mixed than Ward's. After she died Frank told the writer Jane Howard that Dorothy was 85 percent unphony, which he called a very high average. But it isn't really. Dorothy was just a little too theatrical, or too Americanly theatrical for Frank, who preferred her partner, the French hobo Peter Maurin, who was one of God's authentic fools, wise, humble, unself-conscious. Frank admired him with a wondering shake of the head, never quite sure that he was real.

The closest the Sheeds came to a rift with Dorothy, and they never got there, was over the matter of absolute pacifism in World War II. In this she had been counseled by one Father Hugo,* who, along with other sympathetic priests, failed (for whatever reason) to witness in court when Dorothy's conscientious objectors needed them most. Frank and Maisie felt that Hugo had taken advantage of Dorothy's ardent spirit; but this was an emotional time for a couple of Britishers, and they were really just plain annoyed about the whole thing. England was in mortal danger, America wasn't just then, and they weren't in the mood to split hairs or weigh merits. But in every other respect the Catholic Worker and S & W were so far from being rivals that they were practically incestuous.

Having taken the Sheeds apart, let me hasten to put them together again. Frank also visited the Catholic Worker frequently, and even if it was mainly to talk theology, he still had his old Marxist interest in the social issues. In 1936 he wrote what I consider to be his best book, *Communism and Man,* the first half of which was later used in Communist study circles and the whole of which was praised, in an anonymous review, by George Orwell. Frank's response to the Depression was typically cerebral, but he knew very well what he was responding to: after the dialectic has been wrestled to the floor, *Communism and Man* rounds on the Church as Maisie might have, demanding from it social action at least as thoroughgoing as communism, and much more compassionate. Short of that, it didn't matter

* Father Hugo, a Christian-radical retreat master at the *Worker* from 1940, was himself silenced in 1944 for extreme pacifism. He retained a curious influence over the strong-minded Dorothy for the rest of her life.

how theoretically superior the Church might be: the search for justice would simply bypass it, or trample it down.

The anticlericalism of the Spanish Civil War was just bursting into flame, and as so often, I wish Frank had been just a little bit less abstract: I never knew a man to read newspapers so thoroughly—and use them so little. To write a book about communism during the thirties and leave out the thirties was, I think, a mistaken discipline, alien to Frank's natural way of looking at things, which was half legal, half back-fence observation. Owing to some private sense of fitness, of what belongs in a book—a book by him at least (he couldn't have used slang under torture)—he severely rationed the facts in his writing and stuck with abstraction. And granted that few people ever made the abstract so real as Frank, it remained abstract, the Catholic curse.

Catholics then and even now did not need this. They could already start talking "just war" theory before they knew precisely where the relevant countries were. Frank's contribution might have been truly immense if he'd done for them what he did for Rosemary and me: insist that we get the specifics right, the physical facts and the particularity of events, before sounding off. Only when it came to the Gospels, and in his later years, the Book of Genesis, did Frank give reign to the incredible grasp of detail which he displayed around the house all the time. Ironically, Maisie, with her "action now," had more trouble than he with the names and dates she needed for it and had to use Frank as a sometime data bank.

Where his gift for hard detail did show was in his publishing. He knew his books inside out and could, if he had had the time, have done all the copy editing himself, whatever the subject. Even on lecture tours, Frank and Maisie never stopped publishing. They read incessantly, having to make judgments in a strange, uncongenial language. I once told him that one of his nuns' books called *Play It Cool, Sister,* was just too arch for American ears, but he loved it. Perhaps he was right. He picked some pretty good American writers over the years.

One curiosity that Frank picked up early was a young priest named Fulton Sheen. Father Sheen wrote one fairly good book for

Sheed and Ward called *God and the Intelligence* before succumbing to the bright lights. Sheen, soon to become a monsignor, found, like many authors, that speaking was easier than writing—like sledding without the uphill part—and his second book was in the slapdash vein that was to characterize his early, middle and late periods. And since he didn't take the writing enterprise too seriously, he saw no harm in lifting bits of other people's material—he wouldn't mind if they lifted *his*—and he became sufficiently eclectic to turn up at least once in *The New Yorker*'s "Department of Funny Coincidence." Nevertheless, Frank's comment on the second book was probably extreme. "I'll publish it if you'll agree to put the whole thing in quotation marks."

I don't know, maybe Sheen was just absentminded. I worked for him years later, as we shall see, and found him slightly unreal. Meanwhile, his career ran an interesting parallel course to Frank's. For years they worked the same campuses, where Sheen was the unchallenged first banana as an entertainer. But his show became ever more glittery and insubstantial, because once he had learned to work his eyes, it became almost impossible to follow what he was saying. Ask a passing old lady about one of his lectures, and she'd say, "He was wonderful, just wonderful." The subject was all but forgotten. "I think it was about the Blessed Mother." Sheen was the Svengali of what Frank called the "pious trance."

Sheen's eyes were indeed striking, but it was his hypnotic half-mad use of them that made them really jive. Like a pretty girl without her glasses, he seemed to be gazing just at you, if not through you; yet up close, he didn't look focused at all. In fact, if someone had told me he was blind, I'd have half-believed it. Anyway, eyeballs or no, he embodied a style of clerical glamor that every fiber of Frank's old suits cried out against. "Talk prose, man," my father would sneer politely if he were paid a flowery compliment. And he tried to keep his own prose as bare as a monk's cell, with striking effect. Nobody was going to leave *his* lectures without knowing the subject.

"Publish thine enemy." If Sheen's creamy effusions were a symptom of the intellectual mushiness of the Church, another Sheed and Ward protégé, Leonard Feeney, S.J., was a symptom of something even worse. If I linger on him here it is partly because of this exemplary quality, but partly because he loomed large in our lives. This, as throughout, is the view from the Sheeds' kitchen.

Feeney was a blithe young man who wrote light essays and verse, including this haunting little number:

Snails do the holy
will of God
slowly

But he aged sourly. Even among the funny essays there is an occasional note of prudish hysteria, lost at the time in the din of prudishness issuing from the clergy. (For many priests, I suspect, it was just something you were supposed to do; but for some, prudery stood guard over real distress.) Then toward the end of World War II, Feeney became chaplain at St. Benedict's Center in Cambridge, in the very heart of Pagan City, and his delicate nerves were rubbed raw.

The intellectual inferiority that came all too easily to Catholics was turned by Feeney into blind aggression against "cleverness," the Harvard vice. In this condition, he quickly became a natural magnet for right-wing dissidents, émigrés who hated the secular West, à la Solzhenitsyn, but also natives who hated equally the softness of Sheen and the whole cute school of Catholicism—a mixed bag of brilliance and nuttiness which might have made a diverting contribution if it hadn't been for the neurotic core, the alloy of hate. Groups of this sort needed their own pet priests, and the temptation for vain misfits to take on the role has caused trouble in more places than Boston.

Feeney seems to have had a breakdown of some sort around 1945, but already an impenetrable wall of disciples had formed around him and it was impossible to get at the man himself. Rosemary visited around then, and had a carefully measured audience with the sickly sensitive priest, who impressed her, slightly against her better judgment. "Father's health" cushioned him from sustained encounter with the outside world. But from this bastion, the fragile infanta proceeded to deliver thunderous, virile denunciations of just about everything his constituency hated. Evelyn Waugh once visited the center at the suggestion of Clare Luce—the movement was just on the cusp then between prophetic and zany—and for once in his life Waugh described himself as terrified. The whiff of brimstone was unmistakable. Star Chamber, show trial—the disciples had built another wall around themselves, of sheer atmosphere, through which Waugh stumbled in silence to the door.

Feeney's extreme anglophobia somewhat gave the inferiority game away. Once, in his playful days, he had stood between Frank and Maisie at a street crossing and said, "I feel like an ampersand." Sheed & Ward had made him, as a genuine American talent, but now he kicked as only an ampersand can at his surroundings. He twisted his light verse talents into an annual poem of Christmas hate, particularly lashing at the debonair Monsignor Ronald Knox, Sheed and Ward's lead Englishman: then every Sunday, Feeney and his friends would debauch Frank and Maisie's street-corner tradition by pouring bile into the Boston Common (my friend John Simon, the critic, used to heckle them for exercise, and was christened "Brandeis and soda" for his pains); and finally, as far as we were concerned, he wrote an eight-or-so-page, single-spaced letter to my father withdrawing his books in perpetuity, cursing Frank and all that he stood for, and signing off, "Yours in the Immaculate Heart of Mary." If Frank hadn't been half-Irish, the attack might have been even worse.

Indeed everything might have been worse. Frank looked just enough like an Irish monsignor to take the English curse off him—although Feeney's mad acting-out may indicate how nearly English he seemed to some Irish clergymen. Frank's big red nose may thus have been a blessing in disguise, a tool of his apostolate.

When Feeney was at last anathematized by Rome for saying there was "no salvation outside the Church," he went into a very Yankee isolationist schism. Declaring that the pope had been misinformed by that last honest man, (then) Archbishop Cushing of Boston, he turned himself and his gang into one of those cranky New England sects he so disdained, as far from Rome as the Japanese Christians who boycotted Pope John Paul II's visit. Husbands and wives slept in separate dorms at Feeney's place and mated at the whim of the High Command, which by then had little to do with the founder, a gray rather lifeless Dalai Lama by the end.

What did such a one want and what was his appeal? A new

broom, a fresh start, a cleansing from Europe. A Catholic Church swept of impurities, compromise, decay. What he did not want was a couple of English smarties like Frank and Maisie, opening the back door to the Old World. Yet he needed them. And they needed, if not precisely him, something like him. Because like many nerve cases (to use Frank and Maisie's own charitable term) he spoke for a mood it might be dangerous to ignore. There was a wild bitter energy under the American blandness that took many forms, all of which must be considered, as the new Church groaned to be born.

So Sheen, who couldn't get enough of Rome—incense, vestments, curial favoritism and all—and Feeney, the puritan beneath the skin, both made the Sheed and Ward list. And so did all the points between. "I'd rather lead an orchestra than play the flute," said Frank, in modest reference to his own writing. But he meant it. The most mischievous phrase a publisher, or anyone, can use is "Have you ever thought of writing a book?" and Frank used it scandalously often. He was not content to bring European writing to America and dust his hands of the matter; he was going to take something back with him if he had to wring it personally out of every bright housewife, shy nun or glib Jesuit he met.

The punishment for himself and Maisie was excruciating. Even on the most frantic of lecture tours, the pair of them would be found wading or darting through piles of half-baked effort, eternal judges at an amateur open house. "I say, this is rather good," chirps Maisie, peering hopefully over the day's crud. "I think she's onto something," says Frank, of his latest penance. "Yes, [slaps his knee] she's really got sump'n."

He made it a rule, quite indispensable in this case, to add up the pluses and forget the minuses. Obviously, he was not going to get a great literature out of these tattered, sometimes brain-damaged parochial-school veterans and numbed survivors of college theology; but what he did get gradually was a ragbag of witness, as the American Church began to swap experiences and to know itself. Americans uniquely still had to be introduced to each other, while Europeans knew each other all too well. So in this respect at least, the New York operation was quite different from the English one, although I'm not sure that Frank and Maisie, who tended to be country-blind, quite saw it this way. At least, their London people often seemed perplexed by Frank and Maisie's American enthusiasms, and published them with little hope of success.

But the enthusiasms were right for America, and by the forties and fifties, Sheed and Ward had helped at least to shade in the outlines of a counter-Catholicism to which a civilized person could repair. Since this period coincided with the last gaudy parade of the Church of Cuteness, with Spellman and Sheen blown up like Macy's Thanksgiving Day balloons, and Jimmy Durante saying the rosary on the "Father Peyton hour" and topping it with Peyton's immortal "Da family dat prays togedda, stays togedda"—contemporaries still vie with each other at topping these hilarities—it was handy to have such a bombshelter, which could later be used as an attack station.

But this was a long way away in the 1930s, when the *Queen Mary* was still racing the *Normandie* across the Atlantic, and H. G. Wells and Queen Marie of Rumania were interminably disembarking. Observers of that period always remember Sheed and Ward's foreign authors first. "Chesterton ... Eric Gill ... Léon Bloy ... Maritain ... Paul Claudel ... Christopher Dawson ... Romano Guardini ... Berdyaev ... We'd never *heard* of such people." The foreign glamor that accrued to Frank and Maisie demanded an equally exotic list, and it so happened that European Catholics were having their own Indian summer between wars and Vatican councils. But anyway, colonials don't want to hear from each other. They cry genius a lot, but as an Australian editor once said to me, "Couldn't you first become famous in America and England and *then* come back?" (The question Why bother to come back? hung heavy between us.)

So although several young American authors were cheeping and hopping around the barn in the thirties, they didn't come into their kingdom just yet. Sheed and Ward set up shop over here with a backlist of over a hundred titles, and that would be enough to go on with until World War II closed off the Atlantic and forced America to grow its own authors.

Obviously it isn't enough to say, "Let's publish some foreign authors." Again, these vacuous campuses had to be used, this time as markets, and Frank and Maisie were again their own best salesmen, in an absentminded sort of way. Almost anything could be called a textbook in those days, as I discovered in 1950 when I was asked to compile a textbook catalog and found myself stuffing in practically the whole S & W list. The old lecturing-publishing one-two was a heaven-sent setup that no one had quite had the wit to use before.

The schools and colleges and seminaries kept getting bigger and bigger in those days and this included the libraries, regardless of whether there was anything to put in them or not. Since among new titles only Catholic books need apply, Frank and Maisie had merely to recommend one and then back up the truck. The only trouble in paradise was that they had to cope with the unworldly stinginess of the clergy, who wherever feasible demanded a "clerical discount" of bloodsucking proportions ("The vow of poverty means you never have to pay"—FS) but large orders mean large printings and students do eventually graduate and a precious few of them, at least, continue to read. Sheed and Ward began in a small way to flourish, almost to pay for itself, and Frank got to keep some of his lecture winnings.

This whole distribution system—Sheed to campus to book-and-holy-water store—was so finely geared to the Catholic ghetto that the firm had no choice but to specialize in religion. Frank occasionally published secular books to amuse himself—collections of Beachcomber, the English comic genius, *The Mathematics of Esthetics* by Matila Ghyka, who happened to be a cousin and inscrutable to boot—but it wasn't fair to the books. Sheed and Ward couldn't match the sales forces of the secular big boys, and besides you could hardly lay siege to Brentano's with one general-interest title on your list.

Thus, as if any help were needed, circumstances made Frank and Maisie even more Catholic than they were. And it made our home life about as Catholic as you can get outside a religious community. Except for one taciturn brick-faced Presbyterian cousin whom my father dragged round one day, I cannot remember a single non-Catholic that I ever met through my parents. Thank God it's an interesting religion.

"I found I had this extraordinary gift and I wanted to share it." Most people would mean by this their God-given talent, but when

Frank said it to me in his seventies, he meant his faith. Yet despite the intensity of this calling, which is beyond me to convey even to myself, he was determined to keep it light. I don't suppose the theological world had ever undergone a *funny* publishing house before. Sheed and Ward's house organ, called "This Publishing Business" (Pub-bus to its friends), was quite unprecedented in its breeziness. "You become what you read, so be careful" was its motto. Of course Pub-bus only seemed breezy by religious standards. But later it mutated into something called Sheed and Ward's *Own Trumpet* ("You must stir it and stump it/and blow your own trumpet/or, trust me, you haven't a chance"—*Ruddigore*), which, from its pictures and headlines, might have been promoting a line of joke books.

The notion that Catholics have more fun than other people stems largely from Belloc and Chesterton, but it became quickly accepted (among Catholics at least) as virtually an act of faith. This gave Frank all the license he needed to caper. *Saints Are Not Sad* was the revealing title of one of Sheed and Ward's collections. In some profound sense, the phrase must be true, but to me, in my merciless teens it had a smug ring to it. Humor is hard to win with, of course: today's breath of fresh air is tomorrow's worn-out facetiousness, and there were times after the war when Sheed and Ward came perilously close to looking cute itself.

But in the thirties, it was all fresh air. Walter Kerr has written of a perverse sense of exhilaration among some young people during the Depression. After such a housecleaning, new beginnings seemed possible, and they weren't all communism. But they were all borne on the same breeze, and I picture the discussion groups that inevitably sprang up around Frank and Maisie as not so different in ardor and suppressed hilarity from the Trotskyites and assorted utopians of the hour.

Sheen and Feeney were the American Church as Frank and Maisie found it, the Church of the past, both equally sterile. They have left no spiritual children (which doesn't mean they couldn't happen again; such people are cycles not traditions). But there were plenty of other things coming to life through the cracks. And while waiting for these to bloom, Frank could always busy himself with a series called "A Masterpiece a Month to Form a Catholic Mind" or with Walter P.

Farrell's majestic *Companion to the Summa,* or his own translation of Saint Augustine. The man whom I'd come to see as primarily Horley's leading Catholic layman had claims on the title in New York and London as well. In fact his energy during his thirties and ours was so prodigious that it almost made him a match for Maisie, who was at last hitting her stride after illness and childbearing.

I only wish now that I'd been paying attention.

Transplant

MY LAST MEMORY OF ENGLAND—NOT CHRONOLOGICALLY BUT IT has worked its way round to that position—could also have been my first memory of America. Frank, Rosemary and I are waiting for a bus at a Horley bus shelter, and to while away the time, we start to sing. Eventually we run into a song called "Oh by Jingo," in which a girl of that name is pestered nightly by hordes of Oh-by-goshes who court her with honeyed phrases: "Oh by gee, by gosh, by gum, by Jove./Oh by jiminy won't you hear our love?" Between times the narrator intones the words "ta da, tadyadya da, oompah, oompah, oompah, oompah."

It's a very stirring song, much more so than most national anthems, and as we sing it my father begins walking faster and faster, accelerating especially on the oompahs, until we are fairly flying. Hanging on to his hands, Rosemary and I whiz out almost horizontally at the turns like seats on the swings at a fair before resuming our canter alongside the speeding maestro. "Once in good old Sydney Village," he sings, "Every year we used to pillage,/Fight and trample on policemen. Oompah, oompah, oompah," Frank has spliced an old varsity song onto the original just to keep the show going, until inevitably we collapse in a panting clump like Irish reelers, still wheezing our last oompahs. What the bystanders make of this (we draw crowds now and then) I'll never know.

More usually Frank performed his pyrotechnics at the piano, which he could also turn into a scene of riot within seconds. The merriment was all part of our day, like eating, in fact much of it *while* eating, and at first I thought everybody lived like that, until I brought around some lockjawed friends who stood mute around the piano, trying to summon up a single dry-throated "dum da dum." I just wished they would go away; they were making me uncomfortable. I was past embarrassment over my mad father, but by now felt mildly sorry for innocent bystanders.

However, the old man won them round in the end. These red-faced thugs wound up singing "Three Little Maids from School," like everyone else. It was at those moments, I think, that I first realized my father was not the usual washed-out man in the corner who passed for a father in most houses, and that I could have done a hell of a lot worse.

Anyway, let the haunting—haunting to musicians anyway—strains of Frank's piano-playing accompany us across the Atlantic. That would be our one cultural link with the Old World: the manic banging of his stubby hands which prompted his proud mother, Minny, to say, "Just fancy. He never had a lesson, you know," to bemused onlookers.

My earliest memories of Frank are musical. He was simply the man at the piano, perched high atop a stool distended with sheet music. He never came back from anywhere without more sheet music, invariably bouncy and funny: "Two Little Doodlebugs," "The Teddy Bears' Picnic," "You Can't Marry Ten Pretty Girls." These selections hark back to his past, the era of the piano in the parlor, when everyone in the family was encouraged to have a bash, but no one was supposed to sit there being soulful. You were there to entertain: young and old, the pitch-perfect and the tone-deaf, whatever fate sent you through the open-door policy of a Sydney Sunday. The average upright was, or soon became, so tinny that serious music was desecrated on it, and even light music suffered. Your best bet was to sing loud enough to drown out the instrument altogether. At least that was the aim at our place, and Rosemary and I developed the pipes of hog callers.

Even so, we didn't often succeed in drowning Daddy. Frank had teethed on early Irving Berlin's bastard ragtime, which calls for a lot

of left hand, so Frank always gave the bass the works, even on "A Tis-
ket, a Tasket." He would replace the insipid "dum rest dum rest" of
the cheap sheets with a sturdy all-purpose vamp which could transform even Gilbert and Sullivan into a species of rag. Add to this a
strange fondness for the loud pedal, and you can see that the singers
had their work cut out; also the neighbors.

Nevertheless, we did manage to find room for our caterwauling
on the austere ship *Volendam.* This, we were told, was not to be mistaken for a prewar liner where tea music was dished out to you by
syndicated ensembles. The *Volendam* was gray and stripped for war.
We were shoehorned into cabins anyway we fit, and we provided our
own entertainment. In no time, I found myself dancing to something
called "Boomps a Daisy," with a young actress named Jessica Tandy
(names will be dropped in this book with the frequency of sixpences
in a Scotch Christmas pudding). Frank and Maisie had recently seen
Miss Tandy in, I think, *King Lear,* and predicted a great future for her
as did everybody else. Dancing with me was at least a humble beginning for her. The rules of "Boomps a Daisy" were that you bumped
bottoms gently every third bar or so, but my prepubescent notion of
how to do this was to ram my opponent (forget "partner") all the
way to the far wall and through it. Tandy must have looked funny,
deflecting my maddened lunges like a bullfighter and drawing gasps
from the crowd. At any rate, I thought we had the makings of a team.

Nobody had to force Rosemary and me to perform at parties. The
atmosphere was simply such that you felt a little bit more out of place
not performing. To me, not singing and not dancing looked like signs
of mental derangement. I was a raging show-off myself who had to be
dragged off the stage, and I took this to be the norm until I hit the
next age of embarrassment (around thirteen) with a bang and could
barely work my Adam's apple for a while.

But I digress. Several things about that trip stand out fiercely in
the strobes of memory. There was, for instance, my first and only
brush with war. We snagged a mine in our propeller the first day out,
and had to send frogmen down to pry it loose; very businesslike it all
looked from the ship's rail, but also a matter of life and death I was
told. I don't think my imagination was up to being frightened, but

I'm not sure. Fear leaves my memory as fast as my subconscious can get rid of it, but I'm sure there are some scenes I wouldn't remember at all if I hadn't been afraid, and this may be one of them. Obviously we took it for granted that these mines had been strung like a gift of pearls by Jerry (surely the most innocuous name ever given to an enemy), and it was only recently that I learned that they could as well have been planted by the British, with a view to trapping U-boats.

Since we didn't know this, our blood was up over the matter. It seemed like a caddish way to fight a war, typical of those chaps, of course, and besides, our trip was delayed by what turned out to be about two dangerous weeks. We had lost our original convoy, which had been pretty zippy, and were obliged to join instead the slowest one ever to shamble across an ocean. Solemnly we zigged up and down the Atlantic in time with our huffing colleagues, who could have been barges and old paddle wheelers for all the headway we made. We finished the crossing in thirty days, beating the *Mayflower* record by a nose, and found the immigration laws had just been changed three days before; so we were shunted over to Ellis Island while the officials tried to work out our new status.

I wish I'd been taking notes. My picture now is of very subdued, civilized residents on the island all holding their breath. We slept in barracks, and the men around me seemed exceptionally neat about things like folding their underwear, as if this would count in their favor—or as if they would go crazy if they didn't. I had no idea back then what stakes they were playing for. I suppose that many of them would have been content to pass the whole war in this nondescript clearinghouse, if they could have been assured of even that. They played their chess and they took their walks as if they'd been here for a long time already and were resigned to more. But the irony of seeing the Statue of Liberty through a wire fence was quite lost on me. Everything was lost on me. I can grill my nine-year-old self forever, but his eyes wander. He is thinking of the World's Fair.

I have fictionalized and farcified what follows sufficiently for sober memory to be hopelessly smeared. I *was* impressed by the World's Fair of 1939–40, but all I'm sure about is the parachute drop, which I took twice. The national pavilions have since melted into one in my mind, and the curious thing is that the one is always empty. I kept some slides as souvenirs, and they reinforce this impression of sudden abandonment, of a boomtown gone suddenly quiet, as if a neutron bomb had removed the people and left the buildings. That World's Fair was a poignant last fling for the prewar world. There would be no more Belgian pavilions or Greek pavilions for a long time; the wrecking ball was already swinging at this whole elegant facade. But all I truly remember is the parachute jump.

After a few days in our special kind of hotel—I remember one a few years later where Frank and I actually found a fellow prone in front of our room door. "Yes, we know about him," said the desk tersely—we went into the Sheed shimmy. Frank liked to keep people moving: "A change is as good as a rest," Min used to say, and no mother's lesson was ever better learned. "I think we'll see Ross Hoffman [a historian and S & W author]—an awfully good chap," and off we'd go, whipping from friend to friend: Rye, Cape Cod, West Chester, Pennsylvania, where other awfully good chaps awaited us. This was my first inkling that Frank could, like an early Apostle, summon up bedding wherever he chose. In fact, it came to seem part of his fee and his mission to talk all night to his hosts and remember the names of their children.

So my first impressions of the USA were through moving windows. The American countryside in 1940 presented as stark a contrast to England as the outrageous skyline had. Depression or no, the English kept up appearances, like a bum pressing his last suit and starching his one collar. Grass, if any, was cut in England and houses were dingily neat. In America, it seemed, you either had a lawn like a golf course, sprinkled immaculate around the clock, or else a scrawny patch of yard with a tire hanging from a tree and such clumps of brown grass as survived the trampling and bleaching of summer. In short, you either shot the moon on a palace, or you didn't even fix the screen door. Walt Disney had not prepared me for this.

Coming from a country where the most heartfelt motto was "Keep Off the Grass," I found this carelessness gargantuan and scary. In place of the boxy town planning of England with fresh flowers in front of the railway station, one might at any moment run into miles and miles of junkyard sprawled defiantly like a drunk sleeping it off in his underwear. Weeds strangled the miniature golf courses, signs were chipped, rust was everywhere. Nobody seemed to be in charge around here, except in small pockets of prettiness named Elm Street and Maple Street, which seemed to have ridden out the plague by being fussily clean and quarantined from life.

These were not, of course, coherent impressions, merely overpowering ones. It seemed like such a funny place for us to be. The sheer *differentness* of America imbued everything: the swollen frames and tires of the bicycles, the station wagons with kids hanging from the sides, the kids themselves gangly or strangely fat, slopping around in striped T-shirts and knickers, alien from head to toe—but superficially friendlier than English kids, as their elders were.

At our third port of call, the Darlingtons of Pennsylvania (whom I later married into), I got into a roaring tomato fight, with the juice streaming like blood down our faces, not to mention a classic naval battle waged out of inner tubes in a huge quarry nearby. At those moments, the randomness of American life, the improvisation, seemed wildly exhilarating: but then, wading through a stack of *Saturday Evening Posts* in somebody's attic, I found the *strangeness* again, pursuing me through every page. All that smiling, all that charm. To this day I find Norman Rockwell's drawings not cute, but sinister, the court art of a secret society. The boys around the swimming hole are immensely smug initiates, the gang at the Thanksgiving table is as impenetrable as the Prussian High Command. Since I could never enter this holy of holies, I was glad my parents knew so many foreigners: even boisterous Englishwomen in tweeds were my kind of people for those first months.

So now we seem to have done the country; let's try the city again. These things just happened. I had no idea that anyone was planning them. Someone pulls the cord and the train stops moving, and a small boy in shorts and buckteeth stands irresolutely at a street curb, waiting for the lights to change. No one else waits, though. Legs pound eternally toward Ohrbach's and Klein's on the Square, defying cars the size of tanks and drivers with huge contorted faces. A new word for me to learn is "fuckin." Useful: it seems to cover just about everything.

Manhattan exploded—it was the aural equivalent of war. But it has one advantage over the Outback: all the other foreigners are as stunned by it as I am. Every native we meet is loud and kind: "How do you like our country, sonny?" "I don't know yet." "Don't you just love his accent?" And the question that is to haunt me forever: "I guess you must be real proud of your Dad, huh?" At the time I might have said, "Why? I mean in particular?" But as it kept pattering down on me over the years, I began to wonder why these people were so sure I loved my father. It tells volumes about American Catholics in those otherwise Freudian years. They were nice people.

Since I had assumed that Frank and Maisie had been all tied up in the Byzantine affairs of Horley, I was amazed to find how many friends they had over here. When had they done it? While they were home, they were so *thoroughly* home that we had the illusion they lived with us. Right now, they were highly reassuring anchors. They both seemed completely at home here, too, yet they talked exactly the same and looked exactly the same as in England, so that it seemed as if Americans were being brought round to see *us*: we were the stable thing around here, at least in the fastness of Sheed and Ward.

As with Englishmen dressing for dinner in the jungle, the surroundings were just surroundings to them, nothing to change your plumage about. Maisie the Edwardian couldn't have anyway; Frank had changed his once and that was enough. It was mighty reassuring while I was with them, but it only postponed the necessary nightmare of America. Within two years I would be wishing that Frank and Maisie would do something about those silly accents and would try to dress like normal people. Their imperturbability, which saw me through those first anxious days in Lilliput or rather Brobdingnag, now simply seemed like lack of imagination. So much for children.

The Sheed and Ward office in New York was sunnier in every respect than the London branch, which was never more than cozy. There was a flamboyant stag slashed across the wall behind the receptionist by the raffish French muralist Jean Charlot, who would cheerfully decorate your whole office for you while you waited. There was also a painting of a distinguished gentleman whom Frank had nicknamed "Monsieur Cliché" before discovering that he was actually Thomas Jefferson. This giggly atmosphere seemed to pervade the whole staff and I got the feeling that publishing books was not so very different from selling Guy Fawkes (or Halloween) toys. So I was surprised a bit later to learn that Frank had been deeply anxious about money at this time in order to keep his publishing house cavorting, and indeed, to keep his family alive and laughing.

I should have guessed we were poor from the way we did things, but I was still in the magic stage. If we drove funny-looking cars it was because we preferred them and chose them out of glittering showrooms. If we lived, as we were about to, in a large, abandoned house God's distance from New York, it must be for a good reason. The actual reason was that the house was borrowed from good friends (the Darlingtons again), but even that would have struck me as more Sheed magic. There were always houses, there was always food, and I never glimpsed Frank's hands twitching frantically at the strings: the magician's face never showed it, and his patter was incomparable. I believe Maisie eventually told us about the money, not so much to explain Frank as to share her own anxiety with someone less stoical than he, and perhaps to begin teaching us just a little bit about how things worked.

The sea change to America had hastened such confidences. With Europe sealed off, there was no other world for Frank and Maisie to disappear into anymore, no equivalent to America. We were in this together. Rosemary and I obligingly jumped about a year in emotional age, although in my case this didn't get me very far. I probably stopped chewing pencils while people talked. Maisie, obliged to stay at home more than before, told Rosemary she was glad we were finally old enough to chat with. Her appearance of feeling at home here was partly illusory. She was still very much an apprentice, carrying on too much about local customs, such as Howard Johnson's twenty-eight flavors, which she worshiped, as if we were camped out among Hottentots. Frank for his part had a role to play that we didn't even know about. MI-5 had actually encouraged him to come to America to see if he could do something about Father Charles E. Coughlin, the Radio Priest.

Coughlin is a grubby little footnote now, but in the age of radio, a priest with a microphone was something to reckon with. From populist, pro-New Deal beginnings he had, by 1940, degenerated into an isolationist demagogue who blamed most of America's troubles on Jews and bankers, and there wasn't much anyone could do about him. He had his radio and he had his following, and his following could not be reached by normal means.

In a sense, the Coughlinites are quickly familiar: they have surfaced since as McCarthyites and the Moral Majority, though each time, it seems, a little tamer or at least smoother. The Coughlinites were real barn-burners: drawn from every wave of immigrants who had ever resented the next wave, their various hatreds were gathered together and anthologized in the smug person of President "Rosenfelt," "traitor to his class," "cat's-paw to the limeys," "tool of the Yids," and husband of Eleanor "the nigger-lover."

This was America in the raw, rasped to fury by the Depression and the prospect of yet another limey war. If, as critics in calmer times have suggested, FDR had humanely admitted two million Jewish refugees to this country in the late thirties, Coughlin's holy goon squad would have been there at the dock to greet them. Two million unemployed anybodies would have been bad enough. But Jews had not only, somehow, caused all the trouble, they would also undoubtedly get all the jobs. So some of the wraiths on Ellis Island were there indirectly at Father Coughlin's pleasure, or that of his followers, the more brutish of whom were known to rough up Jews on streets and subways.*

Frank's beat was among the relatively civilized Celtic fringe, where isolationism had nothing especially anti-Semitic about it: it was a private matter between them and the British, and outsiders had better keep out. If Frank had come on as a British propagandist, he would have been worthless. His value was as a presence: a distinguished

* To be just to Coughlin's shade, the anti-Semitism seems to have been a last peevish grasp at popularity: that such popularity was to be had that way is the real story.

Catholic of manifestly Irish extraction with a manifestly English wife—there wasn't a lot he could usefully add to that. At one red-faced banquet, where a boozy denunciation of the king was spluttered, Frank rose to say, "You forget, he's also the king of Australia. Maisie, I don't think we belong here," and walked out to applause.

What I did during the war. There must have been more to it than that even on such an intangible mission (eventually, the bishop of Detroit quietly sapped Father Coughlin behind the ear and hauled him off to a humble parish, but no one has ever linked this to Frank), but all that came through on my front was Frank's new and elephantine tact, summed up in the phrase, "It's not my country, my dear," which Frank trotted out sweetly whenever the talk turned to politics. It was a good policy, as I later learned in the alley: guys who prized themselves on being fair-minded flared up like artificial logs if you suggested a better way to run their country's affairs. But Frank stuck to his policy even in calmer times, like the Japanese soldier who didn't know the war was over, and he continued to do it the M1-5 way, repeating, "It's not my country, my dear," to the end of his days.

It all seemed pretty mealymouthed to me. I practically campaigned for Roosevelt among the small fry of 1940, which nobody seemed to mind too much in a nine-year-old. Still it's probably a good thing M1-5 didn't send for me: I was in hot water by eleven.

Frank's diplomacy, which didn't come naturally to him either, was, I now understand, partly the result of publishing, where you have to ease manuscripts out of egomaniacs any way you can, and partly the strategy of the street corner, polished to glistening by his American safaris. Early on he decided not to fight for anything that wasn't worth fighting for. His tongue was a weapon like a fighter's fists, to be used only when the purse was right. And the purse had to be a human soul. He was damned if he would alienate one of those precious things in some dingy political scuffle.

If a weak father turns up now and then in my fiction, his shadow original must have been born and died during this period. Frank, to my pain, could not even throw a ball, but gave it a stiff little flip as if his arm were in a splint. His accent was the same one that got me laughed at at school; so if I was a sissy (that's the way the imitation came out), he must be too. And now, to top it off, he backed off arguments as if they were live grenades.

If Rosemary had written novels the father in them would not have been weak at all, but a snob. Just because Frank was interested in, and could trace, Maisie's relatives, Rosemary assumed he was a title-sniffer. The fact that he could do as much for his own relatives did not help a bit: an interest in the rich is felt to be different in kind. Only when, in his seventies, he pursued the lowly Sheeds all the way to an unknown graveyard in Scotland was it established forever that he was, as he would say, a "slightly mad" genealogist, as he had been a philologist, tracking names as he had once tracked words to their various nesting places. The discovery cost him one-eighth of his Irish blood, and I said to him says I, *that* will teach you to go around playing Oedipus, searching into matters best buried. (After all, I'd lost a sixteenth myself.) But Irish was what he felt like, whatever the tree said, and very few snobs have wanted to be that.

The real snob in the family was Maisie and she fought it all her days, as she fought her slight overweight. After hearing her fill of Biddles and Drexels in our new hometown of Torresdale, Pennsylvania, she exploded, "Anyone would think they were dukes and duchesses!" before realizing the insanity of *that*.

In Torresdale, you did fill up quickly on the great Philadelphia families. Our next-door neighbors, Helen Grace Smith and her brother Kilby, were the offspring of a Confederate general who had sired ten children, none of whom, I believe, married. This expressed the relative values of past and present in the Smith family. Kilby had filled his bathroom with photos of Greek sculpture, male athletic division. He wore a waxed mustache and stood up creakingly every night for "God Save the King." Grace had a dignity about her that made Edith Evans seem like a shopgirl—in fact, when I finally did get round to dukes and duchesses, I never met Grace's match. She still believed in Society, although she was otherwise a humorous woman. It was a shock to find ourselves next to a couple more English, or at least less American, than we were. When I first heard the phrase "the Other America," I thought perversely of Grace and Kilby.

This was our company—almost all of it. A nice family called

Horan lived a day's march away, and I trudged over about once a week to play baseball with the tolerant but older boys, but there was nothing close to hand except more alienated old ladies and the odd, unexplained roughneck kid whom I would play with frantically and never see again. At ten, you're vague about where people come from and what they do. "We must find some friends for Wilfrid," Maisie would say fervently, but there were none to be had. All in all, it was a strange vantage point to study America from, but then, why bother anyway, we were just passing through. The question of becoming or not becoming American never seemed to enter my parents' minds. It was like worrying about a rare disease.

Meanwhile, Frank was commuting to New York, ninety long miles away by such trains as you could flag down in Torresdale. Maisie redoubled her Dickens reading and her free-form knitting, which she would suddenly (since she couldn't turn corners) pronounce a rug or an afghan, and start again. Rosemary went to the local convent school where the bill was a couple of lectures a year by Frank (his lectures were our currency in the walled city of Catholicism), and I went to its humble annex, a parochial school run by the same nuns, where all the riff-raff in the county seemed to be taught in the same classroom at the same time. We were assigned grades according to age, but these were simply honorifics; the teaching was exactly the same for all. American history, simple arithmetic, sentence parsing—which was actually useful.

I objected to the school on the pompous ground that I didn't want to be taught by women. This went down well at home, as I might have guessed it would: I was not without my infantile cunning. So I was shunted off to an eccentric Benedictine school in Morristown, New Jersey, where after a year of Dickens and English war news and Grace Smith's gentle susurrations, I began to learn about America.

On the face of it, Delbarton seemed as unlikely a place as Torresdale for the purpose. It was off the track as usual (by now I didn't know where the track was)—the kind of place that runs small ads between the dubious military schools and the corrective trusses in parts of the paper where no man but Frank has trod.

It was in fact a priory trying to be a school. The monks had signed on to work the fields and pray, but some damn fool had asked them to teach and they were trying to make a fist of it. The best of them seemed slightly amused by the whole thing (Teaching indeed! What will the abbot think of next?) while the worst seemed completely at sea. And the boys were a match for them at both ends. Several were retarded and had clearly been stashed away for convenience, but others seemed much too good to be there. The hulk at the next desk might turn out to be twenty-five, or else one of the three brightest boys in America, sent here for his nerves. Like passengers on a wartime freighter, everyone had his own secret. The one agreement that seemed to run like a spark between us and our ramshackle teachers was that we should leave each other alone. If they would go light on the teaching, we would leave them in peace at night.

And meanwhile we could all enjoy the scenery, which was breathtaking. "Lush foothills," I think we called it in our ad (next to "trained staff" and "full athletic program"), but that wasn't the half of it. We were also on the edge of Morristown National Park, where Washington had spent one of his interminable winters, and we considered it pretty much our backyard.

My first gaudy go-round with autumn colors occurred here and as a true-blue ten-year-old, I thought little of it at the time, simply stored it away forever. The same went for everything I learned here, all of it unintentionally. That flaky gaggle of boys and Benedictines were to prove, like the last deadbeats at a trading station, invaluable guides to my new country; but for the first few months my umbilical cord still wound a circuitous route back to Torresdale and I couldn't wait to get back there on weekends.

Delbarton was a weekly boarding school, connected to our house by a grisly sequence of train rides. But if my luck was good, I would sometimes find Frank smiling at me as his train pulled into Newark station. My heart leaped at the sight; it even leaped at the thought of the sight. He was simply the best company in the world, especially after Delbarton.

Prised from his various special settings, Frank gave you his complete attention, something you so seldom encounter from anyone that it's like a dream at first. Whatever you said became at once his dominant interest in life and he would comment on it, not in a teachy way, but reflectively as if you had just put him onto something fascinating. Since his death I have received countless letters from people who had experienced this same thing and fancied themselves special, and for a twinkling I remembered the five-year-old's irritation: "Why should I share him with all those others?" But I knew the answer by now. I wasn't sharing him with anybody. Like the God he taught about, he gave his full measure to everybody, shortchanging nobody. The imitation of Christ was his guide and he followed it with Australian abandon.

Did he begin at this point to step up the injections of religion, to get the brain-washing in gear? Not that I can remember (though that may be the art of it). On the ship, of all places, he had told me about the Trinity: of how the Father's self-contemplation being infinite generates the Son, and their love for each other generates the Holy Ghost, and I was excited by the neatness of it, although I still don't know what the *second* idea to have about it might be.

Anyway, on dry land, he dropped some of that in favor of the gang wars in Chicago, and the significant part played by the Irishman Dion O'Banion; or it might be the comparative merits of baseball and cricket (How can grown men play in those funny trousers?) and whether a blind chap swinging through the right groove couldn't hit as well as those other chaps, or whether a man of genius could ever be more than five ten (he himself was five nine, but this was beside the point, he said). His interests seemed inexhaustible, though they didn't include plants and vegetables; and we later agreed that neither of us was much drawn to anything you couldn't read about in the newspaper.

Frank's belief in deferring formal education as long as possible carried over in my case to theology. Instead I seemed to be steeped like a tea bag in the stuff itself: learning to serve Mass from memory, and reeling off three in a row one giddy Christmas Eve in the Smiths' private chapel; three hours of splintering knees every Good Friday; and always the murmur of the rosary with Auntie Min. I liked the rosary as other people like mantras. The repetition opened doors. Interesting prayers, like interesting song lyrics, can distract you from the matter at hand. The rosary, since it lasted exactly ten minutes, was also a dandy way to keep track of time on buses.

Dandy. I fell on American slang like an aborigine falling on trinkets. And I have been falling on it ever since.

Just because I loved my father didn't mean I wanted him hanging around my school. If they laughed at *his* accent, I would have to take on the whole student body. And some of those guys were tough.

Fortunately, it never happened. When he did come round, the little sods were quite ingratiating. They even suggested that Frank should allow me to carry his bags. "Perhaps one of *you* would like to try," he said, handing the larger of the two to one of my sniggering tormentors. "No, that's all right, Mr. Sheed." However brutal the kidding, parents were sacred. Even when, the next morning, my father marched up to the Communion rail with the student body, nobody saw anything funny in that. I could be ashamed all I wanted; they thought he was neat.

Rosemary and I used to talk about whether our childhoods had been happy or not. The answer, of course, partly depends on which kind you want to have had, and the kind of statement you want to make about your guardians. Rosemary is, or was, of a cockney disposition which likes to say, "Isn't it all bloody awful?" as one bounces along. But she had solid reasons for discontent. I am naturally sanguine, partly out of thrift—I hate to think of a year wasted, let alone a whole childhood—but objectively I came off better than she did, temperament or no.

Apart from strange gusts of Sinn Feinian feeling, which always headed straight for the limey with the funny name, I recall much more pleasure than pain at Delbarton. I remember howling intermittently for four years over the phrase "Scotland Yard, where all the dicks hang out." "Seventh-grade humor is the best," as my friend John Leo says, and we stretched it forever. But then suddenly, one of two sets of brothers, the Walshes and Fitzpatricks, would remember the potato famine, and feel it their duty to pass the thought along.

The Irish gift for setting the political tone of a group was never better demonstrated. Italian guys would come up and say, "What about da famine, huh?" Germans, Poles, suddenly everyone was up in arms.

Yet Jacky Walsh doubled at times as my best friend. He invited me to Castle Walsh in Elizabeth, New Jersey, and it was my first real look at the modern American home: glass shower doors with fish designs on them, plastic curtains—routine stuff now, but eye-popping in 1942. The Walshes seemed to have come out of the famine a lot better than we had.

I had a special hold on Jacky, because he'd once confided that his middle name was Mary, which more than cancelled out Wilfrid, but his brother Jimmy was the real instigator anyway. For instance he wrote in the eighth-grade yearbook, "Sheed should use some of his extra brain cells to figure out a way to keep his pants up." This was Johnsonianly pithy by our standards. Closer to our usual level of goofy mediocrity was the unofficial school anthem, which Ed Fitzpatrick liked to warble, in season and out. "Cheer, monks, cheer, there's a hell of a lot of beer/Duck, monks, duck, the abbot's coming here/Cry, monks, cry, he's drinking all the beer/There'll be a hot time in the old school tonight." Followed by raspberrys. It was a gentle time.

Yet there was a great veneer of toughness about the place which gave me a roundabout clue to Frank and Maisie's lecture-night *opéras bouffes*. Maisie thought that my friends were just like little English boys, as most little boys were; Frank assumed they were average roughnecks. Neither knew that they were half the stuff of future audiences—those noncommittal Catholic males who would drive them home and leave the talking to the little woman.

All the boys came from, or claimed to come from, working-class families (another black mark for the limey fop) which only recently had come up in the world enough to think about private schools. Theirs was the best of all worlds, as I discovered when Jacky visited us and saw for the first time what real pig farmers lived like. My friends, in contrast, could live like princes in the world's richest country and it didn't matter. So long as their talk was tough and their thoughts were tough, they could be working class forever, like certain proletarian novelists and *Village Voice* writers.

However, toughness demanded its dues, and we had some bloody bare-knuckle fights, with everyone standing round in a circle until someone dropped or quit. They were interesting tests of our only form of aristocracy. Because at a certain point the loser would *know* that the other man had more heart than he. The results were more conclusive than sports scores and were engraved on the group consciousness. The winner was a lord. The loser was just another guy—not a bum, because he had tried. He had gone beyond the "Yeah?" "Yeah," push-in-the-chest phase, and had entered the Irish holy of holies.

I myself was about to cancel a fight on my very first day of school (we'd scheduled it for late afternoon, and only a lion can stay tough that long) when I learned that my rival had beaten me to it and cancelled already. The only real loser who comes back to me over the years was a supermacho kid from Jersey City who backed off, snarling feebly, from a determined farm boy as soon as the yeah-yeahs had ended and battle positions had been assumed. The moment of recognition came too soon: Jersey was a whipped dog.

Although it wasn't exactly coming of age in Samoa, I found Delbarton a useful anthropological dig into a generation turning from faded blue collar to undeniable white. For instance, their code on bullying: no one was allowed to do it too long, or the spotlight turned on the aggressor. Three little guys once took after a big tormentor like the British fleet chasing the *Graf Spee*. The whole student body (which always seemed to be present, there wasn't that much of it) cheered as the pursuers pulled down the villain's pants, the only trophy they wanted, the flag of humiliation. Yet this same bully became a hero a little later when he stood up to a crazy priest who had slapped his head with an eraser, and said, "Don't you ever do that again." Exit priest sniveling.

One point of honor we all had trouble with concerned a spastic kid named Buddy, whom we had all vowed not to laugh at. As for outright imitations, they got you two in the arm, with the middle finger gouging like a drill, from everyone present. Yet the kid did look funny, and all it took was one repressed giggle or aborted twitch to have everyone shaking. Then more vows and the round continued.

Our favorite self-image was, I think, that of a Dead End Kid gone straight. Our guy could still use his fists, but he used them now in the cause of decency and principle: everybody's mother was a saint and a hell of a pastrycook; teasing about neighborhoods had to be light, and reciprocal—unless your neighborhood was London, and even then I had my defenders, especially after Pearl Harbor; as for our handful of German and Italian boys, political kidding was out, right through the war. Sheed might be to blame for the famine, but these guys were innocent. "I'd rather be a limey like Sheed than—you" was the closest to an insult one German lad received.

All these laws and more were generally enforceable on a sort of citizen's arrest basis, the punishment usually being to hear someone braying, "How would you like it if I said that about your sister?" or the equivalent, or else that numbing punch in the arm.

At first I traced this police work to the Walsh and Fitzpatrick machines. But later I saw that it was a melting-pot necessity designed to keep fights down to one a day. There was simply so much to fight about in America ("I hear the boogies have taken over East Orange." Pow!) that consideration for others was a matter of life and death. And my burly little schoolmates were more sensitive to this than many an educated European, who has never had to defend himself with politeness. As they grew up, this might make them seem bland and tentative, but they were seldom as slow-witted as my parents thought: just paralyzed with awareness and an overload of social signals.

What made our code easier to learn, in fact, almost impossible not to learn, at Delbarton was a certain vacuum at the top. Take the priest who hit people with erasers. He had been doing this for years, bang, up alongside your ear until it sang, with mounting ferocity. One day he almost slapped a boy senseless because the boy wouldn't stop smiling. Red-faced and weeping against his will, the boy *couldn't* stop smiling. But the priest pounded on grimly until his own agitation drove him quivering from the room. For a while after that Father X went light on the erasers, then he seemed to gather steam again, and if one of our own ranks hadn't stepped up to him, as noted, and told him to lay off, he'd be pounding people still.

Although we had some wonderful priests, they didn't seem to be able to do anything about each other. I sometimes like to think of them as a gang of escaped convicts dressed up as priests and just trying to get by without fuss. But what they really were was inmates of a dumping ground. Father X, for instance, was some sort of remittance man from Scotland—where did you send him from here? Short of keeping him in a cage, there was nothing to be done with Father X, nor yet with our choirmaster, a Rabelaisian Belgian who fell drunkenly down the stairs one night, screaming words we didn't know priests knew and wetting his cassock.

At that, he gave it a game try, getting up from the floor, spattered in blood, and pushing his way to the bathroom, but the jig was up. Both these burned-out monks were brilliant men, potentially our best, and they were only jimmied out when the boys had seen the worst and might write home about it. Not that we ever did: we, or at least I, covered for Delbarton. We felt sorry for it.*

The better priests were young, and eventually would make a recognizable school of the place. But for at least a couple of years, the students (who were sort of remittance boys themselves, almost as hard to explain as the priests) did pretty much what we liked. We could chase a kid all the way across the vast campus and beat the heart out of him with nary a priest in sight—so we didn't. Or only once, and then we quit at the last second in a spasm of horror. (For this reason, I have never quite accepted *Lord of the Flies,* in which boys on their own turn fascist and worse. We were at least fascist and better.) Thus Delbarton, my lab, my microcosm, put me onto two more things about Americans: (1) the readiness with which they take the law into their own hands, and (2) the ease with which they form ad hoc communities out of strangers and make them work.

Well, it is best to get one's truisms at firsthand. In civics class, right under the nose of this experience, they taught it the old way: the rise of America was still explained almost entirely in terms of rugged

* Frank was always asking to see my exercise books. We had no exercise books, just stray bits of paper, but I kept pretending I'd forgotten to bring the books home.

individualists (half of them called Pulaski in the Catholic version) unleashed by a godlike Constitution. But I knew better. Those bridges and railroads and tunnels came from the massed effort of people called Walsh and Fitzpatrick, who were quickly assembled and as quickly disbanded; and from the glittering phrase "can do." How I got this from a bunch of kids who might have been dragooned from the city pound I'll never know. But by 1942, I was convinced that the Axis leaders would have saved everyone a lot of trouble if they had, God forbid, taken a look at Delbarton, or a thousand such odd, improvised units. Instead, they probably got our civics books.

The one fragment of the school code that stayed with me like a stone in the shoe came from an overheard conversation, the participants long forgotten. "They say Sheed's a pretty good ballplayer." "Yeah, he talks a good game." Those voices still lurk behind every hedge. Boasting, which had been my staff and my rod in a strange country, became henceforth booby-trapped. Compliments were especially dangerous, because they were strewn over the pit, like leaves across a tiger trap. "So you really think I'm that good, huh?" Crash. The phrase "big man on campus" dripped contempt at our place, and an individualist would have had to be rugged indeed to survive. "All for one and one for nothing," as Fitzpatrick might have said. We were team players, even if we had to punch heads to prove it. And we didn't talk too much, ever.

The actual number of consummated fights didn't reach double figures, but the threat was always there and it influenced the boys of that generation wherever they went to school, as the atomic bomb now influences statesmen. You thought twice about making a scene in a store or restaurant, because the punch in the nose was always a possibility—or worse than the punch, the confrontation. We had no rules for real life: if you punched a waiter, would your girl applaud you or walk out? Better not to mess with it. Thus the origins of male social passivity, often taken to extremes by middle-class American Catholics. I had all the clues now that my parents had apparently missed: the reticence, the politeness, even the disarming softness. Those plump smiling husbands at Frank's lectures were, I now knew for sure, like wild animals turned into house pets.

My mother came as a particular shock to me after a few weeks at our animal training center. She had never heard of our bally code, and I used to wince compulsively when she dressed down waiters like a drill sergeant. In a premature Marxist flush, I told her once to take it up with management, not labor, but it was really the scene I was avoiding. Maisie in that one setting* was like a prenuclear statesman, a British consul in pre-1914 Turkey, and indeed nobody ever punched her nose that I know of. She also felt that if one paid for something, one had a right, nay a duty, to complain about it. Quite so. I once saw Frank's head bobbing like mine toward the tablecloth as if to hide, while Maisie was intoning, "I say, look here . . . it's a bit thick, isn't it?" They punch noses in Australia, too.

My one mistake at Delbarton was going home for too many weekends. It seemed like a good idea at the time, as the other escapists buzzed with plans every Friday and the internees looked crestfallen, but it was an open invitation to culture shock, and railway shock too, as I bounced forlornly back on Sundays, passing, between trains, the Little Cinema, immortalized in Philip Roth's Newark, which featured Hedy Lamarr in *Ecstasy* all my four years at Delbarton.

I had nothing to bring from my world to this, not even the embalmed hand the Fitzpatricks once smuggled in in a shoebox from their father's undertaking parlor. (They claimed to have handed another of these things off, still clutching a quarter, at a tollgate.) A Sheed and Ward book would not have had the same effect. For me, every week was a glum re-Americanization, every weekend an unraveling. No border crossing was ever more disorienting, and I got a feeling of always being from somewhere else which has lasted a lifetime.

Yet from Friday night, featuring Auntie Min's Irish spaghetti, to the end of the Saturday night "Hit Parade," solemnly memorized with Rosemary, it was worth it. Unfortunately "we" considered it decadent to go to the movies every week (I have never yet closed the trivia gap), but we saw some nifties. Frank touted me highly on a film that opens with a smoking gun; it doesn't quite, but *The Maltese Falcon* is

* People like the Wards seldom went to restaurants, so waiters were staff, and one's whole downstairs strategy trembled if they got away with anything.

typical of his unerring taste in middle-brow entertainment. So every second week at least we got to know Grant and Hepburn and Davis, all the *intelligent*-looking actors, Frank's weakness as ever.

What I didn't notice as I hoarded my euphoria was the thin war Rosemary was having. She wasn't Americanized in the least, thank you very much, and there wasn't much else to do. Worse still, she and Min had been natural enemies from the very beginning. Min preferred boys, as noted, and Rosemary was "too clever by half," as the English say, a supercilious little pill from where Min sat; but these common-places could not explain the wrestling in psychic goo that these two staged. Rosemary was very English, and perhaps everything Min re-sented could be taken out safely on the child; perhaps she also felt the child was putting her down.

If Min had faced these feelings, she would have gone mad with remorse. But there were always enough trivialities to wrangle about without facing feelings. Min was queen of the kitchen. When she took it in her mind to bake, the room was off-limits for the day, and you had to go halfway round the house to get from the back to the front. Rosemary, rattling about in that big empty house, naturally gravitated to cooking, too, which was the only action going except for me hitting solitary fungoes out back during the summer, or me again listlessly hoeing the victory garden to earn ballpark money.

A kitchen can provide all the material you want for the bloodiest of feuds, and this one lasted until Rosemary left home in her twenties. By then she had forced Min back and back, but there is no joy in such victories. The kitchen *was* Min's kingdom, the only one she had, and it was just too bad that Rosemary couldn't stand her cooking. I liked it fine myself, being a simple little chap, though I wearied of Min's weekly discovery that "you can't hurry the potatoes." She did roasts very well, in both senses ("Incinerate it," Frank used to instruct wait-ers, in memory of his mother), and then we simply worried the meat around in various forms through Thursday, until Friday brought blessed relief in the shape of fish or that weird spaghetti.

That was how she had raised her boys, and we never became so prosperous that it wasn't a good way for us too, but the drumroll of stew, curry, cold was too much for Rosemary, who had no boarding-school food to compare it with. Reeling from the leaden cooking of the German nuns at Delbarton (great doughy women who never spoke), I found Min's food positively feathery. Even when she claimed that her latest passion, junket, was "just like lovely ice cream," I didn't quiver with rage like Rosemary. Just often enough she lived up to her splendid motto, "A little of what you fancy does you good," and she didn't give a Morton Bay fig for diet. At the time, I asked for no more. I was of the Disposal Unit school of eater and even belonged to a group whose members took turns escaping thrillingly from Delbarton to bring back chocolate mocha cakes (the group had no other purpose), so I was the perfect subject for Min's muscular cuisine, and it strengthened my bonds with her just as it weakened Rosemary's.

Anyway, the two were trapped in this great gloomy house called Birdwood—gloomy even in summer: the window screens looked opaque in those days, like crowded flypaper—with Maisie unable to help much. If she sided with either one of them, the other might burst into tears of rage. In such a setup, any tilt of the scales constituted persecution and if Maisie took a middle position, she was letting down both of them. Maisie's relationship with Min was delicate enough without being subject to these constant road tests, and she spent a lot of time working alone on her Chesterton biography and hoping for the best.

As with our school fights, I don't know how many there actually were between Min and Rosemary. World War I veterans sometimes didn't know how many battles they'd been in either, they only knew they'd been in the trenches. Min suffered from crippling arthritis of the knees and could start a fight out of thin air when the pain hit. Rosemary, around thirteen now, had her own brand-new arsenal of moods. Either one would have been a tinderbox without the other: together they were dynamite.

A sad tale of women in wartime. Frank was away almost as much as a soldier, making precarious trips to England in bombers and banana boats in order to supervise his tiny war-torn London branch, and jousting with VIPs for train space so that he could lecture Stateside.

Most of his life he took no income from Sheed and Ward, but talked for his supper (and its); and when he did get paid after the war it was in air tickets. So those lecture trips were crucial.

We were two different families with and without Frank. Quarrels didn't just cease in his presence, they went out of existence, like inconvenient history in *Nineteen Eighty-four*. Min lit up like Times Square. Rosemary and I just sat around laughing. Frank brought out weekend guests, which nobody else seemed quite able to do in those days. Just as he traveled freely while everyone else was becalmed, so he managed to whip out guests, at least relatively hot from England, Japan, Austria and God knows where else.

I paid them little mind, reckoning that they just interrupted our conversation. But I do remember an Englishman named Robert Speaight (author and actor) who insisted on playing Chinese checkers with me until he beat me. But this, despite pulses pounding, his and mine, proved impossible (he couldn't have beaten anybody), and he thus missed the only train of the day. The von Trapp family dropped by to sing, which drove me out onto the staircase from the sheer inhuman perfection of it all: the happy little tykes portrayed in *The Sound of Music* had in fact been regimented within an inch of their lives and forced to wear those fun-loving costumes nonstop, and it showed in their work (one of them later ran away and stayed with us until a truce was struck with the lovable Julie Andrews character).

So many people claim to remember me from Torresdale that our lawn must have sometimes teemed with them, and I only wish I remembered them, but the iron limitations of child-adult conversation made the adults completely interchangeable and forgettable. Two young Sheed and Warders, Robert Lowell and his wife, Jean Stafford, soon to be *the* Robert Lowell and Jean Stafford, dropped in, and I don't even remember *them*, although I do remember Lowell as a subject, someone we talked about. It seemed Sheed and Ward had recently acquired one of its odd business managers (oddness reaching a crescendo in that department) who believed that Lowell was a veritable messiah, someone destined to lead us all out of the paths of sin and war. Lowell by chance found this a splendid notion, so just like that he went off to become a saint and eventually a conscientious objector, while Frank fumed over the loss of a good editor.*

All these things and more may have happened just above my very nose. But "How do you like your school, what's your favorite subject?" is not a line that leads from here to there. Kids like to be in the know, but can't follow anything. So for us, visitors mainly meant watching Frank going off with them for little conferences. He loved to walk as he talked, and he forever seemed to be pacing the grounds with these strangers, on our time, with his head cocked like a confessor. Unless they liked to sing, or play Chinese checkers (up to a point), guests were not much use to us.

The best weekends were those when we had the king to ourselves. On a chirpy Saturday one would find him at the piano, our prevailing symbol, perched upon an apoplectically bulging pile of sheet music, playing his way through the whole crazy-quilt collection while Rosemary and I bellowed happily and the grim old house seemed practically to jitterbug. After that, *we* would get those precious walks with him with his head cocked to one side, and then perhaps a Monty Woolley movie or some Alec Templeton (the blind, comic pianist) records or a trip to the Old Swedes churchyard in Philadelphia, where some Sheed or other might be buried by clerical error. We were always doing something, but we never felt we had to do something.

Sunday lunch was our grand climacteric. Aching, weeping, groaning for mercy, we would totter from the table. "My father is very jokical," Rosemary had said when she was four or so. And if you'd seen him only at table, you'd have sworn that was *all* he was. He might begin by declaring the opening of "All for Daddy Week," to which we'd howl, "That was last week," after which—I forget, except for quivering stomachs and something we drank which Frank called "pigment"—a mixture of ginger ale and grape juice—which he approached with a drunkard's relish.

* Frank retained a blind spot about Lowell almost to the end. He would read a poem of his and snort. "And exactly how does he propose 'fighting the British Lion to his knees'? Where are a lion's knees anyway?" Perhaps he had not lost such a good editor after all. Frank was also convinced that Lowell was jealous of Jean's early success with *Boston Adventure* (a novel) and that he left her in a fit of poet's pique. Frank loved Jean Stafford.

I once told John Updike that in my family, you were punished if you weren't funny, and he said that in his, you were punished if you were. Neither sounds quite true, but at our place you were certainly rewarded. Frank laughed at our stuff if there was the slightest excuse to; and if he didn't, you felt edited for a chilly moment. Since he believed that it was ungentlemanly not to laugh at one's own stuff too (you couldn't foist a jest on the company if it wasn't good enough for you too), an unbroken roar ran through our feeding. What one couldn't do was tell long funny stories. There were too many people waiting in line (only two, in fact, but they seemed like twenty). We learned economy the hard way, and forevermore none of us, including my father, could or can successfully tell funny stories that take more than three lines.

As a painting or faded print, our family meal was as different from Norman Rockwell's gentle, ominously modulated Thanksgiving celebration as can be imagined. "I love to watch the Sheeds eat," somebody once said, and we must have been quite a sight. Frank's unconcealed glee over, let's say, a banana cream pie, Maisie's single-minded attack, Min's lip-smacking pride over what she had just cooked and my own thorough, scorched-earth policy—I ate slowly but would keep going for hours until I reached wood: in ensemble we must have looked like a slack monastery on a major feast day. Rosemary was our only gesture toward civilization, and that only by contrast. The jokes helped the food, the food fueled the jokes—and I still eat slowly. The dining room was the great good place of childhood and I hate to leave it even now.

As for the sound effects, the chomping and clicking of teeth and the stray gurgle, these were just the labor that goes into art. But a word might be said about my father's soup drinking. It was one of the fastest operations I have ever seen not done by machine, and on those terms, it was relatively quiet. It was also magical. Once I surreptitiously matched him stroke for stroke and mysteriously, like a Cambridge crew, found myself eight spoonfuls behind at the end.

I don't know what demons drove me, or perhaps it was just scientific curiosity, but one day at what seemed like a prime, mouth-filled moment—if one can break such a continuum into moments—I said something that I knew for certain would make him laugh; and out it all came, not just the odd carrot, but all the soup in the world. So that was his secret: a spare tank. Beat that, Norman Rockwell—or come to think of it, Martin Luther. Our resident theologian was still laughing long after the soup was mopped up.

Then he was gone again, on a slow boat to Lisbon or someplace,* and we resumed our places. A light went out and the long dark days resumed. I never saw the worst of it, because *my* weekends also brought some relief to the inmates, like prison visits. I could cheer up Min with manic cockney imitations (or did that come later?) or just sit in her room, which looked like a religious-goods store, and chat; Rosemary briefly had someone to confide in and sing with.

When my father came round again, I would feel a little like a prince displaced; suddenly my whole audience had gone, whoring after the new star, the kingfish. But Frank was used to this—he had displaced enough little princes on his visits to Sheed and Ward, and he had a million ways of suggesting that I'd matured wonderfully in his absence and become a whole new thing. And then we'd be off and laughing again, with Maisie smiling benignly—she only got one joke in three, but she loved to be around laughter, it gave her joy of her family; and when she did get her one in three, she collapsed worse than anyone, in choking moans of happiness.

I once literally feared for her equilibrium at a W. C. Fields movie. It was tough enough getting her out of movies at the best of times, because she always took off her shoes and her feet swelled, and she had to fish for the shoes under the next row and jam them on in the dark. But here she was, writhing as well, like one of the possessed nuns of Loudun, rolling and pitching in the aisles of the ten-cent Laff Movie House on Forty-second Street as Fields actually handed someone the driving wheel—well, you had to be there. Fields plus the shoes seemed insuperable. But we got out somehow, looking no worse than the bums who frequented the place.

Maisie was convinced that she was humorless, another fiendish

---

* Frank was stranded for long stretches in both Lisbon and the Azores, superb places for spying if he'd had his heart in it.

Ward legacy, but the very promise of slapstick, the hint of disarray in a dress-for-dinner world sent her into howls of relief.

I identified with her while small, because Rosemary already spoke and thought like a Gatling gun, and Frank said the rosary faster than he drank soup—three minutes tops—but Maisie was a center of peace. She even walked slowly, which a half-pint appreciates. And her conviction that family members could not *really* hate each other kept us all going just as much as Frank's *spritzes*. It also kept her work going. She could not have written her colossal Chesterton, let alone delivered her own lectures or pitched in at Sheed and Ward, if she hadn't believed that everything was fundamentally all right downstairs. Rosemary and Min would eventually team up in a wonderful teacher-pupil way; I would be a genius of some sort; and Frank—well there was no limit on Frank. "Not only a great theologian but a great philosopher," she would say to blushing young academics who didn't know that Frank was a philosopher at all.

Min and Rosemary may have been a tragedy for a while, because they both wanted to be good except in this one respect of liking each other, but Maisie made sure that *she* was no tragedy. She was too busy and too excited. In the interests of sanity she accepted the flimsiest evidence that everything was proceeding to plan for all of us. ("I say, that's rather good," she would exclaim over my schoolboy cheepings. "Rosemary's made a rather extraordinary soup." "Grandmother's Christmas pudding is worthy of the finest houses in England," and so on: all heartfelt, all innocently cunning.)

For someone with her tenacity, Maisie was wonderfully mercurial. She had a fragile heart, quickly mended. Moved to tears by, say, the Polish question, she would hire a Polish farmer that very afternoon, and give a passionate lecture on Robert Browning that evening ("Was I all right?"). None of her interests went away, but just pursued each other like film slides, so that she seemed to have a short, though intense, attention span. Her mind was a searchlight, condemned to keep moving but to return. Her Chesterton took all of eight years, but she'd squeezed a lifetime of other things into the spaces.

As to her farming: besides the garlicky cow next door, there were bees to reckon with now. She had met a wise and saintly Polish priest whose avocation they were, and I remember him wading in, smothered in mesh, to show us how it all worked, the miracle of the hive. As usual, Maisie danced alone. I got stung early on by three of the little miracle workers as I searched for an errant baseball, and henceforth prowled the whole garden with suspicion, like a marine in the jungle. Rosemary, I fancied, found the whole outdoor world rather trashy and second-rate, though this may have been the result of bad eyesight. Maisie cared less than ever what we thought about it: I'm not sure that gardeners really want company, and she was happy enough to get some grudging fieldhand work out of me for a princely quarter an hour, trading vices: her horticulture for my baseball ticket.

The summers in Torresdale were endless, and I got to know the troubling mysteries of boredom. I had at the age of eleven a suicidal spasm somewhat like the one described in *Pennsylvania Gothic*, very much based on this matter of endlessness. If I didn't like eternity now, I would like it even less in the next world. The American summer vacation was a grim forewarning of long afternoons under a clock stopped and broken. Inside the house, the pages turned and turned again; every face was hidden by a book. Maisie would walk into a room talking about a book, only to discover that the room was empty. She would read right through meals and leave the table reading. "Anyone want to play a game or something?" If ever I was in favor of book burning, of capering round a great pyre of print, it was in that dry rustling house.

Outside there were the old bat and the old ball and an ever-fresh supply of time to be killed. And that was suddenly what had to be done with it, all right. Zlit, cut it out, remove it. For one whole night and bits of several others, I knew it would happen, it was out of my hands. I would go downstairs and kill myself. Why? I don't know. Devils like that sometimes leave a clean house behind. Maybe my huge gulps of raw religion had backed up on me, because words like God and heaven made their rounds in my fantasies. But what I wanted to end, felt I *had* to end, was life itself, the lawn, the trees, the still air. God was simply someone who threatened to prevent me from doing this with his fiendish threat of an afterlife. Heaven or hell, I didn't care anymore—I wanted out.

Either I was very tactful or the family was even more than usually preoccupied, because nobody noticed that there was anything wrong with me at all, while I nursed myself slyly back to health. It was like an addict drying out on his own. Suicide of this kind is a compulsion, not a choice, and you have to be terribly lucky and careful to edge away from it.

I couldn't think about it comfortably until my twenties. I couldn't mention it to anyone: it was more embarrassing to talk about it than to do it. But I remember a chat I had with Frank in the first phase of that lifelong summer when I raised the problem of eternity quite abstractly. I said, in words proper to an eleven-year-old, that I was inclined to be frightened of existence as such because it either ended or it didn't—intolerable either way. I wasn't frightened yet, but I was getting ready, and I guess we decided that there was clearly no answer to eternity but to trust God not to hurt us too much. He couldn't have created us *just* to drive us crazy, although he did so often enough to make one wonder.

As I recall, we were talking our slow way through Grace Smith's garden, which was a fair copy of our own botched acres. Frank did not attempt to cope with me theologically, let alone philosophically, because he deeply believed that experience of life should precede philosophy; so God's love would have to do. But in August, when all calmness had fled, I found that garden next door much more reassuring than God. It was the details: a tree in whose crook I had recently sat, warbling "The Breeze and I"; a down-at-heels garage where I had splashed myself liberally while cleaning the car; flowers that would go away and come back and then someday leave for good. Class dismissed. Nature en masse was as threatening as the gasworks I used to dream about, all yammering lights and noise, or as the Nazi army, but maybe deals could be struck with particular objects: that tree, this lawn chair and, above all, the grandfather radio inside. Suicides are collectors, and presumably give up when the collection doesn't respond. "Suicide is an insult to every leaf on every tree," wrote Chesterton, and I could have used this at the time. Yet never before or

since have I given a damn about leaves, trees or any of the above. I had
to leave my obsession the way I came in, through the garden.

Torresdale left us with odd little legacies like that. I know there
are the inevitable good sexual reasons for prepubescent suicide, but I
know for sure that I wouldn't have considered it if I hadn't been so
frantic with boredom. And if that hadn't happened, I would have
missed a glimpse into the abyss, the existential maw, and would quite
likely have spent the rest of my life writing light verse. People who
talk of pursuing art to the very edge of madness usually don't know
madness. If you have had just one lick at it, one taste of the burned
wire, you will do anything to stay sane, even if this includes banality.
So it's lucky, I guess, that madness came looking for me for a few days
in the August of 1942.

Rosemary had her wish and stayed English in Torresdale, which
would have been harder to do in a crowded setting. The school she
went to, Eden Hall, was the last place in the world for a girl to
Americanize in. The Madames of the Sacred Heart were dedicated to
turning out little French girls, which, since it was impossible, resulted
in rather ill-defined, amorphous rich kids with a fragile grip on genteel
nineteenth-century French and wonderful manners. Rosemary at least
got some real French out of the arrangement from a salty old French
nun who fell with glee on this prize student and started her on the
way to being a prize-winning translator. In each case Torresdale's virtue lay in offering nothing much else.

Maisie had much time to think in that desolate village, something she occasionally overlooked in the hum of activity elsewhere.
She once told Frank that she had "something in the back of my
mind," only to be told, "You have no back to your mind." She was
brilliant all right, but all the action was in front. Her impatience to
"get on" with things caused her to deal with ideas by return post, so
to speak, too fast to be deep. But the great Torresdale vacuum fixed
that: ideas just sat there in the heavy air, and she did her most important work on the Chesterton biography at Birdwood.

Frank and Maisie did attempt some street-corner speaking in Philadelphia, but Philadelphia never seemed quite the place for it. The
crowds were small and quiet, as if they hadn't grasped that they could

talk back. I remember standing on a bitter cold night as my father put all his body English into his work (those coiled contortions would one day send him flying off a platform and into a concussion) for a crowd that consisted entirely of two other Evidence Guild speakers. "Reclaiming sinners, so they say, is easier than work," Frank used to recite from some old Communist verse. But it didn't look that way in Philadelphia.

Although his other activities remained cyclonic, I believe Frank's relative abstention from Guild work was good for him too. For most of his grown-up life, he would find himself teaching the same things over and over, year after year—to fresh faces, to be sure, and going round in ever more accomplished circles, but not advancing much. This was all right with him, his vocation was instruction, not pure research, and he had never set out to be a great big theologian; but now he had nothing much else to do. So he polished off a definitive translation of Saint Augustine's *Confessions,* balancing it on his knee in various subways and dictating the outcome to his sometime secretary, Jean Stafford, and he began to give thought to his *magnum opus, Theology and Sanity.*

What Auntie Min got out of Torresdale, I don't know. Her great flowering as Frank's mother—everybody's flowering—came when we bounded from our cells and hit New York in 1943. Before that, I remember much Celtic uproar from her, in the form of groans as she squeezed and kneaded her arthritic knees, or laughter, or requests for her glasses, which were eternally upstairs.

But what child ever checked up on a grown-up's happiness? I do remember two vacations we took to Wildwood, New Jersey, where Min was undeniably happy. She and I, and one year Rosemary, stayed in a hotel full of cheery, classless people, and it must have seemed like the liners Min had taken to and from Australia, where nobody knew more about you than your name. In such a context, she could be herself without being defiant about it, and such was her immediate hold over this amiable, evanescent company that she got half the hotel to show up for an amateur contest and clap me to a second prize for playing "Don't Sit Under the Apple Tree" on the harmonica and singing a wobbly "Waltzing Matilda." When I got back to my seat, I caught the other side of Min's charm. "You didn't deserve it," she said.

This was unusual, but not surprising. Acid honesty could suddenly squirt out of anyone in my family, cutting the sweetness of mutual admiration. I had choked on the third verse of "Matilda," and my three-dollar war-stamp prize felt like thirty pieces of silver. I didn't need to be told.

One late summer day, Min walked the length of the boardwalk with me, as I popped in and out of the amusements: mostly those batting practice enclaves, where newfangled machines flipped pitches at you and you whaled them into a canvas backdrop. By journey's end she was almost dancing. We sat on a bench in the lowering sun and she flexed her bandage-thickened knees and said she didn't feel a thing. Of course, she would pay horribly the next day when the arthritis came roaring back. But Min was a seize-the-day character, eager to make the most of things. She was never exactly a manic-depressive condemned to her own dismal rhythms: give her an occasion and she would rise to it—well almost—every time. The fewness of such occasions in her early life had made her an opportunist of celebration. Announce a party, bang the piano, and Min was your girl.

Why we left Torresdale was as obscure to me as why we had been there. I deduce now a modest boom in our finances; also, the sudden availability of a cheap apartment on Riverside Drive, which was said by the dowagers to be full of Jews, whatever they were. Frank and Maisie seemed amused by the warning, as they generally were with the dowagers, and we pushed ahead.

So we kissed the old ruin Torresdale goodbye. Maisie may have regretted leaving her vegetables, and I regretted just leaving (I cry when I leave hotel rooms), but the overall mood was one of bursting into daylight. Torresdale in retrospect was a pretty little Norman Rockwell village, but the only sign of life there occurred on the odd Saturday, when baby-faced servicemen danced forlornly with Sacred Heart seniors (nothing could have been less erotically promising) to the soupy swing music of the times. Among our four or five shops there lurked an ice cream dispensary called the Pump which actually had a jukebox—still a novelty—and this was the center of our nightlife, *was* our nightlife; because we were also marooned by gas rationing from the nearest town with a movie house.

New York by contrast was apoplectic with possibility. Gas rationing suddenly made no difference; you could go anywhere you liked by trolley, subway, foot. There were movie houses galore and soda fountains to burn, all catering furiously to the kiddie market because everybody else seemed to have left. We bobby soxers (the word was officially confined to girls, but collectively it was the name of a generation) were the ancient ancestors of the Youth Culture, already affecting, and debauching, popular music to our tiny measure. The town was a symphony of jukeboxes, which somebody else always kept fed, so it wasn't even expensive to jitterbug, in our embryonic way. And of course there were the ballparks.

To replace my solitary vigils at Shibe Park, where I had huddled with some of the smallest crowds in recorded history, I now had three brimming stadiums and all the company I could want. It was like going from a Quaker meetinghouse to a Mexican High Mass. All New York's kids seemed to be baseball fans and didn't need to be prodded all the way into their seats like country boys.

The one thing the city *was* short on was legal places for kids to play—you had to belong to pantywaist outfits like the Catholic Youth Organization to get to set foot on the real diamonds. So my friends and I hacked away merrily in Riverside Park, on the narrow strip of green that runs beneath Grant's Tomb and Riverside Church. Pull the ball to left and it crashed onto the drive, where the fast cars screamed by, and was never seen again; punch it to right and it rolled up a little hill and sedately down again. So we became the greatest straightaway hitters of all time, with a rather El Greco view of the game's dimensions. Second base looked to be almost directly in back of first so you didn't exactly round bases, but made trifling adjustments in stride. I gave up shortstop because everything had to be cleared through the third baseman first. So third it was for me.

In these distorted conditions I must have played six or seven hours a day through the hot summer of '44, using the apartment only to hose down and guzzle Pepsi, the only such drink my mother had heard of. Frank and Maisie never accused me of wasting time on sports; it wasn't like reading comic books. Both Frank and Maisie would have liked an athlete in the family, provided he was something else as well—a scholar sportsman for Maisie, perhaps a cricketing publisher for Frank—and, even more than in fields they knew well, they touchingly overrated my promise.

If everything that's going to happen as a novelist has happened by thirteen, then baseball is almost my sole influence. This may not be quite as useless as it sounds. You may not develop much character in sports but you certainly learn a lot about it. The dumbest ballplayer knows precisely who to trust, who's a blowhard, who's a quitter—in fact, all the secrets of a Balzac are there in his fuzzy head. This ragbag treasury can be handy in a new town, because it helps you to make new friends quickly and decisively, and warns you who not to mess with, just by the way they disport themselves on the field. (I'm not sure that these insights are transferable to real life, but I've occasionally tried working the process backward—trying to figure out what kind of ballplayer so-and-so, let's say Henry Kissinger, would make.)

1944 was my sporting *annus mirabilis and I'm glad I had it. I was at peace with each of the Big Three (baseball, football, basketball). My scrawny team had won an intramural basketball title at Delbarton by using my brilliant tactic of leaving the two weakest opponents completely unguarded and doubling up on the two stars and guarding the captain* myself—successfully, because they were the only ones who could hit the basket at all. Mediocre opposition breeds delusions of greatness, and I thought myself a veritable Napoleon.

In baseball I actually made our junior high school team as one of those noisy frenetic little infielders whom coaches consider inspirational and the other guys just think ridiculous. At both baseball and football I could catch anything but the easy ones, the burden of expectation on these being too much to handle. More to the point, I learned the feel of these games, the specific pleasures: the exhilarating spring in the gym floorboards, the grim love affair between a football player and turf, and best of all the relaxed calculations of an infielder as he roams his position—which base to throw to, who covers, who makes the cutoff: a dozen things to check off before he ambles into his set position. Never mind that our relays always came in on three hops, clearing the bases. The best part was between plays.

These textures stay with me still as I watch sports, bringing them to sensual life, and even allowing me a small piece of my first ambition: to be a sportswriter; and as I say, it's a good thing. Because toward the end of that year I came down with polio and that was that.

Polio

I WAS BACK IN DELBARTON WHEN IT HIT ME—THE ONLY KID IN school to get it. That tickled me, which proves I was feverish: a normal guy would have been sore as hell at being the only kid to get it. But everyone in school had to spend days or weeks in terror waiting to see who went next, while I had crossed to the other side, and I found that feverishly amusing.

The other funny thing was that that year's epidemic was believed to be spent by October. It is hard to re-create the fear we lived with every summer until the first frost—not day by day fear, but little bursts of angst. I remember tossing and turning on the odd hot night and thinking I couldn't take it, no sir, I just couldn't take polio, and imagining in full what finally happened in fact. But the panic of 1944 had lifted in the cool autumn air, and we could all take a breather, while the little bugs battled the cold. I went AWOL one Saturday to see the movie *Wilson* in Morristown: and since that was the only time all term that I was by myself in a crowd, it may have been the day I caught it. Drippy movie.

After the rogue virus, or stray sniper, found me, there really wasn't that much more to it. Sore throat, headache, routine issue for any illness: not enough to keep me from playing touch football on the Friday and Saturday. On Sunday I got a lift to Mass in Morristown—I guess I'd slept late and missed the school version—and had to hitch-hike back. I had no luck for all four miles, and a couple of times I stumbled mysteriously. Tired, man. Went to bed that night with my first, truly feverish thoughts and on Monday was sick enough to qualify for the infirmary.

Great. I had been playing a dangerous game all weekend because I was supposed to be writing a report on Bulwer-Lytton's *Last Days of Pompeii* and I hadn't read a word of it, gambling that I'd be just sick enough to wriggle out of the assignment. And I'd made it. So my principal feeling on Day I of polio was petty elation.

Then, I don't know, a few more stumbles trying to make the bathroom: nobody mentioned polio and neither did I. Some mechanism shielded me from the word for a day or so. Then I knew, but I didn't much care. I was too sick to care. I can't remember a single moment of mental anguish over the larger issues. When I got to the hospital, I cried over having to lie on my back nonstop, and everybody must have thought, Ah ha, the realization has finally hit the poor devil. Another time, I moaned over a gas pain and someone said, "It must be tough, huh?" with great melting eyes—more than a gas pain merited. I'll allow that the early going was uncomfortable, what with hot wet pads strewn over legs and belly at regular intervals, giving one the sensation of being forever left out in wet clothes; but to balance that, everyone treated me like a prince. I had all the detective stories I could read, and I was still out of school. Our football team lost its next game 60–0 to a sleek T-formation outfit; clearly they were at sea without me.

I still don't get it. If polio came again I'd be just as scared again. Just thinking about it rattles me: how did I ever waltz through those horrors? Unless memory betrays me, there was really nothing to it. I find this fact vaguely comforting as one faces the abyss. Perhaps one can, after all, even retool for the afterlife and swim in eternity like a fish; perhaps one can get used to anything.

My mother had taken Rosemary to Canada to celebrate the latter's high school graduation, and there Maisie had contracted pneumonia. So when I saw her at last through the ground-floor hospital window she seemed so drawn and anxious that I felt I had to cheer her up. Frank, meanwhile, was desperately marooned in England on one of his wartime junkets, waiting for the next returning freighter, or whatever was available, to bring him crawling back. So in his case I wrote a *letter* to cheer him up. It was easy enough to do, and I was much esteemed for my pluck. It is an embarrassing memory, all that famous pluck of mine.

Only much later, as I marched my own kids in for their polio shots, did I understand what Frank and Maisie had gone through. "Wilfrid was always running, running, running," my father wrote in a letter to somebody around then. Despite everything I know, I would go stark, staring crazy if one of my children got polio today.

Of course I believed I would be cured. Hadn't Nurse Kenny come up with something just recently? And then there was the power of prayer, as sturdy as the British Navy. For several years I made three wishes in new churches and did everything but wear a goat's foot over my heart, until I came to my senses, age seventeen, in the icy waters of Lourdes. If sheer concentration could have done it, I'd have been cured that day as they flipped me in and out of the magic spring like a beach ball. After that I felt I'd given it my best shot, and the prayers trickled off to nothing.

I'm foreshortening this to put it in its right perspective. The disease had been finessed. I expected a cure for just long enough to go on about my business, as serene as at least the next teenager. The score on this is hard to keep. I was spoiled rotten, a necessary evil I think (one needed the cushion), but I got to read a lot. I still dreamed of baseball more than ever, planning my annual comeback and hobbling to games as soon as I could—in fact, I thought of a cure entirely in terms of sports: nothing else one did with the legs seemed that enviable—but there were a lot of hours to kill now, and I turned reluctantly to literature. And when the smoke had cleared, I was just handicapped enough to be considered an expert on that, but not to miss anything important in life.

Even among the minutiae, the balance is eerily even: I got out of some orthodontic treatments, which was as neat as getting out of Bulwer-Lytton, but which left my mouth full of abandoned construction work. The give-and-take was as fussily precise as a good horse race, with the pluses and minuses probably totaling close to zero.

But as a staunch Catholic, I decided everything was actually for the best, and my faith wasn't affected in the least by its many rebuffs. I was like a spurned lover who doesn't know when to quit. A brain-washed sap, you might suppose; but in a way, I had already had my miracle. I had sailed through polio without noticing. And I was ready even then to attribute this to God. In this rose-window glow, the problem of why God allows pain at all was no problem to me. Human life without it would be superficial beyond endurance: people would just lie around and sunbathe. No great thoughts and certainly no art would come of that. Besides, the Problem of Pain was matched by the even more towering conundrum: "Why is good news so boring?"

Nor did I ever ask, "Why me?" which from the start struck me as a weirdly selfish way to look at things. "Why *not* me? Who else would you suggest?" I felt I'd been pretty well favored by life so far and per-haps was due for a kick in the slats. But I wonder now how I would have reacted to a real disaster. My Catholic symmetry might have been badly shaken by a full-scale, all-out, no-prisoners-taken crippling. I once put my "you can get used to anything" theory to a friend who was nearly totaled by polio, and he said, "No you can't." That is ob-viously the great divide, and I had landed on the sunny side of it.

Polio tethered me to my family's respective lives for the next year or more. I petitioned my way out of the hospital, and every day my bed was rolled into our big living room overlooking the Hudson River, where I held court like the Sun King. Every visitor had to come to terms with me somehow. Rosemary's friends had to talk round me, as they used to in the old days. Important foreign authors had to humor me. Everyone was trapped by the monster invalid in the crank-up bed.

But if they had to sit still for me, I even more so had to sit still for them, and this was a blessing I would have gone out of my way to avoid in normal circumstances. In fact, the variety of my parents' friendships was far greater than anything I could conceivably have drummed up on my own rounds. Whenever I hear a classical station on radio, I think of Sunday afternoons on Riverside Drive, where as-sorted French, Belgians, and who-knows-what-all introduced this par-ticular fuzzy-wuzzy to the sounds of civilization.

Wistful, witty, subtle—but the talk seldom strayed far from Eu-rope, which, frozen for that moment in history, proposed itself as a single glory. The soft Sunday voices seemed to wander among cities and centuries, in and out of cathedrals and music festivals and wonderful little restaurants in the Tyrol—these exiles lived in a Europe of the mind, a distillation of high points, so that in some sense their time in America may have been their happiest, a sustained dream of paradise.

But would it still be there when they got back? The war news kept jerking them awake: the torching of Dresden, the shelling of Monte Cassino, the plunder of art treasures by all the little Görings of both sides—not one but two packs of barbarians were stalking each other through my friends' Golden City, trampling through it like drunks in a flowerbed. This was a novel way for an American kid to see the war. (Not that they were anti-American—far from it. It was war itself, any war, for any cause, that was the monster.)

Don't ask me who they were. There may have been only one of them for all I can swear. They were more an atmosphere, chamber music to drift off to in my eupeptic Sunday serenity. It was like coming to from a jolt of chloroform to find yourself kidnapped by a gang of highbrows. The only refugee I remember for sure is a man called Darlan and I didn't meet him at Riverside Drive. Charles Darlan was the son of the admiral who was believed to have scuttled the French fleet in North Africa and who was considered one of the grimier villains among the squalid Vichy French.

Darlan Jr. had been sent to Warm Springs, Georgia, which FDR had made the Mecca, or at least the White House, of polio, with a brutal case of the disease, and in what I have since learned was probably part of the notorious Darlan deal. (As the only son of a war criminal I am ever likely to meet, his story and his father's still intrigue me, though it's a tough one to crack. The admiral had said, like John Mitchell, "Watch what I do, not what I say," but even if you did that, he was hard to follow. The fleet was scuttled all right instead of being handed over to the Allies as promised; but fleets being what they are, it may not quite have been his to hand over. French sailors do not take kindly to British or even American colors, and another admiral did the actual scuttling anyway. Darlan, previously up to his elbows in compromise Vichyssoise,* did come through on the rest of the deal. Oran, Darlan's bailiwick, was the only Allied landing place in West Africa where there was no Axis or Vichy opposition. So he may have delivered as much on his end of the deal as he was able to.)

Anyway, the son had fetched up as my tablemate at Warm Springs, when I arrived there in the summer of '45, and a very droll one he turned out to be. A stocky, sandy, sad-looking man, he must have had few happy thoughts to retreat to: his father, a world-famous traitor; himself an embarrassment (Do you know who *that* is?); his body a wreck, and his soul an exile—for all that, he remained the most sweet-tempered of men.

Darlan had a line of teasing with me built loosely around "ze world fahm-oos Morreestown Academee," which he swore I'd attended but was for some reason too modest to mention. I know this kind of thing sounds tiresome, but his variations on it were so light and ingenious that I frisked like a cat. Morristown Academy had every virtue except existence as far as I was concerned; but he put this down to my Anglo-Saxon reticence, and no doubt cited Saint Anselm's proof for the existence of God: that anything so perfect *must* exist. He also called our other tablemates to witness. "Ave zey not 'ear of zees *nonpareil* academee?" They chimed confirmation. Morristown Academy was one of the glories of America.

Only much later did I realize the extremities the man must have gone through every day not to talk about the war. It was clearly part of his contract as a guest to behave as if there were no war, and everybody he met strained mightily to comply with this—as easy in those days as not mentioning a passing flood or hurricane. So Darlan made it his business to help us out with this facetious, heartbreaking patter.

Whenever he could, he retreated into a game of checkers where his defense baffled me very much as his conversation did. He was a master of evasion, who devoted his obvious talents entirely to putting people at ease and never speaking his mind. Frank, down on a quick

* *Living with the Enemy* by Werner Rings (Doubleday) is the best account I've read of the pressures politicians in occupied countries were under, besides self-interest, to keep their countries intact and free from reprisals.

visit, described Darlan as the most civilized man he'd ever met (although Frank met quite a few of these). As such, he gave me yet another new way of looking at the war. When the French took to snuffing their collaborators, I thought of him. Charles obviously came from what the Irish call "daycent" people. Yet the avengers would have guillotined his father as gleefully as the next cutpurse, if he hadn't by chance already been assassinated by either an OSS free-lance, a Gaullist, or someone from the cast of *Casablanca*. There were no excuses and no ambiguities in the glare of victory.

Otherwise, Warm Springs was just an incident. I enjoyed it but it wasn't getting me anywhere. The therapy was a joke, but I developed a great overhead smash for wheelchair Ping-Pong and a truly maddening bridge system, based on the theory that bidding was put on earth to confuse people, two of whom were enemies, and only one of whom was a friend. So I scrapped the conventions, which I but dimly understood to begin with, and bid what felt good. The result was that only one person knew what was going on—me—and I won some hairy contests, completely out of line with the form book. Opponents would give up on potential winning hands because it sounded as if I had exactly the same hand, or a powerhouse in their long weak suit, or whatever it was a rational person would have been conveying. I would then squeak through with my two diamonds, while they fumed over lost slams.

I thought it was a swell system, but pretty soon I couldn't find anyone to play with, not even partners—especially not partners—and it was time to leave. There was nothing else to stay for. Warm Springs was a gigantic hoax as far as its reputation was concerned, but it had an honest heart. No one there ever claimed it could cure anything.

The snag about all those clever Europeans back in New York was that they seemed to know everything—while I at this point knew nothing. "What *was* the date of the Treaty of Utrecht?" One particular woman was a special torture to me, because she always needed help with the details. Only at Oxford did I learn to mutter "Not my period." Right now I was naked in any period. And any language. You never knew when someone would burst into French or worse, followed by laughter or thoughtful nods. I would smile stiffly. "You understand conversational French, no?" they would say, and I would grunt noncommittally. I realized I could never enter their Great Good Place in this sorry condition, never even croak out a pleasantry about it.

Frank for his part was alarmed when I took a test for an English public school and registered close to "moron." Since I'd been enrolled in this very school, effective from the day the war ended, something must be done every bit as quickly as our troops were advancing in 1945. Delbarton had given me everything but an education: my friends were too tough to want one, and the priests were too obliging to pursue the matter. All I knew was what I picked up around the house: religion, literate talk and my father's flotsam.

Frank shrewdly war-gamed the situation. I had read some English poetry on the sly (I found that Keats was not something you carried on about at Delbarton—not while George M. Cohan's songs were around) and I seemed to be able to write adequate prose—rather sonorous and Churchillian. Every now and then I had to give little talks at school, and they sounded just like the great man's war speeches, whatever the occasion. Well it might come in handy. So we decided to trust English to luck, and get down to a little Latin and French.

Frank became my teacher perforce, and together we blitzkrieged Latin. I have never known such whirlwind teaching. It was like quick-marching in full pack with some kind but tireless sergeant at your heels. "Vocabulary, vocabulary and more vocabulary," Frank would chant. The joys of the ablative absolute and the accusative-and-infinitive he taught in a twinkling as graphically and seductively as he ever taught the Trinity: but these pleasures were not to be lingered over. One must get back to vocabulary: a tick next to every new word, another tick next to an old, forgotten one and then drill, drill, drill them all every day according to their ticks. Hip two three four. Five floors below, naval cadets marched past to the same sort of beat in the last giddy weeks of the war. "Left, left, she had a good home and she left, left. . . ." Which of us was which? I felt as if I, too, were being whipped into shape for some battle. Frank was unfailingly pleasant about it, but there was no time to flag and I became a good enough Latinist in just a few months to get into the top bracket of my class in

England—only to have it all spill out a few years later like hastily packed luggage.

So I learned, firsthand and the hard way, Frank's genius for teaching. We did all the geometry a sane man could ever need in six weeks, and enough French for me to squeak by in that too and this was all that could possibly be done in the small amount of time Frank had to spare in those days. After these sessions, he would go whistling off to work while I lay drained.

I was already an expert on bad teaching. There was a hapless fellow at Delbarton called Father Thomas who could never even get started, because order collapsed at the sight of his face. The ruliest boys would howl and roll their eyes till Thomas himself was reduced to giggles. But between him and Father Adrian,* our best, every shade of incompetence could be found at Delbarton. Now I had a chance to observe a Grand Master.

Energy, concentration, patience, he had all the necessities in profligate amounts, but they avail you nothing if you have not showmanship. I don't know how Frank fitted his famous soft-shoe into our iron regimen, but I felt, weakly, after each bloodletting that we'd had a good time. A sneer at Cicero here (even the ancient world seemed to be divided into Catholics and Others. Virgil was a Catholic, whether he knew it or not, Cicero was an Other), a snatch of schoolboy doggerel there (synopsis of Livy on King Tarquin, who threw the sacred chickens overboard because their livers gave the wrong signals: "The sacred chickens will not eat?/Then let the sacred chickens drink./Next day the news was cabled home:/Sensational defeat of Rome!")—at times a whole library of curiosities seemed to be coming at me.

Who knows how many things one learns from such a man? I realized from those dreamlike Sundays that he had the key to the Golden City of the Europeans all right, from Racine to Ronsard to the Diet of Worms. Yet his idol was precision, not variety. He was sorry I'd missed the day-in, day-out drudgery that makes one get things

---

* Some words of Father Adrian's still haunt me. "You seem to be a nice enough little chap when you're not writing. Then you turn into a scorpion." I was twelve at the time.

right. And I always winced for him when I heard someone mess up an anecdote or a news story for want of a fact. Yet often as not I was that person. With all his force-feeding, he could, after all, only teach me variety.

The hours I spent on my back working out with Livy and Sallust were crucial to my mental existence. Nobody had asked me to do anything of consequence since I got polio. In Warm Springs, the teachers seemed to assume brain damage, as people often do with the handicapped—and they taught us accordingly. What would we need with an education in our condition? Jane Austen's women needed one slightly more. And even now that the honeymoon was almost over and I was just another gimp around town, no outside tutor (and we tried a couple from Columbia and Fordham) could keep up the crackling pace that the clock demanded. Without Frank, I'd have reached sixteen without any education at all.

It may seem perverse to add that, if it hadn't been absolutely necessary, I believe it would have been a mistake, this teaching at home. A student, like a writer, ought to leave the building—or pretend to leave the building—every day. Otherwise, one's work and one's life become gluey and stick to the pan. I know all about great teaching fathers, the pères Browning and John Stuart Mill, who turned their sons into geniuses: but genius is the least you can demand of such an arrangement. Because when the father is the teacher there is no escape from him, physically or mentally.

Even the Christian God tactfully divides his roles into three, and Frank did his damnedest to divide himself into at least two, but he lacked the infinite capacity. On a policeman level, he knew when I hadn't done my homework and why, and *I* knew it was no use calling in sick. As I sat up late of an evening listening grimly to my Gershwin records, he would pointedly *not* say "Shouldn't you be doing something else?" but it would hang palpable between us the next morning.

No one could have done it more gracefully than he: I have never felt so disciplined without actually being disciplined. And I'm sure this would have been the same, son or no son. But we had lost a certain ease. I had learned so much from him before we actually called it learning that it was a pity to formalize the process: but formalize we must. From now on, and for the rest of his life, if Frank straightened out my use of words or frowned over something I'd written, it was the teacher straightening and frowning. Perched eternally over my shoulder, he remains my editor even in death. I wonder what he would think of this particular choice of words? Well, to hell with what he thinks of it—but the deed is done.

I suspect other writers have some similar presence to appease, usually grimmer and narrower. Because Frank was also a great encourager, and I probably stretched myself quite a bit reaching for his applause, which in turn reached down to meet me halfway. On the other hand, there was just the faintest shadow of a clerical collar around my muse's neck: to take an instance at random, he believed strongly that suspicion is a sin, and as a result, I have always felt that people gossiping tend to sound either sillier or more depraved than the thing they are gossiping about: so I grew up missing a lot of good stories.*

As a result of this embargo, and of Maisie's genuine innocence, the outside world, as discussed, seemed at times too good to be true; which meant that, as actually experienced, it gave off a series of rude shocks, almost as much as it had for Maisie's poor brothers. I jumped the first and only time I heard Frank say "bastard" (bahstard) in a fit of pique. I think he did it to show it was all right to. Swearing was no sin in his book, he just didn't like it. In the same spirit, Frank hated people's feelings getting hurt, even in fiction, and I have sometimes distorted things or left them out of novels if they seemed likely to have that effect. Courtesy of Frank, I do not believe that the "Ode on a Grecian Urn" is worth any number of old ladies.

Faulkner's famous phrase† is much bandied about by people who are in no position to find out. But there may be a real distinction here between great novelists and the rest of us. At sixteen, in a froth of Lenten priggishness, I prayed that I would grow up to be a good man rather than a great writer. This was very decent of me, because my

* Well a few. When Frank took a holiday from his principles, he was a wonderful gossip.
† *Writers at Work I, Paris Review.* Faulkner's belief that art is more important than people reminds me eerily of the neutron bomb.

usual dream of greatness at that age was someday to own a villa like
Somerset Maugham's with a thousand steps leading down to the Med-
iterranean, onto each of which my butler, Erich von Stroheim, would
bounce worshipful admirers, students, and so on, one by one, till they
plinked like pebbles into the wine-dark sea. So I knew what greatness
was all about and what I was rejecting.

Even aside from Frank's imperious morality, a schoolmaster is a
constricting muse, and cutting Frank down to the size of occasional
editor, reviewer, finally average reader would become my melancholy
duty if I was going to be any kind of writer at all, never mind the
villa. Oddly enough Frank saw this at least sometimes, while my
mother hardly saw it at all. She was serenely pre-Freudian and could
not imagine two nice chaps using the weapons of art and instruction
to settle Oedipal matters. And as I wrote myself stroke by stroke away
from the family she felt a little betrayed, or rather, since a Sheed could
do no wrong, puzzled. I think a lot of my stuff wound up boring her,
which is the best you can hope for in the circumstances. It went without saying that I was a great writer, but this particular piece, well . . .
she only wholeheartedly liked my stuff if it was ardently right-minded,
which didn't give her much to work with.

Frank understood better the delicate arrangements between fathers and sons, the small areas in which they can meet and be friends,
and after his hectic spell of teaching, he withdrew to Polonius range,
giving, as one chap to another, such tips as I might find handy in life,
such as not saying "hard put to do something" instead of "put to *it* to
do something" ("I don't *know* why," he said, averting his eyes), and
not beginning sentences with "due to." To convey these and other
messages he would lower his face into his hands and groan softly over
my solecisms. Or else he would tactfully say, "I notice you give a
rather unusual meaning to the word 'flair,'" as one might tell a man
his fly was undone. One way or another I was paying for the grammat-
ical sins of mankind. Frank never even seemed to notice other people's
howlers: at least, he smiled bravely through them. But in my case, not
a sparrow fell or a participle dangled without his being on top of it
with blood in his eye.

In the waking world, we were always the best and least complicated of friends, enjoying each other to bursting (at least on my end). But every now and then, for some years, a fear would strike even my waking self, like a wind across a grave, that I hadn't done my lessons: and as for dreams, I once had one set in an office where the loudspeakers had run amuck and kept announcing, "Wilfrid Sheed is a fraud. Repeat, Wilfrid Sheed . . ." but this could have traced to any period of my life. Still the teaching left its light mark. In friendly argument with Frank I tended to feel flustered and outgunned too quickly, and I could never write him a letter without worrying about my whiches and thats. If he hadn't lived so long, things might have frozen in that form. But in the sweetness and occasional deference of old age, we became equals at last, even in dreams.

"Knowledge maketh a bloody entry" indeed. But the bleeding seemed worth it when I got to Rome itself a year or so later and sat in the Forum dazed as by a mystical vision. An intellectual passion other than baseball had arrived at last. And it all seemed worth it passim over the years, as I stumbled through Oxford and into scribbling. But when I tried to write even the most modest of sex scenes . . .

. . . Well, like many of his generation, Frank both was and was not a prude. When he told me the facts of life, or rather mopped up some of the disinformation I'd received from pals, he made sex sound so sacred and God-given that I said, in awe, "So why do people make jokes about it?" "It beats me," he said. But then, after a pause, "You know, there have been some extraordinarily good jests on the subject."

One of them was definitely not Irving Berlin's barnyard song "Doin' What Comes Naturally," which he inexplicably banned from the house when I was sixteen and Rosemary nineteen, a bit old for banning anything. The worst thing about semiprudes is their skittishness. Frank would chuckle over much dirtier jokes than anything in Berlin's simpleminded number. And when I wrote a rowdy college humor scene in my first novel, *A Middle Class Education,* he maddened me by saying, "Shouldn't there have been a bit less lavatory and a bit more women?" This was particularly irksome, because I'd fixed the proportions partly with him in mind—something I would never do again.

Strangely enough, Frank still only remembered at odd moments to teach me religion as such. At one point, he set up a program of weekly classes for me and Rosemary, only to forget the whole thing, or be out of town that day. It didn't matter much: the air at our place was thick with theology and one could hardly help coming down with it. But the first actual religious teaching I ever heard was when Frank was teaching others.

This can serve to introduce Sheed/Ward's other head. With the Europeans safely cleared away of a Sunday, we would frequently open our apartment to a group called "Friendship House," of which we came to form something called "The Outer Circle."* Friendship House was an interracial religious group founded by a flamboyant émigrée, the Baroness Catherine de Hueck, who captivated me right off, in her stripped-down Harlem workshop, with exotic tales of how she had escaped from Russia under barbed wire while Communist bullets practically whistled through her hair.

Despite this, she was a radical of sorts herself, though a bit too volatile and eccentric to be pinned down closer than that. She was wonderful window dressing for her group (one of her captures had been young Thomas Merton in his late pagan, early Christian phase), but a pain in the neck to those within. Bored to madness with dailiness, she was forever planning new branches and whole new approaches for her movement to take. Her lieutenants were probably only too happy to see her leave town (the circus probably felt the same way about Barnum) so that she could tell her Scheherazade escape stories to fresh faces, raise money, and incidentally keep out of their hair.

One tack she did not foresee, or even make heads or tails of, was the one Friendship House and its Outer Circle (or downtown branch) had taken up at the Sheeds'. The notion of interracial meetings in a white family's apartment was "vunderful, extraw-dinary," of course. And to begin with, all comers just wanted to talk about racial injustice, which, too, was "vunderful." But my parents, who pretty much

* This was a truly important movement which, like much else in this book, deserves its own history. My angle, I should perhaps restress, is only on "what I knew and when I knew it," in the immortal words from the Senate Watergate hearings.

took race for granted, began to chafe at hearing the same speech over and over again; and they decided that it would be a great leap forward to talk about something else, anything else than race. Whites and blacks (or coloreds then) were always talking about it, as if they had nothing else in common, and afterward feeling they'd accomplished something. So to have them get together in a chummy elbow-to-elbow and sit-on-the-floor atmosphere, and *forget* race for a couple of hours, would be not just a breakthrough, but the only possible breakthrough.

But naturally, since Frank never missed an opening, the subject had to be theology. And he began to teach it the way he always had, the old Evidence Guild way. Which meant that a young speaker would talk to a specific subject and Frank would heckle along gently or slyly according to the weight of the speaker, and encourage others to chime in as best they could.

Some members never did get it. They'd come here to talk about injustice, by God, and that's what they were going to talk about. The diehards were always given complete right of way: after all, race was still the underlying point of the movement, and these would have been tough people to stop in any event. But a certain impatience could be sensed from the younger crowd who'd gotten hooked on the religious give-and-take. Frank couldn't very well heckle racial justice, so the whole mood changed while one angry soul exhorted a silent room. At the end, the racial speeches always got respectful ovations, but a member of the theological school would usually pop up quickly to change the subject to that old-time, Athanasian, Augustinian religion, which my father made sound like the morning newspaper.

On the whole, the balance worked out pretty well. This wasn't the Evidence Guild after all, and the racial *fervorini* helped to remind at least the white guests that we were not far from the battlefield, and that meetings like ours were charming exceptions to reality, a footnote and not history itself. As if we needed a further reminder of this, the black elevator men in the building lodged a protest against the class of people that they suddenly had to ferry up to our apartment. Clearly, it was a little precious of anyone to carry on about what kind of meetings to have when having meetings at all was still the burning issue.

Of all our theologically disoriented visitors, none was more at sea than the baroness herself when she dropped in one night. She wasn't much of a listener at the best of times, and so what all this high-minded palaver had to do with social protest was clearly beyond her. Fortunately, she believed that Frank must be a great man,* and she knew a live meeting when she saw one and felt she had somehow inspired it. So she left feeling no worse than baffled, never, that I know of, to return. Although a royal fuss was made over her that night, her mind tended to wander when she wasn't on stage.

Despite the odd twitch of tension, Friendship House was eminently the right name for this congeries of dreams. The meetings were convivial with relief, as blacks and whites realized that there *was* no barrier, that the whole thing had been made up, and that they could be friends just by wanting to.

The iron limits to this era of goodwill would become clear a little later when a white woman member wanted to marry a black West Indian, and both races joined in opposing them——whether for the sake of the children, or because the West Indian had a high native polish which made him seem like an operator (he did have exceptional manners, such that Jim Crow enforcers once actually apologized to him and let him keep his seat) or from a vague uneasiness that a mixed marriage would give the movement a bad name, I don't know. I can only report the way it sounded around our house. For whatever reason, maybe even plain humble prejudice, several of these people who had given so much of themselves to bringing the races together balked at this final step, and only my parents and a handful supported the couple all the way.

By "all the way" I mean that Frank and Maisie went on visiting

* He was also by good chance her husband's publisher. Eddie Doherty was a Chicago newspaperman and just the kind to marry a Russian baroness, although she outweighed him a good two to one. He wrote a book called *Gall and Honey*, in which he meditated on no less than three of his marriages: so naturally Frank privately renamed the book "All Gall is divided into three honeys"—a joke which, like so many of his, has gone the way of Latin and liberal education in general.

the couple for years and years as they bucked the roadblocks of housing and schooling, and their children grew up fine and they triumphed over even their own crowd's fears. Friendship House did *not* get a name as a dating service for miscegenationists and the couple endured. But the point here is that it was unthinkable for Frank and Maisie just to give an opinion about a life-and-death matter and leave it at that. They had to back their advice with help for as long as it took.

To the old pros, the Sheeds' role must have seemed like liberal meddling anyway. In the rarefied world of Frank and Maisie, it was figured, the abrasions of street life never got past the tradesmen's entrance. So they had no business using their flashy moral authority to persuade young people to have mulatto children in a racist society. The Sheeds would be gone tomorrow, but the ghetto remained.

What the pros forgot is that the Sheeds, gone or not, were always back the next day and that they never lived in a rose garden themselves. We happened to be perched at that time in one of our few presentable apartments: some of the others could not have housed meetings of any size at all. And although the Sheeds still had something to learn about the physicality of squalor and despair (they learned it), their decision in this matter was not the least bit sentimental. They were simply betting on a man and woman's character.

One unspoken feeling at Friendship House was that the West Indian wanted a white trophy to display, or just ignore, or kick around as the unspeaker preferred to see it. Frank's relative cosmopolitanism may have done him a turn here. As an office manager, he was an uncertain judge of Americans and he hired some lulus, even allowing that few but lulus ever applied at Sheed and Ward. But for gentlemen based loosely on the English model, his eye was uncanny, and why not? He could judge a colonial boy of any color, and he knew that this one was simply too proud to want a trophy. Once upon a time, Frank might have been accused of trophy-hunting himself; so he knew. As usual, the pros were talking percentages, and he was talking people.

It would be wrong to leave Friendship House on this sourish note. I've chiefly gone into the wedding episode to bring back the period—and to show how Frank and Maisie somehow stood outside the period, and any other period, for their different reasons. The meetings seem that much more vibrant to me when I think of the world outside, the frightened elevator men and our nonplussed Jewish landlady, and also the world inside, where even the most radical had placed staunch walls around their hopes.

In the circumstances, it was thrilling just to be there at all, kicking theology around, black and white, in a mood of hot, surprised hilarity. Our overhead fans contributed nothing but noise and I decided guiltily one steamy night that Negroes did smell different, though not necessarily worse. If, God forbid, I should ever find myself at a blind sniffing contest, I would expect the whites to smell ranker, more acid; but either way the smells remind me of the meetings, and the meetings were great. Why not? I had reentered life. Which proves you can be nostalgic about the damnedest things.

By now, I was perched on the sofa, our hostage, it dawns on me, to the world of the disadvantaged. It must have been hard to think of Frank and Maisie as dilettantes while they were shouldering a crippled kid. But I didn't know what they were shouldering. The cost of looking after me, of renting hospital beds and shelling out for physiotherapists and hapless specialists and even installing a galvanic battery which stung like a bee and burned like a cigarette, was all smothered in my parents' optimism.

Everyone, Rosemary especially, had to double at the seamier side of nursing, easing out bedpans and urine bottles and carrying me gingerly to the bathtub (Min insisted that I wear a bathing suit throughout). And the world thought that *I* was having a hard time. The Friendship House gang, brimming with love anyway, treated me as a mascot. And whenever I meet any of them anywhere, the years wash away.

Keeping me sublimely unaware of the psychic cost to them of polio was the family's greatest gift, and it was a pleasure later in life to try to return the favor—to Min first, as she lay crotchety and impatient after two strokes, and later to Maisie and Frank, as time wore them down. But there was no returning this one. I left my sickbed raring to go, as one does from a good dream. If they had never published a book or (in my mother's case) housed a poor couple or sunk a well in India, their works justified them. Because they couldn't have squeezed out this kindness to me from some penurious stockpile. They had to love the human race.

Before I kiss polio goodbye in this stiff-upper-lip manner of English partings, let me add a nullifying note. On behalf of the world's real cripples, I wouldn't like it thought that any experience of this sort is a breeze. Polio may be a bigger event than one is obliged to feel at the time. When I wrote a novel about it called *People Will Always Be Kind*, the experience sounded more harrowing than anything I remembered. Yet the book must have come from *somewhere*. And when I batted out an essay on the handicapped for *Newsweek*, I was accused of all sorts of pent-up bitterness, rage and other fancy stuff. Yet the article, seen from my end, was an amiable, objective exercise written in my usual neutral mood. Writing keeps you much too busy to be angry. The performance itself takes up all your attention, and the subject matter just has to shift for itself—especially in this case, since I was working from somebody else's suggestion.

What happened was that *Newsweek* had asked me to write about the closing of Warm Springs, and I thought it might be fun to have a last lick at the old alma mater. I am also congenitally drawn to subjects that can be handled without leaving the house. I hadn't thought much about the handicapped, myself or the rest, for a very long time, but there it was, a topic like any other. The essay as originally scribbled came up exactly ninety-six (I think it was) characters short, and I decided, ah ha, here's a chance to show off. So I added a paragraph of exactly ninety-six characters—to the awe, I trust, of the copy editor—and it was within that technical finger exercise that most of the "bitterness" was found. People told me that I had never written with such feeling when, strictly speaking, I had seldom written with less.

So subject matter shifts for itself very nicely. Just as you don't have to play Beethoven romantically, only correctly, so writers can sometimes let their subjects carry them—and when they can, they certainly should. (There's nothing sadder than a writer trying to mount his own kite.) Yet obviously the feeling detected by *Newsweek* readers is there, so deeply absorbed into the system by now that it seeps into one's sentences.

When Frank read *People*, he told me he skipped the first, or polio, part because it would be too painful. And I thought, By God, what have I done this time? I had an extra reason to worry, because I had played some low novelist's games with the hero's parents. My own had proved simply hopeless for the parts: with so much faith, courage and love, there would have been no story.

My theme was the effect of polio on sundry onlookers, and the use a natural politician might learn to make of this. And for this I needed something a lot closer to average than Frank and Maisie. Fortunately, anyone who knew anything at all about them could be assumed to see what I was doing—but could they themselves? *They* didn't know what I thought of them deep down or how monstrous they might look to a child: *no* parent does.

When Maisie read my first book, *A Middle Class Education*, she said, "My dear, we should never have sent you to Oxford." After that she came to understand that I was only fooling around, and I can't remember whether she read *People* at all; she was eighty-four at the time and used to me. I had long since wistfully asked both parents not to read my novels, and Frank had complied at first but Maisie hadn't. Then about halfway along, I think they switched, Frank's curiosity overcoming him and Maisie's polite bewilderment doing the same for her in the other direction. But now I had written something too painful for Frank. Another of my bland enterprises had exploded on me.

As I began navigating first the living room and then the city, I found myself encumbered with attention, which distracted me from the exhilaration of simply being up and about. "Take it easy, kid, take your time," kind strangers advised, as if I were hurrying just to please them.

Left to your own devices, it takes a real effort to remember all day that there's supposed to be something wrong with you: but never think that there's not always someone on hand to remind you. Suddenly somebody will clutch your elbow (always the cane elbow, thus immobilizing you) as you cross the street, and all the stratagems you've worked out for that particular operation, stratagems which have become second nature, are rendered void. I almost belted an old lady once on Park Avenue who had flung her arms around my chest without warning, the better to steer me. Not only was I helpless in this position, but she was too, and we floundered into a brief waltz before I jabbed myself free with my elbow. When old ladies help you across streets, you have to fight back somehow.

Being handicapped can make you as mean as having a girl's name, and as timid as a shut-in. For years any offer to help, however reasonable, turned me into a surly brute. Once, at Oxford, I fell to the ground from sheer drunkenness. (I had tried foolishly to match drinks with the big boys, and the ninth pint did it.) The inevitable do-gooder fluttered up and said to my most proximate friend, "How did you let this happen? You must do something at once. You must take him home." "You try it, lady," said the friend, while I rose and fell gallantly in the background.

The approach of middle age takes care of that kind of pugnacity. After a while, anyone can help who wants. In fact, I'll jump on people's backs to cross streets. But time doesn't do much for two other side effects: laziness and stoicism. Laziness, perhaps because you think the world owes you one or, more likely, because the world thinks so too and lets you get away with murder; stoicism, because if you're going to be lazy, you'd better be stoical. Lazy people live lives of extreme discomfort: too lazy to get up and go to the bathroom, open the window, buy a raincoat, we spend our days hot, cold, soggy and covered with infected cuts. A brave bunch, I would say.

Sexual shyness might also be a problem, depending on your ravages. Yet I've known some spindly gnomes who made out like bandits. Here, as elsewhere, the forever missing information is precisely what you would have been like *without* polio. The temptation is to burden the illness with everything that went wrong, which is to overrate it wildly. I believe the time lost from school can make you as lopsided as a rich kid. At fifteen, I knew the secrets of the ages, a very wise old child; yet when I got to Oxford four years later, I fell to bawling dirty rugby songs with the demented gusto of a ten-year-old, all those witless dirges—" 'E 'ad a big this, and she 'ad a big that"—for twenty full choruses. There is a complete blank in my mind as to why I bothered; the delirium has left no trace except for some dingy lyrics which drift through occasionally, picking their noses.

But why did the other young gentlemen at Oxford do it? They had no polio, no missing years. It seems they just missed the army, in which most of them had had to spend the last two sodding years. No one paid any mind to the songs' content, it could have been "Men of Harlech," something to do together before the cold-water flat and the disappointing job. So there are different routes to childishness. And indeed, in considering my own version, I find that polio shrinks to nothing alongside Catholicism, that home of wise old children. I probably sang the songs because I'd decided it wasn't a mortal sin after all. There are probably Catholics who still make it a point to eat meat on Fridays. Which brings us back, I suppose, to Frank and Maisie.

At this point we'll let polio slink out, like some comic-strip villain, muttering curses, and return to the bright daylight of my parents' optimism, or vitality. Right now they wanted to go back to England, or at least Frank did: Maisie *did* want to see old so-and-so again, a lot of old so-and-sos in fact, but otherwise her feeling about going home left no clear imprint on my memory. There was an awful lot she regretted leaving in America.

Whatever Frank planned generated its own gusto, so the house felt excited. Rosemary wanted to go all right, as if she'd been holding her breath for six years. I didn't, but Frank talked me sufficiently around. For one thing, he gave me a book about cricket, which, for dark reasons of the blood, hooked me sight unseen; for another, he told precisely the kind of anecdotes I was calculated to go for about England; and for a third he confided in me why I *had* to go to Oxford.

Outside of the delights of the place, which would be several bloody years away wherever I went, what with my Cro-Magnon education, but unreachable from America, he had a private reason which would have scandalized his fans. He said that he didn't in the least mind sending me to Harvard or some such, but could not bring himself to consider one of those Catholic colleges which he knew so well (perhaps if he'd lectured at Harvard, he'd have banned that too). Professionally, he explained, he would be ruined if I went to a secular American school, but nobody minded about old Oxford. So we would just retreat into the foreign fog from which we had emerged.

His reasoning was self-evidently correct. At the time, it was considered next door to a matter for excommunication to send your boy to Harvard; and a ruined Frank couldn't have sent me anywhere. I was flattered that he'd leveled with me about this: the days of mysterious marching orders were over, although some strange ones lay ahead— strange, that is, even when explained.

Life in America seemed all the sweeter with the end in sight. Barnard girls in bright blue bloomers practiced archery, tennis and hitting golf balls into a sack right below my window, while just beyond them the bells of the Rockefeller Riverside Church (or "rancid butter tower") bonged out shamelessly nonsacral music. "Spurs That Jingle, Jangle, Jingle," "I've Got Sixpence"—the whole place was in a delirium by the summer of '45.

And for our Sunday enjoyment we had our pastor, Father George B. Ford, a famous liberal priest of the period, who tried to speak elegantly for his largely Columbia U congregation and always wound up flat on his back. "It blesseth him who gives and it likewise blesses the recipient" was his version of Portia; it could never be said that Father Ford didn't swing for the fences. But through the garble beamed an effulgent decency. Father Malaprop was a big influence on Thomas Merton and other intellectuals who had the wit to see through the density of his verbiage.

Another small dividend was that, in my semicrippled condition, I didn't have to stand up for the Legion of Decency pledge (a vow to boycott theaters that showed French or other dirty movies), although neighbors may have been puzzled that I stood up for everything else. Frank and Maisie did stand, rather grimly, faces down, and, who knows? moved their lips, Frank perhaps to some old song, Maisie to imprecations. "Preposterous, sheer humbug" and so on. They probably figured that if enough people read their books, the Legion would just lose its teeth and dwindle to nothing, which indeed it did, for whatever reason.

Above all, I had friends now and was in no mind to surrender another set. A genial family called Kennedy would take turns tossing me softballs and baseballs which I whacked smartly from the bastion of my wheelchair and later upright, perched on one and a half legs. All this and Peace too. The atom bomb bothered us all in varying degrees, but not enough to spoil anyone's fun. Maisie thought of brother Leo's love of Japan, and would come to hate the Bomb more and more; but right then, we'd all waited too long. The Sheeds had lost a whole publishing house in the London blitz, and indeed its whole beautiful setting on Pater Noster Row next to Ave Maria Lane. Frank had heard the whine of the first German rocket bombs (if you heard it, you were safe) and it stood to reason that these would be hopping across oceans any day now. So—anything to end this mess.

When VJ Day itself came, I was staying with the infinitely obliging Kennedys in their summer place near Altamont, New York, and the gang celebrated by pushing my wheelchair down country lanes, all of us beating on pans and waving homemade flags. Even then, happy enough to burst, one sensed a certain desolation about this little unit of noise and gaiety straggling through the country silence. Consider it a classic Fellini ending, with us kids pushing and banging along an empty, infinite strand, thinking that we were cheering the *beginning* of something.

It took a little longer, but even the good news of peace became boring in time, and attempts to celebrate it became sadder. But right now peace meant England for us, no avoiding it any longer. Before leaving, Frank shouted Rosemary and me to a short holiday in Curaçao as a postpolio present for both of us. Travel was Frank's favorite gift, and he never gave a handsomer one. Swimming every day in clear blue water, with a lazy eye out for barracuda and baneful sea plants, washed away all the sickroom squalor, the bedpans and pisspots and rubber sheets which had afflicted Rosemary at least as much as me.

At night, we ate jolly Dutch meals, one of them a diplomatic dinner of thirteen courses, until austerity too was forgotten. Our host was a Dutch journalist who happened to be governor at the time— just part of Frank's tatterdemalion network. Every now and then, the governor would review his army, a tiny group of white-shorted natives which fit nicely into his small courtyard, to a muffle of drums. This comic-opera brigade even helped to take the curse off war. They couldn't have beaten off their in-laws. There was serious talk over dinner about the impending loss of Indonesia (which was blamed squarely on America's anti-imperialism), but nothing could happen to our goofy little island in the sun.

At some of these dinners, I made the mistake of questioning our host's opinions now and then, as one might at home. Since his children didn't talk and his wife didn't talk either, I thought he might be lonely, laying down the law like that. And he himself didn't seem to mind (Frank had met him in Dublin where no one talks unchallenged). Unfortunately, his wife did. In fact, she took my feeble banter to be unprecedented insolence, and she had a distraught conference with Rosemary about it. Since she had never seen the like, the governess right away assumed that I was incurable: some sort of animal really, an omen, a hooligan from the future—which left us no choice but to move up our departure date. Rosemary was nice about it, considering that it was her vacation too.

Of all the things that happened in Curaçao this was the only one that taught me anything, the rest was illusion. I had left the land of the Precocious Child and until I returned, I had better button my lip when the grown-ups had the floor. In New York I was a young man, almost too attentively listened to; abroad, I would be a schoolboy until notified otherwise.

As for the sunshine and the white sand and the big meals, I could forget those where I was going. I still had no idea what I was being fattened up for. But the governor's wife would accompany me, taking various forms—monks, shopkeepers, wheezing dinner guests—for some time to come. Because our next stop really was England.

The episode showed how betwixt and between Rosemary and I were. We wouldn't have dreamed of sassing our parents, but we could argue as much as we liked—if one doesn't mind getting into the ring with an eight-hundred-pound gorilla. Maisie especially had a tendency to gang up and form a solid front with Frank, in which case forget it. The governor and his wife obviously offered less formidable opposition and I guess I must have found it too tempting.

England, Then

FIVE YEARS BEFORE I'D BEEN SURPRISED AT HOW AT HOME FRANK and Maisie felt in America; now I was even more surprised to find them at home in England—a *really* weird country.

I suppose if you do enough of your living in your head, travel is just an incident. Anyway, cultural differences that shook me like bomb blasts were, to Frank, simply new conventions to be mastered, and to Maisie, fascinating oddities of no particular eternal substance. The very difficult doctrine of the brotherhood of man was almost too easy for them to swallow: being equally at home, and not at home, everywhere, they found a world thinly covered in a rind of inessentials. Language, custom, things like that: nothing to be afraid of. There was nothing "out there," to compete with, or stand up to, the Good News of the Gospel.

For this reason, they were able to dump me with a clear heart, not just into the strange land of England, but into an English Catholic school remote even from the rest of England, and whole oceans and centuries distant from the Roxy or Yankee Stadium. I felt as if I'd moved back into the world of the Wards, somehow gone rancid. I can't say, with adolescent laziness, that I hated the place; or even, with adult ditto, that I didn't understand it. Part of me understood it all too well. I just didn't want it.

You can't grow up in several directions at once. Many refugees emerged from similar wrenchings and twistings with somewhat weak, indeterminate identities as if they'd been bent once too often in a greenhouse. My horror of Downside, my new Benedictine school, says little about the objective merits of the place (although even other English boys found it spooky) but much about my blind instinct not to be bent again. At first I cried, in sheer confusion, and then I campaigned, and in fact I got out just in time. Because by the end of my second term, I was beginning to like the place.

If I'd stayed, I'd have lost everything I had. English schools were known then to stamp their boys forever, and no school had a more rococo stamp than Downside. To become a recognizable "Old Gregorian" I'd have had to start completely from scratch. And what was bloodcurdling was to realize how easy that might be; one's personality might be much more superficial than it felt, a bad paint job. At least, the other foreign boys who'd just been there a few months seemed to be peeling already. Downside in those days featured a sort of world-weary aestheticism: languor, a hint of make-believe homosexuality, a touch of the fop—all the Oxford hand-me-downs, grimly wrestled over by less talented schoolboys. It would have been sinfully easy to imitate this imitation.

Of course, the understanding was that beneath our makeup we were rock-ribbed Catholics all, capable of prodigies of prayer and fasting, and magnificent under fire. We were just making *fun* of worldliness, because we knew better. Even the monks allowed themselves a piece of this Christian playfulness: for example, our burly housemaster, who would dangle a particular boy on his knee and call him Dolly—which was the boy's universal nickname, but still—in heavily flirtatious tones, until the facetiousness made one's teeth hurt.

These were the Catholic remnants as I found them: snobbish, heavy on Norman names, distantly kind, temperately friendly; pointless. They had kept the Faith, but had no place to go with it. Although Catholics had long since crashed public life, and we were mighty proud of our one cabinet member (Richard Stokes, Labour), our preferred style faced languidly backward to a time when Catholics lived in eccentric enclaves like this and made their own fun. The explosion that was Newman and the Wards had come and gone, leaving this epicene boys' club behind. We had a vintners' society. Fashionable priests gave little talks. On half-holy days, we visited Wells and Frome cathedrals—the excitement lay in guessing which. Or thrilled to the scrawny ruins of a Roman road in Stratton-on-Fosse. Only a savage or an American could ask for anything more.

It has all been blown away long since. The sixties in their awesome house-to-house sweep had no particular trouble with Downside, which at this writing is debating whether to *stop* taking girls. England in 1946 was still too drained to try anything it hadn't tried before, so that much of life was fossilized in the manner of Downside: I just happened to catch a particularly fruity specimen of a school.

Luckily for me, Downside proved equally difficult for me to tackle physically. The classrooms seemed to be acres apart, and the normal school gait was the sprint. So I was always chugging into class on my two canes after the lesson had started. At least once a week, maybe twice, the whole school would fling into military gear and drill with much clatter in the quad. I was allowed to take country walks instead, feeling so far out of it that I was almost ethereal, like a Ward indeed.

But my thoughts were all of America. If my parents had not sent me to this nether extreme, this *reductio ad absurdum* of Englishness, I might have compromised with the rest, and arrived at some sort of transatlantic mix ahead of my time. Now I wanted the whole American hog. Little did I know that I was simply trapped in a religious museum. I thought all England was like this and I wanted out.

No sooner had I gotten sprung by doctor's orders from the crows who blackened the trees, cawing their black thoughts, and their namesakes the "crows" (our name for the monks) who taught us theirs, than I began lobbying to get out of the country altogether. Talk about rising expectations. My rural rambles in Stratton-on-Fosse had turned me into an American for life.

All this must have been trying for Frank and Maisie, but I still think they asked for it. It is important, by the way, here as elsewhere, not to confuse the two of them. Maisie was, as noted, completely at sea with culture shock. Just couldn't grasp the concept. English Catholics, American Catholics—surely they had so much in common, in contrast to the rest of the world, that they should be friends practically on sight (on the same principle, she even expected us to like our relatives).

Frank knew better. He'd gone up against England himself and won, and he expected me to do likewise. He stressed to me the wonderful gains to character in such conquests, as if "conquering" America at nine hadn't been enough. How many more of these would I have to do? What I couldn't say then, because I hadn't yet thought it into words, was that I didn't want any more character if I had to lose the little bit I had to get it. Frank was clearly disappointed, and I thought at the time that he considered me a weakling, which in the circumstances I certainly was. Downside had routed me.*

But Frank had another problem, more interesting than any worries about my flabby character. He really thought that Downside, as he understood it, represented something finer than America, finer than anywhere. The Catholic England that he had dreamed and willed into reality for himself was the best thing he could give me; and it turned out that I couldn't stand it. I was rejecting his vision. What else was there?

The funny thing was that on the couple of occasions when he visited me at Downside, he seemed as out of place as I did. But that wouldn't have bothered him even if he'd noticed. "So you really want to become an American?" he said at last, bravely, and I could almost see him ransacking the New World for virtues—James Thurber, Melville, Jack London (his hero), Thoreau, Ogden Nash, Groucho; it might not be altogether hopeless. "All right. We'll see what we can do about it."

Maisie had no such difficulties. If a child of hers didn't like Downside, so much the worse for Downside. A Sheed's judgment was the best information you were likely to get on any subject—an indulgence that had us bending over backward to be fair. On her *own* judgment, she had begun to give up on England altogether in a way that

---

* Once upon a time I'd have been tempted to give the old dump some more lumps. But I recently met the headmaster, a classmate of mine, and we embraced like brothers. And that was that. In the interest of neatness, I'd forgotten that I had friends there.

Frank, the English convert, could not. She simply felt that it had lost vitality, which she worshiped as Frank worshiped intelligence. She knew England had suffered—her emotional little book, *This Burning Heat*, written during the blitz, was all about that—but she couldn't see any circumstances that entitled you just to lie down and give up. There was a sourness in the queues and shops, "Nah, we dun' 'ave it, nah, we dun expec' it," which may have tapped the snob in her, the sense of where have all those wonderful people who love their work gone? And a critic might have added that it was easy for her to talk after six plush years in America.

But our life hadn't been plush, and nothing was easy for Maisie. This may be as good a time as any to mention one of the lingering effects of those grueling illnesses that surrounded her childbearing. Her loss of hair around the time of my birth proved permanent and she was condemned to live out her life wearing a wig. I was mindful of this in 1945–46, because while I had been grunting away at my leg exercises, she had taken advantage of our combined incarceration to go wigless around the apartment, massaging and vibrating her scalp with a view to bringing back the old hair. So I felt we were recovering together.

And so we were, and we each got just about as far. I got down to one cane, and she looked like Benjamin Franklin. This wasn't quite enough for the lecture platform, so she clamped the wig back on resignedly, cutting off any further chance of growth up there. Thus disguised, she had to weather compliments about how nice her hair looked—Was she doing something different with it?—and also to make sure that she kept it up-to-date, so that it aged gracefully along with her.

If I throw in the scar tissue on her lungs, the phlebitis that racked her legs and the pain in her feet, it will sound as if I'm entering her for "Queen for a Day" (an old TV show which scoured the country for the most miserable specimens to shower gifts on). But to Maisie these things were just nuisances, "bothers," and not to be carried on about. Even having to pretend one had hair was no worse than a nuisance, if she thought about it at all. What for most women would have been a wound (men are expected to grow bald, but people can hardly stand the sight of a bald woman) was reduced to an embarrassment as her wig occasionally tilted or threatened to come off with her hat.

But losing one's vitality was on a different order of things from losing one's hair. This was a sin against the Spirit and it made her angrily unhappy. Her immediate and absolutely original response to it was to hire more Poles. Nobody else would have thought of that. For the purpose Maisie bought herself a small farm in Essex and manned it with Polish refugees, who had fought the Germans for at least as long as the English had and didn't even have a country to show for it; yet they hadn't given up, but were as usual planning a comeback. Now there was vitality for you—in fact, almost too much of it for her at first. The manager she hired was one of the most impressive men I have ever met: tall, handsome, rugged, articulate, all the usual stuff, plus extraordinary presence. Before the war, he had taught economics at Cracow* and, in the normal course of events, one had to assume for him a distinguished career in whatever field he chose.

As it was, and with all his ambitions shattered, he confined himself to teaching the Sheeds economics, brilliantly and unforgettably. The farm, under him, was beautifully run, a showcase, and Maisie cheerfully pumped in her American earnings, which towered above the sickly sterling of the day. All Maisie wanted in return was to provide some jobs plus a little extra food for family and friends. Still it would have been nice to make a little money—or at least break even. Mysteriously, this did not happen. The Sheed and Ward accountant went over the farm's books looking for possible leaks, and found none. In fact, he said he had never seen such elegant accounts. The manager blamed the government, which suited Maisie's mood just fine and settled the matter for now.

And so it might have gone on for a while, with Maisie's money disappearing inexorably into the magician's hat, if it hadn't been for a scene one night at the farmhouse, somewhat different from the time the Irish boys stayed up saying the rosary until the cows came home. This time around, one of the farmhands took a butcher knife to his employer and chased him round the kitchen table, accusing the latter

* I have since learned from Polish friends that the postwar immigrants often shouted themselves to lordly pasts. However, this man had done *something*.

in fevered Polish of stealing his girl. I believe our economist sustained a slash or two in the arm and, there was no way round it, the police had to be called in. I never learned the details, but I gather it transpired that the farmhand's girl was not the only such item to be whisked out of sight whenever Maisie toured her model farm. Dr. Cracow had been living the life of Riley—the life he would so richly have deserved if it hadn't been for the recent unpleasantness in Europe.

One more look at the books, then; and this time our accountant had to amend himself slightly: these were the most elegantly *cooked* books he had ever seen. Whether our man had been warped into anarchy by the war, or was just a natural-born crook——maybe a little something in politics might have settled him——he had bitten deep into his patron's hand. Maisie was desolate—and immediately hired another Pole, to take the taste away.

It never occurred to her to blame Poland for one scumbag. But when the dust had settled she and I had a mild argument which revealed another and I think touching prejudice. Could she like a really bad person? No. Even if it were a member of the family? Well. A member of the family *couldn't* be a bad person, she blurted.

Of course she knew better, and came to know better still. But this was always her impulse. She believed ardently in hero worship as a simple necessity of life, and she flinched and defended whenever she heard anything bad about one of her pets, especially Chesterton or Browning. "I believe Cardinal Newman may have been a little *vain*," she would confess unhappily. Or "I'm afraid that GK was drinking *rather heavily* toward the end."

Such a one would seem like inexhaustible shark-bait, but there was a hardheaded countrywoman side to Maisie which functioned in the day-to-day, blissfully unaware of her schoolgirl philosophy. Anyone so earnestly virtuous needs such a side to do the dirty work: to be selfish or blind or even a little mean when the occasion warrants, and even to doctor one's memory of what precisely happened. Maisie could drive a merciless bargain (before, often as not, giving away the proceeds) and on the few evenings we prevailed on her to play the revealing game of Monopoly, she would turn before our eyes into a brutal rack-renter, humorlessly demanding every last shred of paper till the last foe had caved in. Close to tears by then, she would insist on hewing to the beastly rules of this beastly game which she couldn't understand why people played in the first place.

With such subconscious equipment in her corner, Maisie's record for picking winners in life was quite respectable for a saint, or whatever she was. ("Of course I want to be a saint. Don't you?") She knew that absentee landlords are fair game. Yet among her farmers, she scored two impressive successes out of three, and it can be argued that Dr. Cracow would have fooled anyone. Misery Farm, our prewar folly, had been so expertly transformed by one Mr. Rosier that she finally deeded the joint over to him in acknowledgment.

But her new man, Mr. Zaleski, was her special joy. A stubby slightly mussy-looking peasant of the school of Brueghel, he talked to her vivaciously in fractured French, fractured English and presumably normal Polish, as if they were all one language understood by everyone. "Madame, let us *partage*" was his phrase for "splitting the difference," after which warning shot he'd be off and jabbering. His other particular gift besides the linguistic was coaxing pigs off cliffs on foggy nights to get round the official regulations concerning the slaughter of animals for home consumption. We dined well off Mr. Zaleski's late-night doings.

Maisie's ebullient Pole did little to reconcile her to the overall grayness of England. She dutifully went back to her Evidence Guild chores, or rather fell on them hungrily, as a last symbol of authenticity and life. She even got herself involved in the petty politics that blotch even the purest organizations, trying, I believe now, to get more out of the Guild than was there.

It was a perky little outfit, and its parties were as much fun in their way as the Friendship House bashes (Rosemary and I once did a heartrending version of "Baby It's Cold Outside" for the Guild), but Maisie had been there before. Despite the constant threat of new blood, the English weakness for repetition always won out at the Guild, making it more comfortable than exciting, a good place to watch new blood age.

Maisie's burgeoning soul rattled around restlessly in this teacup, and although she wasn't quite ready to do it herself, she saw no harm whatever in my heading, once and for all, for America. "We are what you were," a smug Australian said to her around then, and the fiery Maisie accepted it meekly. The Ward who had once lured Frank with her sheer Englishness was about set to go colonial herself.

As it turned out there was nothing "once and for all" about my American dreams. I was about to enter a dislocating period of shuttle education which gave me some stories and a deeply puzzling accent, but did no real damage, if you don't count profound social unease with all groups, classes and nations. Otherwise, one man's fragmentation is another man's eclecticism, and as the years have passed, New York/London has become more like a nation to me than, say, New York/Texas or London/Bradford. My cell has also filled up with company, other mutants on the same wavelength. Besides which, I now knew who I was: I was an *Australian* (said the lunatic brightly).

The reason behind all this transatlantic shilly-shallying had to be, at bottom, Frank's abiding romance with England. Despite a wanderlust which was such a reflex that you could hardly call it lust anymore, he liked things to stay roughly the same wherever he went. Just as he had once counted on the laughter and cheer of the Maloneys in his dizzy rounds of Sydney as a kid, so he expected the Guild still to be singing the old songs in London and making the time-honored speeches.

"What are the four marks of the Church?" each beginner would pipe in the training sessions Frank ran. "The marks of the Church are as follows: that it is one, holy, catholic and apostolic. The Church is one because ..." Frank, alert in his interlocutor's chair, and primed with heckles old and new, never tired of this rigmarole, though I could stand no more after a few months of kibitzing the classes.

Professional speakers had better not mind repetition too much—like comedians they have only so many routines—and both Frank and Maisie kept a stock of pet phrases which reduced Rosemary and me to occasional whimpers. "You can't be at your best all the time," Frank said to me once in uncharacteristic appeal when I'd poked fun at some set response of Maisie's, and I've been living with this sad truth ever since.

But it wasn't just the ritual with Frank. He drew sustenance from the people in the Guild, even while avoiding its politics. In fact its politics tended to avoid him too, so regally did he rise above them, a big fish in a little pond for sure. Intellectual equals who talked back were a chore which he seldom ducked, but for ordinary human contact, which he relished in ungovernable quantities, he seemed more and more to prefer something a little less challenging. He liked intelligent people all right, but intelligent people he could *teach*. Teaching was a relaxation, jousting with equals was work.

As for people who could teach him, his attitude was sometimes startlingly reverential. Lunching one day with him and Monsignor Ronald Knox, the aging whiz kid of English Catholicism, I saw for the first time the star-struck Australian boy dazzled, like Marco Polo, by ancient glitter.

Knox was indeed a clever and witty fellow, but nobody could be as witty as Frank found his guest that day. Poised to laugh at every sneeze and cough, or else nod thoughtfully, Frank found gems in what was in fact quite a humdrum performance by the monsignor. "He's not that good," I wanted to shout like Nick Carraway. "In fact, you're better." But Frank would have been uncomprehending. Like many an Irish dandy he secretly overrated the English and underrated himself. (I never once saw Frank overimpressed by an American.) For once and only once, since childhood and its web of misunderstandings, I thought I saw through him that day with Knox.

Perhaps what I was really seeing through, though, was his profession. To a publisher, Knox really was that good, or had been. For once, the Protestants were partly right about the dire effects of Romish conversion: Knox had been a brilliant young satirist and wordsman as an Anglican, but as a Catholic he felt called upon to defend the Faith virtually nonstop, which is rather like patrolling the beat on foot, plodding work for such a mercurial talent. And I think he only made it worse by trying to do it with a light touch. He had preached at a girls' school during the war, and his sermons were undoubtedly perfect models of how you do this. But Frank published them in great big grown-up books, where they seemed whimsically insipid.

Yet they sold a lot of copies, especially in fat comfy America, and a publisher has to see gold shining in the very soup such an author has for lunch. Later I read not only these wartime chores of Knox's and the early twinkletoes stuff when he was the toast of Oxford, but an extraordinary novel he wrote for Frank called *Let Dons Delight* (about an Oxford common room visited at fifty year intervals from 1538 to 1938) and I began to feel a little reverent toward him myself.

Anyhow, Knox right then was our transatlantic meal ticket, little though he looked like one with his vast collar and his little turtle head threatening to disappear inside it. His translation of the Bible was Sheed and Ward's beefsteak mine. From World War II to Vatican II the sales of that, and the missal that was spun from it, gave us illusions of vast prosperity. So this was definitely a man to court, and Knox, clearly if shyly, liked to be courted. He once boasted of being at a party with three of his current publishers (Frank said sweetly, "Belloc used to come with thirty"), and he was always likely to slip away and elope with some other flattering editor. Hence the sense of moist palms under the table that day. I'd seen Frank do a little light truckling before, but nothing like this. One mustn't think, though, of a businessman unmanned by greed, but more of a collector afraid that his favorite piece will get up and walk away.

Also: when a publisher truckles, he is partly doing it to reassure himself. His praise is not directed just at the author but at some invisible sales conference which must be sold right now on this person's genius. When Frank was asked at a lecture to name the three greatest minds he'd ever encountered, he came up immediately with three of his own authors. That sales conference in the head never disbands.

Finally, there was some sociology to be learned at that dull but instructive lunch. Knox as an object represented something beyond the ungainly wooings of commerce, and the panting ones of hero worship. Ronnie was at the very nexus of those two great civilizations, Rome and Oxford University. Wherever he went, a charmed circle formed about him. And I sometimes wondered how that circle felt about Frank. In his biography of Knox, Evelyn Waugh called Frank "an energetic American publisher," which in the *lingua Evelyn* meant a well-meaning pithecanthropine. And later in a private letter, Waugh talked of Sheed as never quite being part of Knox's set, while "his son [me, who had just panned the book lightly] was educated largely in America, I believe."

No one else was ever as blunt as Evelyn, who was a bit of an outsider himself (Knox told Frank he did *not* want Waugh as his literary executor, although biographer was quite all right) and who, in real life, was outstandingly courteous to Frank and Maisie on the rare occasions when their paths crossed. The few shadows whom I identified as belonging to Waugh's idea of the Knox circle *liked* Frank all right, oh Lord yes; they just didn't seem impressed by him. And he, in turn, seemed slightly less sure of himself with them, a little more eager to laugh and to rattle the latest small talk about bishops. I felt he wasn't trying to impress them so much as to find out what they wanted. Because these people were finally as impregnable to him as they had been to me at Downside. There may not have been much to them, but they guarded it with their lives. Contrariwise, their opinions of others they wore on their faces, and in Frank's case I fancy it was something like "Oh yes, wonderful popularizer, damned useful man. Now what do you hear from Ronnie?"

If this makes Frank sound a bit like an intellectual Gatsby, I've gone much too far. Many men are Gatsbys to their sons, but Frank neither wished to shine nor to be around shining people, as he proved after his publishing life was done and he returned gratefully to his "nobodies." It was just that back then I wanted him to impress "them" as much as he impressed me and anything short of that was magnified grotesquely to abject failure. When I hinted to my father my uneasiness over the Knox luncheon, he said, "Oh, I treat him the way I treat everyone else."

So the difference was probably perceptible only to the distorting lens of a son, who feels that if Daddy fails, he fails; if Daddy can't stand up to them, I certainly can't. Using this same lens I had at first found Downside much more intellectually formidable than it turned out to be. Frank's respect for educated Englishmen as such had seeped through, like mustard gas. Only when I left did I discover that these titans wanted me to stay very badly indeed——because I was the son of Frank Sheed. As the headmaster wheedled away at me, I realized that not I but my father sat across from him, and that together we were quite a prize for this pretentious backwater.

So Frank stood very high in the English Catholic world at large, whatever the talk at the clubs. Yet even at Downside, where *Theology and Sanity* was used as a text in the sixth form, his true position was slightly blurred by his profession. Because there wasn't a single crow, or monk either, who didn't nurse a secret manuscript (although only one that I can recall, Hubert van Zeller, a miraculously human crow, ever nursed any good ones).

I had never thought of Frank primarily as a publisher but simply as a great man at large. Now I began to see him more in the tight little uniform he wore for authors. Sheed and Ward was one of merely two Catholic houses in England, and with its American branch, it was much more dashing than its rival, the semiofficial Burns & Oates, which included hair shirts and knotted ropes for self-flagellation in its catalogs—a far cry from the jokes that filled ours.

The most snobbish of Englishmen had to vote for the American dollar over Burns & Oates' hair shirt in those scruffy days, and even for the loathsome American lecture circuit (which one could always satirize later), and Frank had the key to these things. Feelings about such middlemen tend to be mixed: as equals they would be unendurable, but as "the best of their kind," they become assets. Thus, Frank might be a mere publisher, but he *was* Ronald Knox's publisher, whether or not he was in his set (I think he was more in that set than Waugh knew. But Knox was a great gamesplayer, and could easily make *you* feel like the insider while the other "chap" wasn't quite. He also had more sets than any one set knew about).

If Frank was a tradesman, he was at least Tiffany. As a theologian, he never claimed originality, and such modest self-assessments are always quickly and gratefully accepted. None of this mattered much at the time, but later when fashions had changed and neither he nor Sheed and Ward stood quite so tall, he was perhaps easier to dismiss than he would have been if his early status in England had been clearer and firmer.

Bernard Shaw maintained that you have to keep telling the

English how great you are until it finally sinks in. Frank leaned if anything in the other direction, toward self-deprecating irony. Maisie
liked to tell of an exchange between him and Sir Arnold Lunn (father
of the slalom and a big noise in the Catholic raj), which concluded
with Frank saying, "You see, perhaps I'm just provincial after all," and
Lunn nodding, "Perhaps that's it." Maisie thought it hugely funny
that anyone should consider Frank provincial, but I find the story a
sad little thing. Maisie thought Frank's gifts were self-evident and
blinding. But to the Lunns and Waughs he may have been just a
bouncy fellow from the Outback, surprisingly clever, who published
one's books, as he might make one's boots.

Perhaps the real difference was that he didn't lecture in England,
except for that funny outdoor stuff, and anyone who hadn't heard him
lecture had encountered less than half of Frank. Significantly, anyone
who had passed through the Guild, including brilliant strays from
Oxbridge (Norman St. John Stevas, the parliamentary *wunderkind*, cut
his teeth there), tended to idolize Frank, and they would tell quite a
different story about a quite different man. Otherwise, Frank's quick-
silver presence in the forties had left a trail of secondhand books and
funny friendships and private legends, but nothing to build statues to.
Any of those would have gone by then to Maisie, who became more
respected every year in the land she had spurned, while Frank's myth
had to settle for that colony-gone-wrong, America.

There were other, more theological and churchy reasons for his
relative eclipse in the seventies, but for the moment, I am haunted by
a phrase from his last years, "I should have known all along that
America was my country." *All along.* This means that my 1940s ap-
prehensions were not just projections of my own bafflement with
England, but a blind sense of something wrong, of a picture hung mi-
croscopically askew. There was finally this something, impossible to
name, unrequited about Frank's love for England. He was simply not
a clubman in any sense, he wanted no part of inner circles, and
England is made up of inner circles.*

* I once asked him if he would accept a royal honor, and he said no, it wouldn't
suit his style; it wouldn't suit his hat. Rosemary believes he could have had
England by the tail if he wanted. But perhaps his terms were too Australian.

But little or none of this met the naked eye in 1947, even mine when I chose to use one. I can still picture him lunching at the Café Royal with such blithe friends as J. B. Morton (the great "Beach-comber") and D. B. (the Good) Wyndham Lewis, who had a ten-dency to get thrown out of the better places in tandem for bellowing Provençal folk songs; then the pair of us descending to Regent Street and taking a squint at the latest cricket scores on the hoardings, and deciding on the spot to hop a cab to Lords to check out the South Africans or the Pakistanis and to hell with publishing for the day—I have never seen such hastily generated happiness. London on my own already seemed gray and unprofitable; but sitting with him at the Nursery End of Lords, munching on cherries and taking turns with the crossword, it seemed like a garden of wonders. Merely watching him sprint onto or away from a moving bus quickened the scene. I learned on sundry trips with him that Frank could do the same thing for Dublin, Paris or Rome, but London seemed the greater achieve-ment.

There are enough witnesses to his electricity to establish that this was not some private circuit between him and me. "I loved his hat and his hug," wrote my splendid cousin Hester after Frank's death—and the hat was certainly part of his secret. He was always arriving from somewhere or about to leave: one must make the most of him. And he in turn acted as if God had granted him just these few min-utes with you. So he always left you tingling.

A couple of times he returned from America with frozen steaks, dinner for one in a Texas restaurant, and invited hordes of relatives over to share them, while Rosemary and I looked on in equally frozen horror at the dwindling slices. But the relatives would have loved him anyway.

It was always fun to see Frank work a new room, and the English gentry brought out a side of him that few Americans ever saw. For a man who claimed to treat everyone exactly the same, the shadings of his performance were extraordinary—unless it was the audiences that made them seem different. Anyway, here he was, the perfect English gentleman, "one of us," considerably more at home with Maisie's rela-tives than she was, so that she and they probably prayed equally for his arrival: and shazam! there he was in his funny hat, with the back brim bent down instead of up,* ready to entertain and be entertained.

There was no conscious trick to it that I could see—he actually seemed to enjoy these people. "You see, I don't *mind* the rich," he once said thoughtfully, at a time when the public was baying for Patty Hearst's blood. They were just more souls for his mill. If they lost all their money tomorrow, it wouldn't make a scrap of difference. He still wouldn't mind them. (Not all our relatives were rich by any means but they were all gentry, which goes something like this: I once told Rosemary that I'd met an officer in the Guards and she said, "You mustn't say 'officer.' It suggests that you know people in the Guards who *aren't* officers." That's gentry.)

At the end of the war, he had touched base in Australia and re-Aussified himself slightly. Antipodeans seem to need to do this even more than other people, because it is so easy to imagine that one has dreamed the whole place. Frank's first dose of Australia had held up for twenty years. From now on he would need his fix more and more often until he seemed like a man in a revolving door.

But in 1945 (while the rest of us were still in America), one was enough. He came back bursting with songs, which we dutifully learned in the Sheed parrot factory, and stories and atmosphere. His only dark moment came, he said, when he met a girl he used to go out with and she burst into tears at the sight of him. "If I hadn't been a gentleman, I would have cried too," he said. He had indeed changed shape and his thick black hair was now strandy and gray, but I couldn't see anything to cry about. *We* had to look at him, and that's the way he had always looked and always would.

So it was as a born-again Aussie that he hit postwar London, and perhaps some of his unearthly jauntiness can be put down to that. Since his Australianness included a passion for England he could play the English gentleman to his heart's content without compromise. What he was *not* that year was American. When the Australian cricket team came over in 1948, they seemed like sunny, strutting versions of the same spirit. There's an old saying that "an Englishman looks as if

* He claimed this was an Australian custom, but when I got there the Australians thought the hat looked funny too.

he owns the street [that year he looked more as if he expected to be arrested for trespassing], while an Australian looks as if he doesn't care *who* owns the street."* An admirable sentiment: obviously the thing for me to be was an Australian in America. A complicated destiny, as Henry James might say.

Don't ask me how I got there. In fact, I'll skip over this and a hundred conflicting daydreams, which at sixteen and seventeen pretty much have the run of one's head. As long as you keep them clean, even the Church doesn't mind. In its ageless wisdom it must know that it is sometimes easier to keep away impure thoughts by imagining oneself playing cricket for Australia than by thinking about the Virgin.

Rosemary was, and was to remain, the most rooted of us, because she really liked England, postwar or not. This could be the difference between a twelve-year-old refugee and a niner (she remembered for instance what our cousins looked like when we got back, whereas I was poleaxed with surprise) or it could be the slightly different situations we came back to. She had just finished high school, and was of precisely the right disposition and comely appearance for a London Season, or what had to pass for one in that year of Spam. She ravenously loved to dance, as Frank had, and although she thought Englishmen danced funny, bobbing up and down like wind-up toys to such postwar synthetics as "They've Got an Awful Lot of Coffee in Brazil," and "Her Bathing Suit Never Got Wet" (music took a long time to come back from the war), she found them between sets better company than the large, bland, beautifully behaved Catholic boys of America who seemed to be the lot of Sacred Heart girls.

Rosemary always thought and talked very fast, so it must have been bliss not to have to wait for these fellows to come panting up behind every sentence. English Catholics (it was still all Catholics for us) were allowed, even encouraged, to be clever, and Rosemary fairly wallowed in anyone's cleverness. Operating out of our convenient West Kensington flat (which we'd got for a song from some realtors named Chesterton), she must have cut a mighty swath through May-

* The same saying has been applied to Oxford and Cambridge and no doubt to Swaziland and Zambeziland too. It is always correct.

fair every night—or so I imagined as I chewed moodily at the bars of my Downside penitentiary. I'm sure it wasn't that good, but it was quite good enough to keep her from returning to America till the fun blew over.

As for Min, she had the American bug for the least or most philosophical reason of any of us: to put it symbolically, she loved Fats Waller. "Choose your poet early and stick to him," said Disraeli. Min chose hers late, but when she did she found that this fat, bubbling incarnation of laughter, song and animal spirits, part Ariel and part Caliban, was what she had been waiting for all along. Our flat in Oakwood Court may have been a launching pad for Rosemary, but for the less agile it was a genteel mausoleum. The only signs of street life I ever saw there occurred when the aging Queen Mary drove through in her hearselike limousine. Every curtain lifted a few inches: eyes appeared in windows we'd thought abandoned, until the ghostly rigadoon had passed through. Then the curtains dropped. "Play 'Your Feets Too Big,'" said Min—if not that day, any day she could catch my eye.

Next to Fats Waller, she continued to find the English chinless and mumblesome. "An Irishman's entitled to speak twice and an Englishman till he's understood," she'd say. And then, "Play some more Fats"—a generic term which came to cover Count Basie and any jump song from Goodman or James. During the cold winter of '46 and '47, she and I formed a hot club of two.

Not that year, but the next, 1948, I would be accompanying Min back to America, where she flourished and grew moody all over again. Frank's policy of keeping people moving was modeled on his own impulses, and it worked wonderfully with Min until he sent her to Australia once too often in the fifties, and after a boisterous trip out—quite her fourteen-year-old self again—she found her beloved sister Sarah (Aunt Sar to us) cancer-ridden and estranged. Frank's merry-go-round ground reluctantly to a halt, and when Min returned she was, for the first time, an old lady.

So our ensemble creaked along, but the end of it, strictly as an ensemble, was in germ. On rereading some of the blessedly few letters I wrote at the time, I find that Maisie's impatience with England was alleviated by frequent trips to America and France. So she barely had time to get angry.

To me, 1946–47 was our English year, but each of us no doubt had a different epithet for every year after the war. Rosemary had so many English years there had to be some other way to distinguish them. For Maisie, it was always the year of the book: *France Pagan? The Young Mr. Newman, Browning*—and the locations determined by that: Marseilles, Birmingham, and in the last case Baylor, Texas, which boasts (oh, how it boasts) the world's finest Browning collection, lacking only—and I'm told they're working on this—the poet's bones. For Frank every year seemed to contain the elements of all the others, writing, lecturing, publishing, *moving,* so that the decade becomes his smallest unit, if not the lifetime.

But for me, that was the English year. And if I'd never gone back, I wouldn't have cared much for the place. Any adolescent is lucky to get away with just one bad year, but it's too bad that mine had to occur entirely in England, which was also having a bad year. V. S. Naipaul says that Hindus judge a period entirely by how they felt at the time. And in this sense, every teenager is a Hindu. If 1946–47 was not quite my first year on the sexual griddle, it was by far the worst, and one wants decent weather for that; but by evil chance, that winter was the one when the rails froze and electricity was rationed during the daytime, so that one had to study incomprehensible muck under fifteen-watt bulbs. Since I was also racked with the English disease, constipation, I felt myself in a state of lonely siege all winter.

Contemporary friends in England, and probably elsewhere, are something you find in schools and nowhere else; so I had none to speak of and the clammy solitude of Torresdale was replayed. To improve myself, I was busily swotting up for the London matriculation—which is one of those worldwide talismans that you can probably pick up in a back street of Bangkok and which gets you into any undiscriminating university anywhere—at a tutorial body shop called Davies. The only student remotely my age was a little chap alleged to be a child movie star, hot from a triumph in the film *Oliver Twist,* who was driven up every day in a limousine and whisked to some private sanctum, wrapped (memory plays games here) in blankets and shawls. And the only gossip concerned the alleged actor and a famous nymphet of the period, who was presumably delivered to him also wrapped in blankets.

Otherwise we were too insubstantial and transient for gossip. The tutors themselves were nice oddbodies: one with black hair and a red beard who argued after-hours about theocracy (he, though an atheist, was strongly for it); another who looked like Dr. Watson and took snuff, so that his great purple nostrils groinked and quivered constantly over his deep-stained mustache (one wanted to take the mustache out and have it cleaned), and a third gloomy genius dressed entirely in gray who cured me forever of fine writing with one offhand sentence. "This sort of thing is much easier to do than many people suppose."

Davies was clearly the French Foreign Legion of teaching, and the only quality these shadowy men had in common was that none of them changed his shirt more than once a week. My parents had found me another doozy, but in this case they had no choice: I was hell-bent on America, and I had to be stuffed somewhere in the interim.

My pocket money went entirely into amassing phonograph records, which seemed to be made out of chalk in those days so that bits came off in your hand if you gripped them tightly, and my collection has long since disintegrated without trace. Even my one reward from the welfare state was cruelly denied me. As a sixteen-and-under I was entitled to one banana a week. But when I got home on the appointed day I would find Frank wearing a guilty grin, with a banana skin practically sticking out of his pocket. It was his one, unrestrained vice.

The records had a purpose deeper than pleasure, which was to keep me in communion with America. These plus the late-night American Forces network broadcasts from Frankfurt made me feel I wasn't slipping irretrievably away. (I was though, and so was the network: American music had already changed on us quite a bit since 1945.)

Having thus made up my mind, I couldn't very well afford to like England; although as the pubescent glooms lifted with spring and then a gorgeous summer, it wasn't easy. People who insist on unhappy childhoods have to edit fiercely, and now that my calendar year of discontent (May '46 to May '47) was up, I really had to grope for grievances. To wit: I don't know what the irreducible minimum is for cricket—it can be played with one arm or one leg, but probably not both—but I was able to make a fair fist of batting and even bowling, and I cajoled various small fry to humor me in these matters on the bombed-out lot in back of our building. I also found myself giving batting tips, genetically acquired, to some lads at a youth club where I helped out.

My only cricket complaint concerned some genuine pint-sized Brahmins, who talked like Peter Sellers (embassy kids I guess) and who suddenly withdrew from our pick-up games for reasons of caste. I didn't mind Englishmen anymore, because they seemed sort of natural around here, the only possible thing in fact, but imitation English was awful: another good reason to get out of town, cricket or no cricket.

My English year sounds, as it felt, rather empty of people. Yet faces loom up now, until the tent is quite crowded. The world of the Wards seemed to buzz just above or behind my head. Cardinals Newman and Manning were much discussed, along with Baron von Hügel and poor Father Tyrrell—all the latest from the Modernist crisis. All my cousins but one were older than me, which gave me a sense of running after a parade trying to keep my pants up. But the Nevile cousins in London absentmindedly accepted me as a Bohemian *flâneur* or cracker-barrel philosopher, or whatever I wanted to be that day, as they accepted each other (they were great performers themselves); another cousin, Antonella Lothian, christened me "Old Trenchant," which I liked the minute I looked it up. Tetta's daughter Hester, who had proposed to me when she was nine and I was seven, continued (despite an unfortunate incident with a seltzer bottle; as a two-reel-comedy fan I thought it might be funny to spray her in the moosh) to be a soulmate. And so on. Byronic melancholy does not preclude a busy schedule, but in this case it was almost all in the family, which made for a kind of echo-chamber effect. There are only so many ways of being a relative.

The one totally new experience, protoplasmically different from anyone I had ever met, was with a gnome called Caryll Houselander who wrote spiritual books for Sheed and Ward. Right after I got polio, Caryll sent Frank a note comparing me to a field of golden corn struck down in its prime and I thought, there's no way I'm going to like a woman who talks like that. And when we finally met she offered to do a portrait of me, which had to be scrapped because it kept turning me into an effete Polish airman of her acquaintance. But in no time I was posing for the sake of the conversation.

Converts have always vied with each other in accounts of their previous sinfulness (not realizing the envy this rouses in us born Catholics—couldn't we have just a few years like that?). Caryll seemed to have been a *real* Bohemian, who had done everything and known everybody before seeing the light of Rome. Now in atonement, she apparently dipped her face in flour every day, treating herself to a hobgoblin appearance, which sounds as humorless as Isadora Duncan, but was in fact Englishly funny.

Besides being a retired sophisticate, Caryll was an amateur psychic and graphologist, or whatever you call someone who reads handwriting, and she mixed magic stories of ESP and prophetic dreams with thirties gossip so casually that they became a single entertainment, take it or leave it. She didn't mind a bit if you didn't believe a word, as long as you enjoyed the lantern show. So I was surprised when Frank told me that he had used her services on a couple of handwriting specimens, and that she had flushed out deeply buried secrets which later checked out. Frank must have had mixed feelings about coming even this close to bugging his employees, and I believe curiosity as to whether it worked was the decisive factor. Anyway, Caryll asked him not do this to her too often because it gave her terrible headaches and depressions, and he certainly never did.

I sometimes wondered where the Sheeds found their authors. Caryll the witch was the farthest possible cry from Ronald Knox, yet he once wrote her an ardent fan letter. There were connections in this whole circus that I couldn't see. All I knew was that this prim little woman who never showed her teeth, because she thought teeth looked silly, and who lived in a faceless, endless apartment block and used no special effects but her powdery face managed to generate an *Arabian Nights* atmosphere in the engulfing grayness of 1946–47.

Frank and Maisie were quite gullible in the realm of the uncanny (which is rare among bright Catholics) and they bought Caryll's whole catalog down to the last talking statue. I both believed and didn't believe, as I suspect Caryll did and didn't. In the swirling psychic mists, who was to say?

What I most liked about Caryll, though, was that she never once played the spiritual author with me. Her published essays and verse could be tender to the verge of soupy, but she knew better than to pester a sprawling teenager with that stuff. If I had had to guess at her métier I might have said, writer of risqué novels, or Scotland Yard's ace in the hole. For our portrait sessions, she was earthy, funny and rather creepily flattering. No doubt she thought I needed a boost, and for a while I would bask in her compliments (don't ask me what they were; they melted like snow in my pockets) until I felt suddenly sick with myself for enjoying them so much and conspiring in them. "I'm really looking forward to being old," I think I said once. "I'm sure you'll be wonderful at it," she replied. I hope it never got worse than that.

Her goblin face told me nothing at sitting's end. "The patient responded well to praise" I imagine her jotting afterward. "Perhaps we can take him off it for a while." Certainly she had brought out a great flubbering weakness to a point where even I could see it, and taught me from ludicrous example how funny and undignified vanity makes you look. ("Sheed talks a good game" is a lesson that has to be repeated after ocean crossings.) But whether the goblin had that in mind I'll never know. Caryll was such a mixture of mischief and affection that her flattery could have been anything, even honest admiration. Otherwise, she told terrible and hilarious stories about her friends, and made no attempt to love everybody. Being a saint would have cramped her style. Yet that she was one I have no doubt. Her love of God was positively translucent.

Caryll's prosaic manner and quirky imagination almost redeemed England for me, if I'd wanted it redeemed (or if it cared): the hellfire club grubbing along in a Chelsea bed-sitter. And there were other characters that year: Gertrude Warrington, my parents' dearest non-relative, who always wore black, from her feet to her velvet Erasmus hat, and took at least three baths a day for fifty years and reread Dante every year without, I trust, getting it wet—again this sounds impossibly affected but it wasn't, it was exactly what she felt like doing.

Gert (she was never called anything else) was also better at taking teenagers to good restaurants than anyone I have ever met. And while we're on baths, there was a Cousin Reggie Huddleston, an old salt, who always contrived to get discovered in his tub swigging at a gin-and-lime on visitors' day at his stately home. I don't know: some Englishmen do these things right and some don't and Reggie could even lift a skirt amusingly. Yet in retrospect, I can't even stand the sound of him. As for Aunt Tetta and Uncle Herbert, they both seemed for now slightly the worse for the war, as indeed did so many people, but they both lit up at the sight of Frank, the old lamplighter, and I realized how merry the Wards must have been two wars ago.

Anyway, the clarinet's opening blast in *Rhapsody in Blue,* which I liked to listen to on rainy nights with the lights out, blew England away, relatives and all. New York was the dream I lived in, all painted and glistening, with Gershwin piping from the buses and from the bell tower of the Riverside Church, an America manufactured abroad, as much as Henry Luce's was made in China, depending on an obstinate act of will.

One thing that helped in this respect was a wheezing anti-Americanism which was in the English air back there, as sour as bad breath. Like the ignorant hecklers who made Frank and Maisie look good, the anti-Americans were so invariably uninformed and wantonly, childishly rude that they enhanced everything they bashed. With a brutish disregard for a poor conqueror's feelings, they would blame me and my fellow barbarians for destroying all culture and civility in England: after which the American "How do you like our country, sonny?" seemed splendidly civilized.

Although I was to return the next summer and on other ad lib occasions (Frank the travel agent was at his inspired zenith as restrictions came off and everyone could move as much as he), it wasn't till I made it to Oxford in 1950 that I got the taste of 1947 completely out of my mouth.

If I hadn't done so, I would still think of England as incurably second-rate: the BBC, of course, the dreary little royal family (whose real name I was sure was Jenkins), the wonderful wave of postwar comedies (so damned cozy), the clubfooted attempts to play American jazz (we being to the British what the Negroes were to us) and again the BBC—"Workers' Playtime," and the dreadful old literary men on the Home Service; special reports on the vanishing art of crofting; Midland accents, West Country accents, posh accents, the lot. Even the chorus girls couldn't kick straight, as Frank pointed out one surprising day.

My dream in 1940 of returning to England had been hammered so far back that I couldn't remember what I had ever liked about the place. In 1950, some of it came back. But by that time, a new generation had surfaced, some of whom felt even uglier about BBC England than I did and a small number of whom would proceed to kick the starch out of the old lady, on stage, in print and finally on screen. That was my one serious misjudgment of England (the rest stands): I should have known that the Osbornes and Sillitoes would turn up eventually. In retrospect, my own list of peeves sounds quite banal and middle-of-the-road compared with the great roar of rage to come.

One thing I didn't mind a bit was the Labour government— partly because the Blimps didn't like it, and made fun of its members (Attlee, Bevan, Darwin, and the others) as if they were bloody Americans. Class distinction had survived the war like a tetchy old relative. When it finally goes away for good, it will be impossible to describe, because it was just an atmosphere. Americans can visit England and not know it's there: but once you pick it up, it's like a dank smell in an old house that permeates every room. Sheeds seemed to be immune from its effects, like theater people with titles. But what did I know for sure? I do know that even Maisie would refer to someone as the salt of the earth—but not really a gent: a distinction that vanished mysteriously when she was in America.

Beyond that, England was a painting that was finished. I could add nothing to it. One more brushstroke would be extraneous, a smudge. Since America at that point looked as if it would never get finished, it seemed like a good place for a young man to make his mark.

So in September 1947, I returned to the U.S. to spend a peculiar year at Fordham cramming at Classics, and after that we all fell to just shuffling about.

The Whistling Theologian

FIVE PEOPLE IS NOT REALLY ENOUGH FOR A DIASPORA, BUT THAT'S what we began to feel like from 1947 on. Frank and I flew to America, in the company of an old lady who simply wanted to get off the plane. Methodically she would gather her things and pack up her knitting and stand by the exit waiting for it to open over the Atlantic. In my half-sleep it seemed that the planes we flew in were becoming like the hotels we stayed in.

After a few weeks, Frank left me to go on about his business, and from then on we all seemed to meet and travel in odd combinations—me and Min, Maisie and Rosemary, or any of us solo, as if Frank were frantically pushing pins around a map. We never knew when one of us would turn up in Australia—or which one. So only by a species of montage did we still seem like a unit. Over the years we did put in several more stretches together, but there was always a sense that someone had just checked in or out. We developed certain migratory patterns. Rosemary saw no reason to budge from the European Theater, though she did so anyway. Min would hop any ship that was going anywhere, and Maisie went looking for the action, which in those years meant France. (I, then as now, went to wherever the ticket said.)

If I was ever going to feel crushed by famous parents, I had better hurry. Frank and Maisie were now as big as they were ever going to get, kings of the Catholic world from John o' Groats to Borneo, where I fancied their arrivals to be announced by tomtoms and bushfires. Certainly in America they loomed enormous, and I was Frank and Maisie's boy if I was anything. So let me recollect precisely how Frank at least looked to a quivering teenager ripe for awe and suppressed resentment.

"I'm wicked and bad/A contemptible lad/And I *hope* to get worse by and by."

Frank was to receive, during the great postwar, an honor that no lay Catholic had ever come close to: a doctorate in sacred theology from Rome itself, entitling him to wear a four-pointed biretta (priests only rate three). One more funny hat for his crown. He was on the very brink of being a sage. Yet nothing could knock the jingles out of him. The great theologian would launch into one like the above, muttering the words absently and then, as if they reminded him of something, end with a bang.

"It was on a bank holider*/The sea came and swallowed her/And *that's* why I'm fond of the Navy." Mutter and bang.

Where he got this stuff, I don't know—although he usually had a trace of a memory. One specimen he managed to track all the way back to an old Navy captain in Sydney, only to find that the captain himself had forgotten it. So Frank was the sole repository, a veritable Vatican archive, of bilge.

"She is my Lulu from Woolomoloo/She is so strike me pink or strike me blue/Oh I take her for a walk and show her around the shops/And if she gives me any lip I *smack* her across the chops."

It isn't true that he only did this during sermons—crowded buses were another favorite setting—but wherever he erupted, the last line always got the same fervor, even if he had to whisper it. Unless of course the poetic stress belonged elsewhere. For some unimaginable reason, my stately Aunt Tetta fancied a brief snatch of his from the twenties, to wit, "She went from the Indies to the Andes in her undies," which had to be done in one breath and then forgotten. A more rounded performance was the following spoken duet with (he swore) a duchess over dinner: F: "I eat my peas with honey" [pause]. D: "Oh, do you?" F: "I've done so all my life." D: "Really!" F: "It makes

_____
* "Holiday" to the infidel.

the peas taste funny—" D: "Yes I suppose it would." F: "—but it *keeps* them on the knife." D: "Oh, you're joking."

It wasn't the joke, it was the meter that clued her in. Note particularly the cadence of the duchess' alleged answers, as she plays against the verse. If Frank hadn't given it all away with that knee-banging last line, she never would have known that they'd done a number together in the middle of a normal conversation.

So this must be what people meant when they said, "You must be very proud of your dad." I'd taken a squint at *Theology and Sanity,* Sheed's own *Summa,* and found it just the kind of stuff one heard about the house. But only a great man could produce on demand or without it, "Take your girlie to the movies, if you can't make love at home," or "It doesn't matter, it's only me and I'm sure that I don't mind," with all its haunting variations, such as, "If I hadn't been there you must admit/You wouldn't have had any face to hit/Perhaps you'll never meet the man you want and if he dies/It's some satisfaction to have hit someone—so don't apologize."

And when Doctor Sheed wasn't singing, he was whistling. It used to be commoner, I believe, to hear grown men in actual hats and suits whistling in the street. But by Frank's prime, it turned heads. He might as well have been talking to himself or eating an ice cream cone in church. Never mind. The man had a beat. However properly he was dressed, in his gray suit or his blue suit, his blue tie or his red one (he never owned more than two of either garment at one time), there was always something going on in there.

So we follow our whistling theologian as he enters his Golden Age. By 1947, when I got back to America, he seemed to be Mr. Chips to the whole Catholic nation. After one swing of forty lectures in twenty days, strung together by mail planes and anything else that would move, he said, "I'm too old for this sort of thing," but he wasn't by a long chalk. I can still hear him on the phone. "Oh, God. Is he? I trust it's not serious." It seems the featured speaker has a head cold. "Lord! Poor devil [sigh]. All right. Is there a connection from Newark?"

Like those legendary old doctors ploughing through rain and flood, Frank couldn't turn down a house call from the faithful. "Lec-

ture, my boy," he would say to me; "it's the easiest money there is."
But it wasn't, if you did it his way. Half or more of his lectures seemed
to be given for nothing, and I was genuinely surprised when he
turned one down on the following grounds: "I suppose," he said,
"that you're giving me the honorary degree in place of a fee? I'm
sorry. You see, I already have a cupboardful of the damned things."

But he was talking that time to a rich university, and it touched
an old Marxist or Wobbly nerve in him. *He* hadn't taken a vow of
poverty, he must have thought as he gazed around the million-dollar
auditoriums of the nouveau riche Catholic educational plant. But the
struggling, inadequate little places could always command him. One
particular such won his heart forever because all the faculty wore different colored gowns, tippets and tassels. "What do they stand for?"
asked Frank. "I don't know," said the president. "We bought them in
a bundle."

As Frank went, so went his publishing house. In the forties he
was still publishing full blast, as well as lecturing, but he was always
happy, even eager, to delegate the book business to anyone who
seemed even mildly competent. By the fifties, he began to luck out
and attract some real professionals, but this, too, was partly a chain result of his lecturing, which, while still resolutely unpoetic, was in-
formed by that foot-tapping, follow-me beat. "He was such a change
from the nuns" (or the priests) was the line I heard most often. He
may have been the only businessman (he always used the term laughingly) in history whose staff had all heard him lecturing first. So the
set was complete: the Pied Publisher had attracted a trail of readers,
writers and finally assistants, using nothing but his tongue.

Beyond that, there was a Catholic boom of which he was only a
part. World War II deserves at least some of the credit. Suddenly, the
march of the converts was on, with Fulton Sheen ushering in the big
fish (his given name was an appropriate Peter, but for some *"raison de
snob"* he had traded it in for this *"nom de fish market"*) and with Sheed
and Ward functioning as, not precisely a delousing or debriefing center, but more as an intellectual Welcome Wagon.

From there they went, intellectually speaking, straight to Jacques
Maritain, the Thomist sage of Princeton, to encounter an actual

breathing European, a piece of the tradition. Some confluence of prejudices led me to underestimate Maritain at the time. I felt that like Paul Tillich the theologian and Herbert Marcuse the philosopher and sundry hot dogs, he was over here to dazzle the aborigines, and that back home, he'd have been lost in the crowd. Also Maritain had a beautiful spiritual marriage with an intense Russian called Raissa, which struck me as somewhat un-Australian, not to mention an affront to Groucho.

How did Groucho get into this? It has something to do with French philosophers. I had already met Maritain's great coeval Etienne Gilson, and he had told me how reluctantly but genuinely impressed he had been by the bayonet-glinting Nazi march into Paris in 1940. Primed on *Animal Crackers*, I suggested that it might have been even better with the Marx Brothers marching just behind: and I suppose French philosophers still bring out this association. At any rate, I pictured the pair of them, Jacques and Raissa, weaving burlap vestments in which to renew their marriage vows every Candlemas, and all I could think of was a scene from *A Night at the Opera* where Groucho and Harpo are disguised as a mad old couple who might well have been doing the same thing.

Heaven knows, there was plenty of both kinds of imported fraudulence, intellectual and aesthetic, that year, with minor-league Europeans scavenging the small campuses, and all sorts of people baking liturgical bread in their homemade dirndls. But in the case of Maritain, I hadn't realized how much the intellectual balance of power had shifted recently, particularly in the direction of Princeton, so that to have a Catholic thinker operating on equal terms in and around the Institute for Advanced Studies was bracing and valuable. The intellectuals who had dreamed of Europe right through the war had perhaps taken one look and, like the English Americaphobes, found their old home missing; but instead of blaming America for this, they went to Princeton. Also, Maritain paid his hosts the honor of lucidity, so that one could judge for oneself just how good or how limited he was. His honesty shone among the European carpetbaggers.

As for spiritual marriages and all that—a few years later, I would be drawn to liturgical groups myself, though never to dirndls. But in

1947 America itself seemed exciting enough without these bits of dead skin attached. "Welcome home, son," said the big immigration man, causing me to jump. How did he know? I still had a big blue passport and only a little green card. But the card was the key to the city.

"Straighten out dem magazines, kid" was hardly the greeting I'd counted on, and something dreadful had happened to the music. A monstrosity called "Near You" seemed to bray from every storefront. Never mind about that, or about Vaughn Monroe either. A believer walks straight down the aisle, blocking out the bad hymns and the creepy statues to see what he came to see.

I hopped a Number 5 bus around Fourteenth Street and passed the whole slow trip uptown in a delirium close to mystical. As we swung onto Riverside Drive at Seventy-second Street, I was fairly frothing. The Gershwins lived over there, and Babe Ruth in his straw hat took a cab to the park along here and nothing, down to the last cornice, had changed. I was heading right now toward a pen pal, Chris of the Kennedys, who lived near 119th Street, but he was out when I got there and so was everybody else. "You should have called," said the person in residence, and the air whooshed out of my surprise visit. But what the hell, the Dodgers were at home and in a pennant race. The new guy, Jackie Robinson, was in town. I hadn't played my last card.

Sheed and Ward seemed exciting too, if only as part of the general excitement, a thrum in the air that I can no longer feel or hear, but which was everywhere then, drifting through office windows, car windows and those special Sheed hotel windows which almost rattled with it: a compound of buses, voices, river breezes, everything that *can* fill air. It was as if the city had forgotten to stop celebrating the end of the war, but had composed a "Symphony for Five Senses" in its honor. Blindfolded on a quiet street, a man could tell he was in New York a hundred ways: no one smell, or one sound, but the residue of the lot. It was a hell of a long way from Stratton-on-Fosse.

I only marveled that everyone else seemed to take it so calmly. Finding myself being driven over the swirling Triboro Bridge, I

thought, "Hot damn. This is *incredible*," but everyone else seemed to take it for granted. One hugs these loves to oneself out of necessity, because everyone else thinks you're nuts, or feverish. Except for other foreigners. Nowadays when I hear a late arrival babbling about the wonders of New York I listen patiently, trying to remember. But nothing comes. We've been married too long.

Long before the 1960s, this kind of open-throated America-worship put one at odds with the more vital side of the Church, the Left to which I thought I belonged. My comrades weren't just unimpressed by the Triboro Bridge, they were sickened by it and all it stood for. The late forties was for Catholics an age of movements: family movements, pacifist movements, interracial movements—you could always pick one that matched your temperament, but they were all against the country I'd dreamed about in England.

Friendship House still flourished, especially in Chicago, which was a blast furnace of movements; the Catholic Worker would soon be staging public sit-ins against fake civil defense drills, but at the moment what it was doing preeminently and quietly was attracting talent: John Cogley and James O'Gara in Chicago, Ammon Hennacy, and later Michael Harrington in New York, a flow that had begun before the war, been slightly clogged by the pacifist issue, but had now resumed itself. And the talent all ran the same way. These people were already fed up with the feast of plenty—and I'd only just got here. Finding themselves safely parked in the world's only winner, all they could talk about was poverty and injustice. Spoilsports. After austerity England, voluntary poverty was just too damn much. I hadn't come to America for more anti-Americanism.

It was a tricky position for a young Socialist to find himself in. I clucked with the gang over the amount of steak that Americans threw away—but my eyes lingered on the steak.

Only some time later when I dragged my eyes over to the America that the Catholic radicals were looking at, a land of sleek pastors in box seats seated jowl-by-jowl with fat cats voted "layman of the year"—the understanding being that "the business of the laity is business"—did I realize we had been talking about somewhat different things. Gershwin was dead and the Marx Brothers were retired, and I was welcome to them. My dream America was as far away as the Catholic Worker's.

However, we foreign-born America-fanciers (if I may invent a group to stuff some generalizations into) occasionally ran to a taste for vulgarity and a craving for streamlined trash: we would not have liked an America as pure as the native radicals wanted. The worst of us were not even embarrassed by salesmen called "Elmer," although we could do without historians named Chauncey Truslow Adams, Jr. The authentic tended to put us to sleep, but swing and bastard country music revived us. We liked, when it slunk onto the scene, Las Vegas much better than Williamsburg. Americans believed we were putting them on, or down.

The fact is, though, that after the war, a perverse quest for the un-European seized a few of us, and there was nothing condescending about it. Europe could once again be left to handle the business of being Europe, while America must be itself, though our notion of that might be quite unreal. I remember a cultured French landlady of mine installing a super-duper pressure cooker that would have turned civilized Americans pale. Labor-saving devices, gadgets, gizmos—after six years of hell, America couldn't seem silly enough.

Or even after one year of England. It was while still there mulling on my Spam that I first read the purest of all new movement publications, a magazine called *Integrity* which positively scourged labor-saving devices, and which even denounced people who wore pretty clothes to church of a Sunday. After kneeling amidst the English in their mustard overcoats and faded bandanas and frocks weary from scrubbing, I yearned for pretty clothes, with pretty women inside them.

However, *Integrity* was not easy to dismiss, because, among other things, it became one of the noticeable strands in Sheed and Ward's postwar thinking. Of course, everybody was beating up on the piggy materialists right then, especially European lecturers who found a gold mine in it. (For every America-fancier, there were two professional deplorers taking their turn at the whip, flailing the fat nation until the guilt ran.) So there was nothing sensational about that. Even Bishop

Sheen in his twinkling robes gave the back of his hand to Godless materialism and conspicuous consumption. It was a terrible time to be a hedonist.

What distinguished *Integrity* from the rest of the gang at the wailing wall was a certain intellectual structure and continuity. Before the war both Belloc and Chesterton had preached something called distributism, based on small independent ownership of land, while a third, Eric Gill, had actually experimented with a species of commune where one could be fully Christian and worship God with the work of one's hands, mind and, in Gill's case, sexuality. *Integrity* took a piece of each of these and ran.

The mother-foundress of the group was a large, dreamy lady called Carol Jackson who looked as if she were listening to birdsong while she talked to you and whose hatred of modern American life verged on the lubricious. Of the three women leaders, Dorothy Day, Catherine de Hueck and Jackson, Jackson was easily the most headlong, consumed by a need to say something passionate or bust, even if the content might change in a year or two. As an educated convert she had a turn for all-or-nothing rhetoric of a kind that attracted young people, though once they were in the tent they tended to go their own ways; like the baroness, Jackson was at her best as a recruiting poster.*

Integrity was soon carried beyond its Cotton Mather stage by a charming couple named Ed and Dorothy Willock. The group had already been living a liturgical life in New York, eating monastic dinners with candles, and so on, but the Willocks and others decided to add a distributist touch to this. New York was as Godless as it was expensive, and all the candlelight in the world couldn't make it a good place to raise Christian children. So they chipped in to buy some land which they called Marycrest, near Nyack, New York, there to raise their families in real Christian community, though with the independence of distributists.

Maisie was thrilled by this. It was as if the books she had helped publish were coming true. In fact several Sheed and Ward books led to action in this way, and the action led to books: the Catholic Re-

* Having once denounced TV as the work of the devil, Carol Jackson went on to marry an ex-producer of the "Today" show.

vival was a whirligig of words and deeds chasing each other, and books weren't supposed just to sit there. To Maisie preeminently, publishing *was* action, and Sheed and Ward belonged more to the genre Catholic Worker than, say, the genre Houghton Mifflin. So in this spirit, she personally advanced Marycrest $4,000 (where she got it, nobody knows) and proceeded to watch over it avidly as one of her finest publications.

Perhaps the best thing that can be said about what followed is that she learned a lot. In fact this dry run of the sixties might, if properly studied, have saved quite a few people some time and trouble. The participants were about as bright, sane and dedicated as can be hoped for anywhere and they certainly did the best they could. And the fact that the community did not last in its original form forever does not make it a failure: every good year was a value in itself.

Yet the strains came inexorably, and Maisie noted them with resigned dismay. Since birth control was frowned on at Marycrest, some families ballooned, and needed more of the pie (and what was the matter with those childless couples anyway? a little weak in the spirit?). Ed Willock, who had one of the largest broods, suffered a debilitating stroke, but sired more children anyway, which must have put his disciples in two minds. As a leader of sorts, Willock was on the spot either way. Catholics were expected to consider the lilies of the field and trust God to provide. And if this was good enough for people in the slums, how could Willock indulge in more prudence for himself? Compromise had been ruled out by his magazine before the Marycrest experiment had even started. Indeed, being a fool for Christ was the whole point, although how foolish you had to be, Christ only knew. Anyway, it was Dorothy who had the children.

Behind all the little strains (and there had to be a lot more than I knew about) was a megastrain which made all of them worse at once. In brief, and as Maisie saw it, several couples seemed to consist of one enthusiast and one mostly along for the ride, and the resentment in such cases had to slash viciously both ways: every scenario one imagines seems more bloodcurdling than the last.

Since I believe the same sort of problem arises in wife swapping, it wasn't finally a matter of sacrifice or sainthood, but of taste. Some communards missed the outside world too much, others may have wearied of the inside one. I don't know the details. Maisie learned a lot of general lessons about how much you should do for people and how much you shouldn't, but one particular lesson stood her in good stead when she got into her own major work of housing poor families in London: she learned to assess *both* sides of a couple, to gauge just how much the strong one could carry and the weak one drop. From a slow start, Maisie learned more about human nature in her sixties and seventies than seemed strictly speaking possible.

Marycrest taught, and learned, several other things about men and women. One of the more revealing was that it was often the woman who wanted to give up and get back to nuclear living and the man who preferred to linger in the distended family. Ed Willock was a patriarch, and in this he didn't foreshadow the sixties at all. He believed that men and women should play their appointed roles in the Christian family, which led to a cruel irony, as this truly wonderful man became steadily less able to support his family while his wife struggled without labor-saving devices to be the complete Christian parent.

But even without this gruesome example, the sexual strains of the sixties must have been felt in advance by these people who had so stripped life of clutter that relationships had nothing to hide behind. A man can't become a patriarch just by wishing it, nor can a modern woman accept him as one without deforming herself. Places like Marycrest (and it wasn't alone)* were like primitive labs where this kind of problem had to be worked out in the dark. Because the rest of America was launched upon Macho's Last Stand and offered no illumination.

Sheed and Ward was the bulletin board on which one followed these things. *Integrity* calmed down under a new editor, Dorothy Dohen, and naturally she completed the cycle by writing for the old

---

* I'm taking slight liberties with Marycrest, using it mainly as a symbol. Maisie had various things to say about various communities and I'm lumping them together under one name. In her "up" phase, Maisie wrote a book called *Be Not Solicitous* about such matters. Later, she might have added, "Well, maybe just a little bit" to this title.

firm. Frank did not commit himself to any one stage of such a saga. His readings in Hegel and Marx had long since sold him on the dialectic, an excellent thing in a publisher. Even in theology, he would sometimes find his authors running on ahead of him but it didn't bother him at all in the 1950s. "Every intelligent man is four-fifths right," he once said to me in reference to, of all people, Sartre.

Nothing, to my memory, bothered him much, at least in the early 1950s. The Catholic consensus was still sturdy enough to support any amount of eccentricity. So although you couldn't have got him to live in a commune on a bet, Frank smiled on any new way of being a good Catholic; let a hundred books bloom from it. Which brings to mind a possible team secret: if Sheed and Ward visited a place such as Marycrest, Maisie might burble over the work being done there, while Frank would say, "I think there's a book in that fella." She would see a subject, he would see an author. Well, sometimes.

Finding new ways to be a Catholic might almost be called the theme of the fifties, if the fifties had a theme. The converts and bright kids that Frank and Maisie had at least partly influenced found themselves heir to a 5-and-10-cent Church. So in a great fury they set to work redefining spirituality, putting life into liturgy and simply finding things to do commensurate with their excitement. The divine afflatus they experienced was enough to burst the rib cage of the sturdiest institution—but this they were determined to avoid. After the recent global bloodletting, the Brotherhood of Man was the only game in town. The Protestant churches were beginning to cuddle, and the UN instantly sprouted agencies covering everything an agency can cover to bring us all together. So if you already had a world religion you'd be a fool to let it go. The revolutionary fervor that poured from this generation of Catholics into the children of the sixties now went mostly, as Frank's had, into holding, and redecorating, the fort.

"Rule the obedient with a rod of iron," was Frank's description of the official Church's rule of thumb. Only a revolutionary can expect concessions. These respectful zealots got nothing. Their mildest requests for social action or a rethinking of birth control were treated like scratches on an oak door. "Imprudent." "The time isn't ripe"— anything was good enough to disperse the urchins. Later the mob would break in and get much of what it wanted. But for now, the energy raged in a straitjacket. What can we do within the regulations, the tradition? I have never sensed so much genuine spirituality going nowhere as in the fifties.

A lot of it petered out quickly in discussion groups and little movements made of nothing but enthusiasm. A lot of it also went, for better or worse, into intense private experience, with Catholics tending their own gardens ever more elegantly. High above the coarse self-improvement of the marketplace, where the likes of Norman Vincent Peale and Billy Graham and our own Father "Three-Minutes-a-Day-with-God" Keller hawked spiritual beauty tips, a line of ingenious new prayers, meditations and liturgies was providing roughly the same service for the sensitive, or Sheed and Ward, type. After all, the hero of the decade was a Trappist monk named Merton, and you couldn't get much more private than that.

Some of this may have been a bit precious, but the truth was, there *wasn't* that much to do publicly in a strictly Catholic way. "Remember all those movements?" one veteran will ask another. Because the movements actually began to thin out as the flaccid fifties wound down, while private spirituality flourished right through the sixties. Sheed and Ward's biggest seller in that decade was a book of "prayers for our time" by a French priest named Michel Quoist.

By that time, the old movement hands were likely to have segued into civil rights organizations, and they were less likely to want to do this "Catholicly" than before. In the fifties there was a Catholic way of looking at everything, and a "theology of baseball" would hardly have seemed farfetched. If our current social concerns had existed then, we would undoubtedly have had a "League of Catholic Environmentalists" and "Catholics United Against Cigarette Smoking." Today, significantly, even the Right-to-Life movement doesn't call itself Catholic: it figures to travel farther without the label. And only the venerable Catholic Worker, older than time, survives intact from all the postwar bustle: like New College, Oxford (founded in 1357), its name is part of its quiddity, and nobody stops to think about it.

Obviously Sheed and Ward thrived on all this Catholic self-consciousness, although it was not so sunk in self-interest that it wasn't also first in line to publish the ecumenical books which would later dilute the chauvinism that greased the wheels that ran the press that paid for the house that Frank built.

One turns to a limp phrase like "period of transition," and the fifties were certainly that, like the chest-beating phase of a new nation. But that's aftermath. This was also an invigorating time in itself, especially since the rest of the nation seemed hopelessly bogged down in boredom. To be Catholic was to be alive, or at least to have a shot at it. Our very own little Right and Left could even join hands occasionally and jeer at the insipidity of the secular consensus. The fatty deposit known as the Eisenhower Years could be attacked from so many angles (including even my Gershwin bastion) that revisionists have since claimed that the attacks *were* the decade, the real story. But this is because words live longer than atmospheres. At the time, the live ones, Catholic or otherwise, stood out in bold relief against a background of Jell-O.

"Some liberals make me feel like a cad," Frank would say. "I feel unworthy of such decent fellows, of so much sheer virtue" . . . take that, Eleanor Roosevelt. "But," he would add, "I much prefer the company on the Left."

It was hard not to, back then. The Right can be smug even in defeat, but in the fifties it was fat in the saddle and positively purring. From preferring the company of the Left it would have been a short step to preferring the positions of the Left, but Frank stubbornly refused to take the step, partly because he didn't want to stop the flow between himself and his many-headed audience, but partly, I think, because he liked to keep politics as a playground where whim and prejudice could gambol without answering to the Holy Ghost.

He remained an imperialist and favored the Suez adventure, claiming that Nasser was cutting Britain's jugular in seizing the canal. ("What's our jugular doing way out there?" I muttered. No bones broken.) He wasn't really happy that Pakistanis could now enter England with the ease of Australians—though if he'd met a Pakistani, he would undoubtedly have sponsored him and become godfather to his child. He still liked Belloc's notion that monarchy was the only form of government where you didn't have to get your hands dirty to reach the top, and in the one book he never referred to in later life, called *Society and Sanity,* he criticized the welfare state as "Caesar with a milk bottle." He had an indiscriminate horror of bureaucrats, no doubt from having his passport stamped once too often (it was an Australian one with a unique visa dating from 1812, so he was asking for it), and I never heard him speak well of a politician, so he expected nothing from government.

These were defensible positions, but Frank didn't like the people who usually defended them and it didn't mean that much to him. "You don't understand about Man and you don't understand about God and you don't understand about the meaning of life—now let me tell you about birth control" was how he parried temporal questions. If you were going to take away Caesar's milk bottle, you had to have a just society all ready in place: but for this you had to go back to the beginnings, as long as it took. The Fatherhood of God, the Brotherhood of Man, the whole chain of being.

Maisie could never wait that long, and she shrugged off her Toryism impatiently in the fifties and waded into the Present. On reconsidering her disappointment with England, she seemed to decide that the welfare state was probably better than nothing, but that it needed a good shaking. Where was all this welfare when the homeless and the aimless needed it? she demanded. What use is welfare without a roof over your head? When she took on the bureaucrats herself, she found them far from Caesars. In fact they trembled before her, even as parish priests had. "*Why* can't you do this?" she would explode: and lo, it was done.

But she was still feeling her way in the forties and fifties. Her great discovery back then was the French worker-priests, men who went into the factories and mixed it, a group of whom practically adopted her as a mascot. In their steamy quarters in Marseilles, Père Jacques Loew, a lawyer turned dockworker, and his equally improbable colleagues were as far from her hated Jesuits* as possible, and they welcomed her with love and dialogue Masses, the ardent little

---

* Her latent dislike, dating back to her brother Leo's early troubles with the "jebbies," was rubbed raw by what she saw as their tendency to be café intellectuals while the Church in France was dying.

Englishwoman with the atrocious accent. For her the idea of priests actually working was intoxicating, and she only worried that in their youthful fervor they would become Communist apparatchiks and lose their special magic. She understood that they couldn't avoid union politics, but as priests they would have a fatal tendency to lead, or be asked to lead. And as union officials, they might as well be Jesuits.

Her excitement over this came back with her to New York, and was fed into the bubbling stew out of which would later emerge the Berrigans and who-knows-what-all. She herself was leery about politically prominent priests, because it was one more opportunity for them to showboat and spread their tailfeathers, but she did believe in getting them out of the damned seminaries and into the street.

Did *Maisie* impress me then? Only in retrospect. Her enthusiasms were always just too big for a small apartment. The style that could rally crowds at will backfired badly in our sunken living room in the Bronx, where we killed the second half of that winter. Her intensity had a slightly off-putting effect from up close like someone sticking his face in yours. To this day I cannot read Browning, and it was touch and go with my hero Chesterton for a while.

Because of this, I also found her public speaking overdone, and for a while I was embarrassed for all of us. Yet I always felt its power. If I had stuck to hearing her *lecture* on Browning, I'd have been hooked on the fellow. It was her private self that was unconvincing, no doubt on some principle of consanguinity: the nearer the relative, the greater the disappointment.

Or perhaps it was something else altogether. Maisie had been so awestruck at having children at all—especially me, the last throw of the dice—that I think she felt uneasy with me. At least I felt that she was trying awfully hard for me to like her (love went without saying), and the strain made her seem artificial, not quite herself.

Then, not later. Both Frank and Maisie were to change surprisingly in the years to come (as Mark Twain observed of his parents, they seemed to get smarter as I got older). But for a moment I'd like to hold them in amber, Frank forever jaunty and arriving from somewhere, Maisie brimming with her French priests, and the whole Sheed and Ward office humming with youth and suppressed laughter, with a staff that could get laughs out of Holy Week.

A nomad becomes a connoisseur of welcomes, and Sheed and Ward's New York's were of the finest. Dusty-eyed from all-night flights from London this was a place of steady cheer, and not because I was some boss's son (nobody needed a job at Sheed and Ward that badly) but because they always seemed to be having a good time, to which one simply plugged in.

Faces changed from time to time, but this sense of entering a winning locker room remained. Beyond each individual's reasons for merriment was a larger feeling that the Church was on the move, and that this office was helping it to get there in a small way. No one could have said quite *where* the Church was going: the reforms of the Second Vatican Council would have seemed much too much to hope for. But on every front, something was stirring: Catholic education was lumbering out of the stone age; psychiatry had just been discovered after the usual Catholic cooling-off period, and priests were examining themselves for neurosis as strictly as for sins of pride; and from Europe rumbles of mighty theological warfare could be heard.

The official American Church at first wanted no part of these foreign entanglements, but America wasn't quite the Outback any longer, the European connection had been made and the days had gone when you could hide a schism in, say, Holland under the rug:* and it was clear that a schism was in the works if Rome didn't mend its ways convulsively. Sheed and Ward passed this on neutrally because it did not monkey too much with the bulletin board. Watching all this upheaval from America was exciting but confusing as conflicting reports came in. The idea of a bishop "protecting" a favorite theologian from Rome, as Cardinal König protected young Hans Küng, was so far from American practice (we had no theologians to protect, and our bishops would have been the first to turn them over if we

---

* The Dutch who recently heckled Pope John Paul are attached to the same fuse that almost blew the Dutch Church apart in the sixties. In fact, the possibility of schism in that country may have prompted Vatican Council II almost as much as John XXIII's "open windows" policy.

had) that it was hard to weigh the seriousness of what was happening. What was defiance and what was local politics? Allowing for these difficulties in conceptual transition, Sheed and Ward probably ran the best bush telegraph in town, and published the most significant European voices.

Where the Church was heading was indeed Vatican Council II, during which some fairy godmother of dubious origin granted us almost everything we wanted, after which nothing was quite the same. So into amber goes the time of expectation, the faces frozen in curiosity and hope, the publishing house with the fixed smile.

Scrapbook

HERE IS NO REAL NEED TO FREEZE THE REST OF OUR LITTLE troupe. Rosemary had her own affair with France, and translated a book for Sheed and Ward called *Priest Workman in Germany* by Père Henri Perrin, a landmark of sorts, and from then on she played the unsung translator's part in shoveling French ideas at the Anglo-American audience—these being the best and *chic*est available after the war. Pères Henri de Lubac, Jean Daniélou, Yves Congar* et al. were among the first to get the Church moving again after the great idea-freeze, or rather communication-freeze of 1939–45 (World War II was actually an excellent time for thinking—especially in France).

Rosemary also married English in the fifties and her husband went to work at Sheed and Ward, but that isn't a story yet, just a satisfied burble. So I'll leave my sister in peace for now, with babies roiling all around her as she types and checks her Larousse.

Min came to America around then, which always gave her a lift, but the pain in her knees combined with, by now, explosive blood pressure just about nullified it this time round, and I find from one of my rare letters home (home being here used in the relative or Sheedian sense, as the place where I am not) that I spent much time humoring the old girl and wresting her mind off her knees, and off the crime in the newspapers, which she had come to take personally.

---

* It was an omen of headaches to come that both de Lubac and Congar, superb theologians, had their troubles with Vatican authorities. Publishers like Sheed and Ward were being dragged, along with America itself, into a European caldron.

This would continue on and off until her death in London in 1953, mainly because I seemed to be the best at it. Not that I possessed any special nursing skills, beyond thinly disguised irritation, but I was simply the right animal for the job. She still loved young men, and once, after she'd had a stroke, she confided in me sternly that Frank was getting very fat, as if I were the father and ought to talk to him about it. Since her idea of a compliment had always been "You're looking nice and fat," the reversal of values puzzled me. But by then, she had little to thank fat for. Partly owing to her bulky build, she had fallen one night and broken a hip, which at her age you just left at that. In a grisly way, it was a relief, because it meant that she was bed-bound and couldn't get into any culinary mischief.

Or so we thought. But somehow, while we were out one evening, the lion-hearted creature managed to work her way into the kitchen and, packing the frying pan tight with lard, to cook herself the greasiest meal in Sheed family history (no mean boast). Her blood pressure must have been simply sitting around waiting for something like this to happen, and the punishment was swift and inevitable: a truly massive stroke which left her woolly and helpless from there on in. Although her tough pioneer body hung on as long as it reasonably could, I have always attributed her passing to "death by frying pan." Min was finally a martyr to her own most precious belief, that "a little of what you fancy does you good." It was like a Roman falling on his sword.

In her very last days she whispered to me that her real age was ninety, although everyone else thought she was eighty-five. I accepted the revised figure immediately and passed it on; and Min, satisfied on this point, died serenely soon after. I was there for the death rattle, and I saw the years roll off her like a cloud passing, and suddenly she was a strong and beautiful woman of about sixty. It was very calming to watch a death and see what a matter-of-fact thing it can be. And later, the Latin funeral service deepened the calm. I had lost an old lady and gained a memory that could be any age I wished; just as when Frank died, his worn-out carcass would give way to a young man prancing the streets of Sydney. My occasional dreams about Min are good ones.

As for me, I got into Oxford by a series of back alleys. On the way, I took a terrible drubbing from a Corpus Christi College scholarship exam. In those days, I must have looked brighter than I was because I was always being thrown in over my head, but never deeper than this. Never mind my attempts to write Greek and Latin verse without knowing the stresses, or to turn Macaulay into Cicero, or the other petty humiliations of that week: what really hurt was a delta (or D) double-minus in the English essay. (By the time I left Oxford I'd improved this slightly to a gamma delta, or CD. I guess Oxford just didn't like my stuff.)

The topper was a late-evening interview with an old man called Livingston, who ran the place and had never heard of Danny Kaye. For a moment, I could have been back at Downside, sipping tea in the Twilight Zone. I didn't want to go to this place and start all that again. Finally Livingston asked me which I preferred, Greece or Rome. Everything about the man screamed the right answer, but I crankily gave the wrong one anyway. "Rome? Why Rome?" he asked incredulously. Just at that moment I hadn't the faintest idea. "Because it worked," I said.

On this barbarous note, I washed my hands of Oxford ("*Worked.* The chap said it *worked,*" haw haw), and announced that I wanted to go straight into journalism, where glibness was properly appreciated. My parents, who were still unwilling to grant a defect in a child of theirs, whipped up a new category for me, "brilliant but bad at exams," meaning "too brilliant to express himself in three hours," a likely story (maybe every family has this category in reserve), and they set to figuring out how to maneuver me past the exam system, like smuggling somebody over a border. Frank wanted to shuffle me off to Fribourg in Switzerland, but I had him on that one: my living languages were even worse than my dead ones. Then they remembered an old family friend—and the tortuous approach to Lincoln had begun.

Lincoln College had been having a very good run at talent-spotting, and since it was hardly anybody's college of first choice ("You might as well go to *Queens,*" growled my tutor of the moment), it had to do it all on intuition rather than records or references. A stammering wizard named Harold Hanbury was, I believe, the man most largely responsible for peering through our layers of mediocrity to our small inner sparks, and in my first year Lincoln wangled ten first-class degrees: chicken feed for Balliol but a banquet for us.

Lincoln's recruiting exigencies required it to beat the bushes and hedges for talent, rather than the posh schools, so we had a splendidly various student body, like Wellington's "scum of the earth"—rugby players, calypso singers, scientists: we had no type, no college style *except* variety. The only type we didn't have was the Downside type. I was home scot-free.

England, perhaps even more than other countries, becomes an entirely different place in the right company and Lincoln was it for me. Austerity was only a little less severe than in 1947, and the beer was watery, and the cafés had always just run out of eggs, so superficially England was the same old dump. But in my little Catholic corner of it, I hadn't seen how many ways there were to tackle the country. It may not have been precisely what Frank had in mind when he steered me away from Notre Dame, but meeting non-Catholic, non-Establishment England was probably the most magical single thing about Oxford.

Not that I became less Catholic myself, far from it. Having at last engaged the ancient enemy, I could finally drag out all the old halberds and crossbows of argument that every Catholic keeps in his cupboard, and I found myself set up in a small way of business as an apologist, in the old family trade. I suppose that talking to a papist must have been part of the Oxford experience for some, like joining the Socialist Club. Unsurprisingly the chief difficulty my new friends had with Catholicism—outside of sex, which made the whole thing academic—was that it seemed kind of preposterous: an objection old enough for even my ancient weapons. One lapsed Catholic told me that I obviously belonged to some special Church which sounded quite sensible, but which wasn't the one they taught in Manchester. So much for Sheed/Ward's attempts to raise all the boats.

Anyway, my special Church seemed quite intellectually respectable, especially since the reigning school of Oxford philosophy, linguistic analysis or whatever the phrase for it that year, had so tied its disciples' tongues that, at least as practiced by freshmen, one could only quibble, not assert. "Do you really mean to say . . . I take it that what you're saying ... Aren't you making a category mistake?" (this last in naked appeal. *Please* tell me you're making a category mistake).

Fortunately for the Faith, all this tortured jargon was filtered to me through beginners, who were grappling with it themselves and were even more cautious than their masters as to what could or could not be properly said. The result was almost an embargo on discussion. "That's a synthetic a priori proposition," they would say; and to this day I don't know a better conversation-stopper. Yet Catholics reading philosophy quite often left the Church in their first term, so the dons must have packed some secret weapon which I was spared. So I simply leaped into a callow neo-Wittgensteinian a posteriori posture and decided that if philosophy couldn't talk about certain things, then we'd just have to get along without it for now.

Actually, I read quite a lot of philosophy at Oxford on my own and found that the stolid linguistic sentries out there made metaphysics all the more exotic (the name "positivist" still conjures up heavy footsteps). Oxford is a good place to be a Catholic, as Frank must have known, because, among other things, you don't meet too many dumb ones. At a Catholic college I might well have cracked—as Frank also might have known. But when the secular mind is on top and sure of itself, *it* says the silly things, and you can sit back and think of other matters.

All sorts of other matters, including even a little history, my chosen field. A reviewer once complained that I had written a novel about Oxford in which no book was opened and no lecture attended: but one can only write about what one knows. Actually, I did open a book and I was also tutored briefly and well by a man who may or may not have been the original of George Smiley (John le Carré and I overlapped at Lincoln, both under different names), whose identity would probably be of interest in the dark corners of Fleet Street where the men who talk about these things talk about these things. But the bulk of my Oxford education came from conversations which could have happened anywhere, especially with two fellow historians, John McHardy and Michael Butler, who knew more even about *American* literature than I did and more about everything else than I know yet.

One tended to change friends, as the day wore on, in lieu of clothes, as in the days of *Brideshead:* all roles had to be played in the same patched jacket. In the evening the scholars repaired to their book-lined nests, to be replaced by louder and thirstier souls. "You must have been quite a 'hearty,' " sneered a don to me recently, invoking the sternest of all English class distinctions, that between the hearties and the arties, and after dark I generally was, making up for lost school years, and singing those ludicrous songs, rowing energetically away from gentility and into middle-class naughtiness, a journey of about ten feet. A Sheed will sing along with just about anything, so maybe Frank had done the same at Sydney, though he'd have choked on the lyrics. As always, he was trying to be more civilized and I less so.

However, for a couple of nights a week I would tear myself away from the roustabouts who lurked in the college lodge looking for action, any action, and take in a political or literary meeting. At the former, I found it much harder to defend America than it ever was to defend my improbable Church. On the Left, it was taken for granted that the Korean War was an imperial venture, perhaps the first of many. I did manage to score one off a visiting Communist speaker who swore that there were no Russian weapons in use in Korea. "That's funny," said I. "I saw some on television." I hadn't actually, but I felt for the moment that truth was a bourgeois indulgence that I couldn't afford. Curiously, the speaker bowed to my authority: television was still comparatively rare in England, and people hadn't thought much about how to evaluate it.

But the running sore picked at by Left and Right was of course McCarthyism, first as manifested by the House Un-American Activities Committee and later by the senator himself and his madcap assistants Roy Cohn and David Schine, who whipped through Europe like Tasmanian devils, yanking Dashiell Hammett books out of Army libraries. (I know there were other authors, but Hammett was always the one that came up.) "Does anybody want to talk about papal infallibility?" I felt like bleating. Because I couldn't even think of some sophistry to keep the political argument going. Not that I wanted to defend McCarthyism, but one doesn't want one's adopted country to make a complete ass of itself.

As for the other perennial, American racism, I would have to wait several years for England to develop a race problem of its own before that one was answered for me. Just then, the English were all aglow about releasing their own colonies, and in this heightened state of purity even the vaguely pro-American element felt themselves superior to the dirty old USA. To make matters worse, the inevitable American servicemen seemed to be everywhere, not misbehaving themselves as such things go, but simply being rich, hulking reminders of Britain's new dependence. "Why are all Yanks either enormous or tiny?" raved an undergraduate friend. "Aren't there any normal-looking blokes like you over there?"

Well, that was the good part. You were always the exception, the civilized Yank. And as the very best type of fuzzy-wuzzy, one could cross class boundaries with unfair ease and make friends who made each *other* uncomfortable. However, I never claimed to be anything but Australian myself.

Oxford memoirs usually include a dithyramb to punting and the spring term in general, so we'll consider that said. We, especially Catholics, fell in love a bit because we weren't allowed to do anything else, and it's my impression that we got more out of the specific pleasures of Oxford in this awesomely heightened condition than the operators did. Oxford was thin pickings for operators.

Perhaps what interested me most about the place was the way that Oxford, by its sheer differentness and without force, severed us all from our pasts. Working-class guys tended to fight against the process, even thickening their accents defiantly. But accents weren't the half of it. Unless you came from a family of dons, and not always then, you could seldom go home again from Oxford.

In my case, we had a bawdy junior common room at Lincoln which was about as far away from Sheed and Ward as one could legally get and I plunged into it gleefully. By chance, our cleverer undergraduates tended to be college rather than university men, so that such wit as we could muster was consumed on the premises rather than dispensed around town. One result of this was that nobody else ever heard of us; those brilliant Oxford careers that one reads about could simply not be conducted in such a shoebox as Lincoln. But we had a fine time of it, until the wit ran out sometime in my last year, and for a spell before that our common room was rumored to be the liveliest in Oxford. It was the least we could be, since we didn't do much else except win games.

After losing two elections by squeaky margins—which is infinitely more painful than I'd supposed—I became secretary of this outfit, delegated to the writing of minutes which were supposed to be travesties of the meetings they described. Since the meetings were themselves travesties, one could only turn them into *different* travesties, an interesting exercise for a beginner.

My custom was to labor over these monstrosities for the best part of every Sunday, and then march down to the bar and announce that I was just about to start on them. (No one was fooled, it was just what one did.) For years I remembered those old minutes as comic triumphs, so I was abashed recently to receive a set of them and learn the sad truth. Fortunately, they are so dense in parochial allusion that one would need something like a key to *Beowulf* to get through them. Nevertheless, I keep them out of reach of my children. I had been lulled by the sheer obligingness of English laughter, and had forgotten that nothing could be as funny as the chaps made one's stuff seem at the time.

Still, I learned something about writing from those minutes, which is more than I can say for my history essays, which remained puzzlingly flat and unformed, as if in this one respect I was still a raw American schoolboy. I needed, it seemed, to put spin on everything to get it to move at all, so I stuck to comedy, not out of choice, but of necessity. Humor, as even some of the Englishmen had discovered, also covers the gaps in one's education wonderfully.

Frank and Maisie dropped in at Lincoln from time to time, and it was a pleasure, particularly as one remembered the strained psychic readjustments of school visits. I had no mistress to hide and my friends behaved themselves more or less, content merely to whistle or hum the dirty songs, and Maisie thought that this was exactly the same place her brothers and grandfather had been to: hence her mild shock when my downstairs novel about it, *A Middle Class Education*, appeared.

Frank was not particularly shocked by the bits he read of the novel but was always politely surprised by my sweeping ignorance of history. "Which *is* your period?" he would ask with genuine puzzlement. Just before I went up, he had mumbled something to me about working on my character rather than my intellect, but then had added quickly, "Oh, God, that sounds awful, doesn't it." I, of course, compromised by working on neither.

But it wound up no worse than he expected. Universities were to be enjoyed and it was all too clear that I was enjoying myself one way or another. As a petty campus politician or wardheeler, I was helloed by a lot of faces in the quad; and since I was struggling vainly with budding myopia, I could only peer back dimly, thus giving the impression that more people knew me than I knew back. Capital stuff.

But my memories of Frank at Oxford are mostly mellow ones, just of strolling with him through that incomparable town, himself mightily pleased at how things had turned out. His Downside had been rejected, but this was vastly more important. It was his *best* dream. In family folklore, Oxford would always be Catholic, whether there were any Catholics actually there or not. It *looked* Catholic. And the congregation at the chaplaincy sang the Credo as if it were "We Shall Overcome." We seemed to be within inches of our birthright.

Frank startled me, one Oxford day, apropos the sacrament of confession (we had exhausted cricket, which I used to watch five days a week during the summer term), by saying, "I have nothing to confess these days but sheer mediocrity. That's it. Just a great dull grayness." It wasn't a melancholy moment. He was just comparing notes. In fact, on that particular day he could have been talking about the weather, which was as gray as any soul. But it haunted me.

Once before, when I was sixteen or so, he had told me in the same matter-of-fact way that "up until about forty, you think you can do anything. The world is your oyster. And then you realize that you're running out of time, and that you'll never do half of those things." What things hadn't he done? What was so gray about him? In each case it seemed half-warning, half-apology. "The years the locusts have eaten," he liked to intone at me, especially on days when I slept late. But no locust ever ate a year of his, not while he was looking. Yet there must have been some opportunity missed that he couldn't quite put his finger on. He'd felt it at forty and again now at Oxford in his mid-to-upper fifties. Oh, well. Rum business. Now——I think I'll be off.

He and/or Maisie would thereupon leave me, to the Jesuits at Campion Hall or the Dominicans at Blackfriars, and I would slink back to my average sensual life. Talk about shades of gray: anyone who has drunk, and randomly evacuated, the beer of Lincoln College 1950–54 can never talk about mediocrity again. But the friendships* at Oxford were solid gold, and built to last, and although all of us would have been hurled out of *Brideshead* in a body, we too lived in Arcadia in our scruffy way.

I remember walking along a particularly uninspired part of the Iffley Road, in a particularly fine evening light, and realizing with dismay that I could be happy here forever. But that was just Oxford, and they send you down, and if you try to go back you find Arcadia is closed and boarded over.

During spring vacations, I usually went to Rome for Holy Week to repair my soul, and batter my liver, and in the summers, my parents tended to toss me onto assorted American lawns like a newspaper. In those days, a resident alien had to check into the U.S. periodically or go through the humiliation of getting a new visa: which involved, the only time I did it, sitting in one's shorts for an hour and a half prior to being tapped on the chest and given an eye test. (The shorts business was obviously just to make you feel unworthy to enter *any* country.) "Does it matter if I flunk the eye test?" I asked. "I don't think so," I was told.

Then I had to swear I had never been a Communist, anarchist, flat-earther—I doubt if anyone has ever gotten to the end of that list. When I came to syphilis, I said, "That would be rather like taking coals to Newcastle, wouldn't it, sir?" and for a moment, I thought I

---

* Nothing is duller than a long list of unfamiliar names, so I'll just mention two: John Maxwell Brownjohn and John Stockton, who still pierce my laziness to keep in touch.

would be down to my shorts again. "You're under oath, son," growled an official. I felt like a huddled mass.

So the kindness of strangers had to be better than risking that again. Clare Luce,* whom I've written about elsewhere, was actually part of a sequence, although no one expected me to stay the whole summer at Clare's any more than the others'. Come to think of it, the inertia that kept me tethered there may have been part of the system, the thing that made it work. No host got rid of me without a struggle. A splendid couple called the Woods practically had to rent my room to somebody else to get me to move. Or so they say.

The Woods were just the latest example of my parents' ramifications. Nancy Wood's father was the poet Allen Tate and her mother was the novelist Caroline Gordon, and the whole shebang had up and become Catholic recently. So naturally they had met the Sheeds, and naturally I spent the summer there.

"Your faw-ther thinks," said Allen Tate southernly, "that I do nothing but fall downstairs." It was true. The two times Frank had dined with the Tates, Allen, top-heavy with bourbon, had toppled down a full flight. Although Tate swore to me that this had never happened to him before or since, it was no use telling that to booze-phobic Frank. Even without falling bodies to worry about, Frank was never really comfortable in a hard-drinking atmosphere, which cut him off from a lot of American writers. So the Tate-Woods were not his closest friends, only the best, at the time, for me.

This business of farming me out seems rather bizarre in retrospect, but it was all part of Sheed/Ward's higgledy-piggledy pattern. People were always staying with us for no discernible reason, and we expected an open world in exchange. Frank and Maisie didn't have a place of their own in America just then, and they were used to staying with people, in tacit exchange for services—lectures or help with problems—and for their esteemed company. The trouble was I had nothing to offer save my unwashed presence (after so long in England, the roguish Woods claim they had a devil of a time coaxing me into

* Playwright, congresswoman and so on, and wife of Henry Luce. Also a convert of Fulton Sheen's.

the tub). Twice, Frank shouted me to trips across the country in the car Clare Luce had given me, first west and then south, where I could light on his friends for no more than one night at a time, but inevitably I would come to rest and have to be put somewhere.

Three summers were spent this way, and Frank knew it was awkward ("Throw the brute out," he would tell my new landlords, "the moment he gets on your nerves") and he never exactly planned it. I was just like some rogue evacuee out of Evelyn Waugh. The only thing Frank could do about it was to choose my victims wisely, which he certainly did. He had always spared Rosemary and me as much as he could from the rich dull friends who were part of his mission, his cross. And the ones I got instead, the Luces, Spaeths (rich but interesting) and Woods (poor but well-bathed), have all remained, if we skip Harry Luce, lifelong friends.

On my car trips I was no longer surprised to find that all the names he gave me, even in the deep South, were Catholic. In sinful New Orleans, I stayed in a rectory (a lively one, but still—). In Kentucky I checked in with the university chaplain, in Charleston I bobbed in the water with the segregationist, but otherwise charming, Bishop Russell. (He didn't *look* segregationist.) In Rock Hill, South Carolina, I met his opposite number, a ribald Oratorian father who had integrated his parish by building a shack for the whites, while the Negroes used the regular church. To hammer the point home, the whites' only Mass was scheduled at dawn. It may be worth adding that he was a giant of a man, a far cry from Cardinal Newman, the most famous Oratorian and prototype, and could probably have gotten the same integrating results with his bare hands.

Priests everywhere. Priests gossipy, priests irreverent, priests saintly, but all from the same shop. And as they talked I realized that their shop was Frank's shop too, that he had immersed himself so deeply in it that clerical small talk was his second language.

On my western swing, Frank had appealed to yet another priest to supply me with contacts, but these at least turned out to be lay people. In the South, there didn't seem to be any lay people at all, at least in my parents' world. (There were plenty of lay people of all descriptions in the bars and honky-tonks, but that's a story for a scurvier memoir: I led a double life on these trips, which amused Frank in the slightly modified telling. *He* didn't expect me to hang around priests all day. He just didn't know anybody else.)

Frank's friends like the Luces and Woods and, in Hollywood, Jane Wyatt introduced me to all the non-Catholics that even a maniac on the subject could want—a Sheed introduction was never more than a step away from the outside world. But Frank left the step to me. Even his priests knew more non-Catholics than he did. He certainly had no need for them: like Saint Paul, whole communities of fellow believers rose to greet him wherever he went. And these exhausted all his social time and energy. Any visit to or from a Catholic could turn into a parish call, and he would have to don his invisible biretta to advise about an annulment or a Pauline privilege. (To cut down on the matrimonial guff he finally wrote a pamphlet on nullity, which he could pass round soundlessly. His inner lawyer enjoyed the workout.) In this respect, I think he found time spent with incurable non-Catholics to be time wasted. Curable ones, of course, got his fullest attention.

In a world like Frank's, full of clients and potential clients, there was no need to go looking for more company. But it still seemed strange to know *nothing* but Catholics. I believe there was something clannish beyond the call of duty about Frank and Maisie in their pre-ecumenical primes, and I'd like to propose a couple of possible reasons. To an English Catholic bent on saving souls, Protestants could be just as big a headache as atheists, and heartbreaking amounts of ingenuity went into arguing with them about who had persecuted whom the most in the distant past: as if straightening out the sixteenth century would bring everything back to normal.

The Protestants were just as pigheaded about this as we were. Peter Glenville, who went to Oxford in the 1930s, told me that the only prejudice he found there concerned the teaching of English history, in which antipapist smugness had not moved an inch in three hundred years. Twenty years later I found it in much the same place. "Official history," as Belloc sneeringly called it, hinged on an unspoken belief that England had turned out in the best possible way, so that whatever had happened, however regrettable at the time, was a step in the right direction. For obvious reasons, "official history" has not lasted into the Thatcher era.*

However, it will probably last forever in the mouths of hecklers, which Frank and Maisie had to stare into constantly, like dentists. For the more than thirty years that they worked the street corners, my parents listened every week to the garble of prejudice which results when bad teaching hits the streets. If the history seemed a little simple-minded at Oxford, it was gibberish by the time it reached Hyde Park Corner. And that, for Frank and Maisie, was quite enough of that: you don't go looking for it in real life.

Frank and Maisie were much too civilized to use social occasions to convert people. Yet they lived in—dread is too strong a word—mild apprehension that something silly would be said at a mixed gathering which would require a Catholic answer. Frank believed (and in this Maisie was a rubber stamp) that Catholics live in the real world and the rest don't and that this has implications far beyond the religious. So every conversation was a mine field. And the danger faced both ways. Outsiders might admire Sheed/Ward from afar, but if they got too close to it or went too deep, they would have had to find it insane (as they would Dorothy Day or Mother Teresa). Those crazy claims must be symbolic, aren't they? Virgin births? Resurrections? No, I'm afraid they're not. If Rome *was* the true Church, and there was no if about it, Catholics were right and the others wrong, except insofar as they agreed with Catholics. Discussion is difficult on these terms.

Of course *any* truth has these implications of exclusion, but the wishy-washy seculars seemed to want everybody's truth to be as good as everybody else's, even the pope's if he liked; and they only bridled when told that the pope's truth *couldn't* be like that. This was the hey-day of the word "relative," and Catholics preened themselves on despising it, and indeed of being out of the swim altogether. I remember once hearing my mother debate on radio with the famous critic John Mason Brown. The subject was divorce and for once the fluent Brown was tongue-tied, because he had never heard such arguments before, at

* Fairly recent British TV series on Henry VIII and Elizabeth I have come much closer to Belloc's own version than to the official history which scorned him.

once primitive and morally subtle, and completely off his daily track. Here was a bright, possibly even sane woman showing him a world as bizarre as Dante's, which apparently carried on full blast right behind America's (and England's) back.

There were Catholics at that time who seemed to go to parties just to be out of the swim. Christianity is *supposed* to be a scandal, went the reasoning, so they were doing the Lord's work simply by startling people. It was a funny sort of apostolate, requiring many changes of clothes, but who knows? It may have made some daffy converts who were looking for something different: a way out of gray bloody England, or Babbitt's America.

My parents, in contrast to the exotics, were flatfoots, street preachers. They wanted a Church as sturdy as a house, and bent every effort into making Rome seem reasonable, which is much harder than selling the decor. People in heat for conversion are either not looking for reason or looking for so much of it that the off-the-rack, ready-to-wear arguments of the Evidence Guild sounded thin and unsatisfying. The Guild was a halfway house, even more so than Sheed and Ward, where people picked up the first glint of an interest and moved on.

In sum, I don't think the Guild was anywhere near as important as the publishing house, although of course one had led to the other. No scores were kept on unassisted conversions, but my hunch is that lapsed or lapsing Catholics, who'd given up on defending the rigmarole altogether, got the most out of the Guild, Protestants the least.

I was able to measure my own drift away from this battlefield when a South African friend at Lincoln told me he'd heard this bimbo making pretty good sense at Hyde Park. I told him, that's funny, my parents talk there, and he said, well, that explains it, it must have been your mother. And I felt one of those sharp jerks of alienation, as if I'd read about this in a "Believe It or Not" cartoon. My parents' speaking was a private affair, even if they did do it next to the Marble Arch, and I was stunned that someone from my world had stumbled into it.

Sheed/Ward did not mind venturing out in a world that thought them cranky. But it was only by the seventies, when many things had changed, that they did it for fun; and only at the very end of Frank's life, when I introduced him to non-Catholics as consistently as he had done the opposite to me, that he ceased noticing which they were. Relaxed and off-guard, with no need to defend anything, he became his old self—the Sydney boy whose two best friends and whose favorite male cousin as he grew up were as non-Catholic as could be. What I had reluctantly come to see as a major prejudice was really a minor convenience—with a pinch of prejudice.

After bagging an undistinguished third at Oxford ("All great men get thirds"—FS), I decided to go looking for the ghost of this boy. Sydney was a five-week boat trip from London, which gave me plenty of time to settle at least one question: I was definitely not Australian. I might have been, if I'd taken the trouble to live there: I picked up the accent immediately, and the phrases that go with the sounds soon after. But the same matter of language which had cut me off from England now loomed between me and Australia.

It sounds like an odd problem, but I knew instinctively that I didn't want to *write* Australian. I liked to read it all right, so long as it wasn't catching. But just as the camera steals your soul, a new prose voice threatens your very head: the way you put things, the way you look at things, the way you think, finally your face. Knocking around the English-speaking world is like snake-dancing through these risks, the worst risk being a pan-colonial voice-view, emptied of all particularity. The only homesickness I still felt by twenty and up was embroidered around the phrase "they talk funny around here," as if menacing noises were gathering like insects outside my tent to steal my last heirloom, the contraption that makes the phrases, and replace it with some local gadget. But I was here to look for my father, not myself, and to track down some of those elements of culture and style that combined so strangely in him, to produce this most sophisticated of true believers. In some respects, Australia reminded me of a good Edwardian school cut adrift in the Pacific, using the same library and the same chapel, but stranger and farther from the source every year. The famous *Sydney Bulletin*, with its nineteenth-century layout, had a weird aesthetic attraction: it was old-fashioned and yet it had never happened before. On the floating school, it had developed a manner that belonged to no time or place.

And the same was true of Australians in general. Being so far away from so many world capitals, they were free to pick and choose among the goods that washed up there. One poet, for instance, the splendid James McCauley, wrote hauntingly in the manner of Dryden; a jazz man called Spike Hughes so identified himself with Jelly Roll Morton, down to a slight and painful-looking stoop, that it was beyond imitation: it was duplication. In his heart, mind and voice, the Sydney boy *was* Mr. Jelly Lord playing up a storm in a New Orleans whorehouse. Well, goddamn. Even Patrick White the novelist gets some of his strength from the fact that you don't know where the voice is coming from. Again it is old-fashioned and completely original. And that is, or was, Australia.

Great virtuosity could come out of this freedom, but there was necessarily something secondhand about it, as if the boys in the prop room had decided to combine Restoration wigs, Elizabethan ruffs and business suits. Not that the effects were necessarily calculated: Frank, for instance, was always completely himself. It was just that some of his parts were made abroad and assembled along unusual lines in Australia. (For this reason perhaps Australians have a special fascination with their own identity. "Who *are* we anyway?" was a burning question in 1954 and I'm told it burns on today. One could always turn a quid writing pieces called "What Is an Australian and Whither?")

The lanky, slit-eyed bushranger image that I had rather coveted was particularly out of favor with the university crowd I met. One might as well wish to be John Wayne singing "Waltzing Matilda." "I was disappointed in your old man," said a student in the shy local manner. "He seemed just like your typical hard-nosed Aussie." He did? I'd never noticed it in London. He must, I supposed, have reverted briefly to the Australianness of his youth, the last gasp of the bushranger, not knowing that it was out of style. His old friends were mostly gruff, jocular men of the same vintage who confirmed him in this, and he was off and dreaming.

When I saw him in Sydney I thought he had a jauntiness and a slightly baiting expression round his mouth that I hadn't seen before, and I wondered if as a scrawny kid lying about his age he hadn't had to adopt a swagger all his own which had come back to him now, long after the danger was past. There's an immortality to exile: the home crowd expect roughly the same man to return someday young and intact, be he Chou En-lai or Frank Sheed; and the exile expects to find the same country.

Anyway, it was good to meet Frank the Australian, after all the other Franks. It completed the set. He might not be quite the thing for my sensitive young friend, but he was just right for the middle-aged set who ran the place. He seemed to come back just often enough to get a hero's welcome each time, and not as Frank Sheed the Catholic but indeed as Frank Sheed the Australian. And he responded in kind: whereas in other countries only Catholics seemed to exist for him, *any* Australian would do. Here at last was a category grand enough to stack up against Mother Church. Thus, Australian actors were just as noteworthy as Catholic actors, and so on. I even wondered if Australians *needed* conversion, they had so much already. Frank would probably have laughed if I'd asked him this, and then with a dreamy smile, have said, "You know, there may be something to that."

So the big fish came sailing back into the little pond—and out again. He never stayed very long. He must have known from suppressed memory that dailiness in Australia was not so much better than elsewhere, and he didn't stay to find out. A life composed of landfalls and departures suited this scion of sea captains well enough, especially since he didn't have to scrub the decks.

I did stay to find out about dailiness, and had interiorly the most rewarding year of my life. Exteriorly the year was a mess because practically upon arrival I developed a rash as wide as a sash, sometimes around my belly, and sometimes draped from shoulder to hip, which persisted the whole time I was there. I had it in the mountains and I had it by the sea and everywhere in between, until I got back safely on ship. Any Australian who may remember me as, perhaps, a rather jumpy fellow should be apprised that I was on fire with itches under a blanket of calamine even as we spoke.

It seemed silly in a room full of Australians to call myself an Australian. I would have been the least of them, the last in line. They didn't *need* another Australian. A pretty test was put to me that year, because an English cricket team had come over practically on my heels, and I had always rooted against such. But as a lone Englishman in the Outback, there seemed something wrong with this. Whichever way I faced was a betrayal of sorts. So I decided that cricket had been put on earth for our pleasure and not to pose gruesome moral dilemmas, and I cheered for England, which had a very strong side that year. Nobody noticed.

By chance an Oxford contemporary called Colin Cowdray was on the English side and he must have wearied of seeing my beaming face as I, hitchhiking from Sydney to Melbourne to Adelaide, loomed up on him in each pavilion as if we were the closest of friends (we'd met twice). He was very polite about it, providing me with beer and introducing me to all the players on both sides. Meeting so many athletes at one time is like having a bucket of ice water thrown over one's youth. Although several of them were quite amiable, they were no amiabler than anyone else or more interesting, and there would henceforth be no good reason to go looking for athletic heroes in the flesh. They are best viewed from about a hundred feet away. This set my mind at rest—although I was still surprised some years later to find that the same thing held true for meeting writers.

Purged of cricket by these forced marches, I no longer felt that Australia was merely an appendage of cricket: in fact, several natives didn't know there was an English side over there at all. Stripped of my brochures, I had to face the country on its own terms. Only to relatives and old-timers was I "Frank Sheed's boy"; otherwise, I was just a bloke, species "pommy." Having been American in England, it was a nice change to be an Englishman in Australia. It brought home the full asininity of these luggage tags.

There's something Kafkaesque about trying to figure out why people like you or not in a strange country. Maybe it's because one is paying more attention, but Australians seemed to make their preferences starkly clear, though not always their reasons for them. Friendship and antipathy presented themselves quickly and irrevocably. Frank grew up in a world where if you knew anything it was who your friends were. He had always talked with strange admiration of the ease with which Australians took to their fists (strange, because he barely knew where his own fists were), but what little I saw of this consisted mostly of one group of mates challenging another group of mates, or more rarely and drunkenly, of one mate saying to another, "You've never really liked me, 'ave yer?" In a world unadulterated by women until closing time, mateship was a complicated and demanding code, and though I felt it, I never fathomed it.

The Catholic intellectual world tipped its cap to me right away and moved on. A visiting English hot dog grilled me* about recent developments in Catholic thought, and later pronounced that "young Sheed is not serious." That I consider a close shave. My Maloney relatives were delightful, but I only saw most of them once or twice apiece. Australians give you your freedom, however bleak it may sometimes be. (I dream of returning, and none of the phones answer. Everyone has either moved or died.)

Bernie (Carrick) and Diddy (Reid), who had so comforted young Frank, were equally solicitous of me. But they couldn't imagine I would want to be bothered with them much. Frank, to his mother's relatives, was an unaccountable freak, an intellectual, a reader, and they admired him without even attempting to understand him. And I was just a curio he'd picked up abroad. His own later skill with everyday people, talking family and shop and do you remember? must have come originally from bridging this gap. As for me, I have never felt so rigidly, pointlessly English.

On the Sheed side, however, the "sarcastic bastard" Alan Stafford became, with his wife, Betty, and his daughter Binky, the first of my friends. Lunch, dinner, singing at the piano, why stint oneself with a new friend? Alan was Frank's other side, dry, literate, amused. He was also, for his own good reasons, quite irreligious. The Staffords had been implacable Presbyterians at the tail end of the fire-and-brimstone era, before hell became a metaphor, and no one ever escaped lightly from such households.

Of the three Stafford boys, each had taken a logical position. Douglas went along staunchly, though I found he had unbent a bit with the times and was, anyway, nice enough to get away with being

* This figure of speech has no name and will not occur again.

staunch; Wal was a rabid atheist, a jovial unhappy man, and wonderful company for everyone but, in the end, himself (he killed himself not long after this period); Alan, a skinny unassuming fellow,
simply slipped away from the Presbyterian God, which is no easy task,
and it wasted years of his life and tired him. A Calvinist maketh a
bloody exit. And as a relic of his struggle, Alan still, in his fifties, kept
his liquor in a false bookcase, which could be whipped around in case
the wrong relative called.

Although Alan's hard-earned indifference seemed the exact opposite of everything about Frank, Frank understood it perfectly and
loved Alan. They had both been raised in the same school where you
played religion for keeps. The subject was eternal damnation, and not
for one spring day were you allowed to forget it. After such a fiery,
high-stakes religion, you were lost forever to the tame ones. Just as a
Catholic used to see no point in becoming any kind of Protestant, but
usually sailed straight into atheism, so a Stafford could not believe in
anything that didn't feature hellfire. So Alan had no place to go except
the humanitarian void.

To show the bond between Frank and Alan in this matter, I sub-
mit the following: I once asked Frank what particular doctrine or
combination of doctrines could cause him to lose his faith, and he
said, it wouldn't be anything like that. It would be more like waking
up one morning and deciding just like that, that the whole thing was
absurd, every brick of it, and the game would be over. No more religion ever again. In later years when Frank seemed almost too heartily
assured of his faith, I thought of that.

Anyway Frank and Alan came out of the same furnace whose
smoke could still be smelled faintly on both of them. The Stafford side
of the family had once angled for Frank's soul too, but had lost by a
whisker to Mary Maloney, who was all of their match in ardor and
concentration, and to Frank's own temperament. The Apostle of the
Street Corner was born, and I was going to say "braised," amid religious passions hard to imagine today.

In lieu of relatives, I adopted, or was adopted by, two families
with Sheed connections. Norman Nelson had been a student of
Frank's in Sydney long ago. Niall and Elaine Brennan of Melbourne

had camped with us in London. To my surprise, the road to the Australian Frank led for me through friends rather than family, who seemed, outside of Alan Stafford, to block it.

For Maisie, Australia was altogether a simpler matter. As the only outdoor Sheed, she fell in love with the Outback, and as soon as she had smiled her way politely through Sydney like the queen, she would be off to some station (or ranch) to drink it all in. She loved the resourcefulness of country Australians who with ham radios and airplane-hopping sustained a mate system over thousands of square miles. There was a touch of the boy's adventure-story fan about Maisie, and nothing could excite her more than, say, a priest covering the bush by pogo stick or a farmer parachuting reading matter across state lines.

A woman of action was such an oddity in our family that it was nice to find a continent for her. More to the point, I believe the Outback reinforced her own swinging spirit as she returned to her social missions in London and later India. Australia was what Frank had been, a jolt of adrenalin in socially clogged English veins.

To the Aussie relatives, she must have seemed as strange as Frank's career: something that happens to you in England. Although proud of their nation's beauty spots, as one must be, they were no more pioneers than other sensible city folk are. To a Sydneysider there is no more beautiful sight than the nearest beach, unless it is a winning horse, and the botanical glitter in Maisie's eye probably just had to be humored. The Barrier Reef? We keep meaning to go there. They say that Perth is lovely! Maisie, being really English, did not feel English and was not in the custom of wondering what people thought of her, so her trips to Australia were unalloyed bliss.

To me it soon came to seem home, which doesn't necessarily mean comfortable, but just a place whose contours fit. It was the right color in the right light, and the people were made of the right material. I felt for the first time in this Anglo-Irish melting pot whatever people mean by racial identity. Four generations isn't enough for a single root. But I cried when I left Sydney Harbor, as I have only cried since over deaths. Just looking at Australia and touching it brought me closer to a sense of what Paul Tillich and others have called the ground of Being than I thought was in me. Maybe that's what brought on the rash. It was a creative year out of which nothing came, at least for a while.

It occurred to me, therefore, on the way out that perhaps Frank did not come here simply out of sentimentality but for spiritual refreshment. In the great Australian silence, no idea seems too big or far-fetched, even the Catholic God. Just as any aesthetic style is yours for the taking, so is any philosophy, short of flat-earthism, which is clearly wrong. Hitchhiking along a dirt track, which in those days *was* the Melbourne–Adelaide Highway, with a runaway schoolteacher (wife desertion is the great Australian vice), in a car whose door came off at the turns, and then plunging with this man and his lizzie into the silent dark, and looking, dear God, for one bloody tap to slake our thirsts, I found my thoughts careening between mad and noble. Alienation, integration——why the hell not? Gissa glass of water and I'll sign anything. The driver and I kissed the tap when we found it in a lonely backyard and rolled under it like children.

Frank's theology struck many people as pretty cut and dried, a series of legal briefs, and he made no effort to disabuse them. He gave you the words, and you provided the music, the excitement yourself. But for such a dedicated career the preacher needs some excitement too, however house-trained the acting out of it may later become. Frank, unlike the ultra-house-trained Ronald Knox, always had sympathy for religious enthusiasts and he ended his days writing for Pentecostalists. So I like to believe that his mission began with a touch of the divine madness, whether received in the Outback on a camping trip (his talk lingered over those) or in Methodist Sunday school, and that he went home like an antipodean Antaeus to touch it and feel its force.

On the way back to America, I got one last jolt of culture shock, almost as unhinging as real shock treatment. Our ship stopped off at Fiji, a frumpy, charming British protectorate, untouched by "this so-called 20th Century" (E. Waugh), and then at Hawaii, which had been touched all over. The American slickness and professionalism which I had once furtively liked suddenly looked like all the menace that Graham Greene said it was, creeping across the globe like this and strangling it in neon. Even in San Francisco, which is supposed to be so "real," I thought, Yankee, go home. All I could see now were the office buildings and first-class hotels. The quaint parts of the Bay Area seemed this time shrunken and self-conscious. The truly old-shoe atmosphere of Sydney had wrenched my tastes around. I wanted *everything* to look slept in.

It was a little late in the day to become anti-American, so I was relieved to see New York again in all its shabby splendor. The skyscrapers still looked like dowagers compared with the upstarts I'd seen lately, and the streets were as moth-eaten as ever. I have been hanging around it ever since. My parents' itchy feet were not handed down to either Rosemary or me, or perhaps we burned them out too young. Anyway, New York provided anything a man could want—even Australians if necessary.

There is nothing drearier than accounts of "how I became a writer." (I can only say that being turned down by an Australian newspaper hurts.) Frank assumed his usual position of cheerleader as I began to send things out in America. Both parents were convinced that Rosemary would be a writer too, and a damn fine one, and no doubt all our children after that unto the seventieth generation.

I've described this elsewhere as akin to coming from a long line of dentists, and I only yielded to it at last when I found how truly unspeakable the alternatives were, and how unfitted I was for any of them. Frank promptly introduced me to a far-flung friend at *The New Yorker,* which led circuitously to my having a story taken there, which in turn was good for one full year of confidence. But otherwise, his efforts consisted mainly of trying to foist a couple of my long shapeless essays on Sheed and Ward, which resisted good-naturedly (I thought he was a little nuts myself), and in his judicious chorus of "damn good" after each piece. "But what was the point of putting a 'ly' at the end of 'single-handed'? What does it add?" he would say, to show he'd been paying attention.

All this had nothing to do with earning a living, an ugly business which had to be faced sometime. Frank had always made it clear that he would not press me to follow him into Sheed and Ward. "I won't

play Mr. Dombey to your son," he said. Of course, if I *wanted* to follow him ... in fact, being the combustion engine that he was, he
couldn't really see why I shouldn't write full-time and keep an eye on
the family business at the same time, like some Jane Austen gentleman
who "does something in the City."

Luckily, the professionals at Sheed and Ward knew that even *he*
couldn't do that anymore in the postwar business world—a knowledge that would cause some strain between him and them as the era of
the one-man band receded. But they got quite used to seeing me
around the place, not keeping an eye on anything, but making a fast
buck reading proof or writing ad copy. Sheed and Ward was always
my employer of last resort. But as a profession, publishing had no
more appeal to me than the priesthood. I preferred, to use Frank's
image, my own flute solos.

Pity. Perhaps Frank would have liked a crack at playing Mr.
Dombey after all, especially since I did pass through various related
jobs on my way to what I unwaveringly saw as early retirement. One
of them was with the strange Bishop Sheen and his Society for the
Propagation of the Faith (the receptionist always answered the phone
with a sprightly "Propagation?"), and this is perhaps worth pausing
over as a second chapter in the strange story of Sheed and Sheen.

Nothing but greed and curiosity could have persuaded me to
work for this man Sheen. The first thing I can remember about him is
laughing at his radio show, and I'm afraid I was not alone in our living room. And his TV show was, if anything, worse. As Uncle Fultie,
a pioneer in the field, he had not learned to tone down his effects to
box-size and he overflowed the set like Uncle Miltie (Milton Berle, the
effluvious comic) himself or like the spaghetti sauce that wound up
sponsoring him. This, if anyone, was the plastic man, all style and no
content. As I soon learned, he came to the office every day in his
freshly laundered robes, a vision in purple and black, looking the very
antithesis of a priest-workman; and he talked like a recording even
when you were alone with him.

Yet underneath, I was surprised to find a great muddle. His mind
wasn't the least bit streamlined, and when I proofread a manuscript

for him, I stuck him with a publisher's bill for several thousand dollars' worth of author's alterations. I believe he was writing, or at least signing, seven distinct books that year, and I was determined that one of them should be literate.

He didn't really care what came out under his name anyway—he was more a brand than a writer—and he even let me write one of his columns for the right-wing *Journal American*. In the interest of fair play, I dug up for the occasion the most radical passages I could find from his early days and stitched them together, and I'm sure neither he nor his readers were any the wiser. He was, as advertised, a hypnotist, but by then his only trick seemed to be putting people to sleep, in a positive sort of way—a trick which he shared with his president Dwight Eisenhower.

Up close, I found Sheen indeed to be the ultimate show-biz priest, so wrapped up in his own performance that he could barely take in the corporeality of other people. No doubt, he snapped out of it for close friends, but as I knew him, he had no attention span whatever. After a half year around my abrasive presence, he gave me a huge picture of the Sacred Heart, with the heart in bold red relief, the kind you see in lesser convent parlors, and a statue of Mary which lit up in the dark. ("It was like sleeping in a bloody Times Square," said an Australian monsignor after a stretch in Sheen's guest room.)

Both before and after his ascendancy, Sheen was known to be a very kind man: but the creature I knew was so remote that one honestly couldn't tell. His role included doing kind things, but it was hard to discern any emotional transaction, beyond that which exists between an actor and his audience. Sheen was moved by his own characterization, and the donee was moved at being part of the performance. But they never *met* each other. His office contained three automatic typewriters which tapped out, round the clock, his three basic letters to admirers; and his conversation seemed to come out of a fourth machine.

The bishop was, in short, trapped in the celebrity compact; I felt he was not a happy man in repose but restless, frustrated, a prisoner of his own reflexes. He was, I believe, genuinely happy to leave the limelight and rejoin the human race; and in his last years, he confided to

Frank that he, Bishop Clean, rather enjoyed a scatological joke now and then. Maybe the gleaming robes should have told me that.

My tenure with Sheen ended abruptly. He had asked me to write a catechism of the Catholic missions, but neither he nor I had the faintest idea what it should contain, and after several rather desperate drafts, he, or rather "his people," began to wonder what exactly I was for. Meanwhile, I'd written half a novel on his time, scribbling away at it in my desk drawer, the work being paid for by the nickels and dimes of the good people out there who wanted to help us stamp out leprosy. (Our promotion was very heavy on leprosy, not because it was any concern of ours, but because it was great box office.)

Between Sheen's dry cleaning and my salary a certain amount of sacrificial money was diverted, though not as much as at some charitable outfits. Sheen himself must have given plenty out of his own fur-lined pocket, but I had no excuse, and I was happy to crawl of out there, clutching my ill-gotten pages, to work for down-at-heels places like *Jubilee* and *Commonweal* where I belonged.

Sheen was one of the faces the Church showed the world and it may seem perverse to say after all this that he was one of the better ones. He was never a real red-baiter, although he did dish it out to the psychiatrists (I think they frightened him). Despite the damn clothes, which he defended feebly—splendor on the outside, hair shirt on the inside—he lived a spare life, and his appeals for sacrifice were not as hypocritical as they looked. His message, such as it was, was decent and harmless. And having broken with Cardinal Spellman over a matter of real estate* he was his own man—if only he'd known what to do with himself.

Years later, as bishop of Rochester he tried his wings at turning the diocese over to the people, only to learn for the first time what is kept from all superstars: how the world works. The local fat cats explained the facts of life to him and he backed off in confusion and into obscurity. I was sorry for Sheen, and can't imagine anyone not being who knew him well.

* The understanding around the office was that Spellman had handpicked a center for the Propagation Society, but that Sheen got himself a better one. No heresy could have been worse in Spellman's New York.

• •

I had worked for the bishop in order to support my new wife and, the Church being what it was, undoubtedly children. Church or no Church, Maisie believed that every woman should have a baby anyway for her own sake. Just as priests should work, intellectual women especially should procreate, to complete their personalities. "So-and-So needs to have a baby," she would murmur intensely as scurvier sorts might say, "So-and-So should get laid." Once the fulfilling child was in the works, Maisie would become very conspiratorial with the mother. One of the more unexpected sides to her character was that she loved to shop, voraciously, and she could discuss patterns and such for hours at a stretch: patterns in draperies, cribs, maternity clothes, as if a baby deserved a new world in every detail.

As for Frank, he had always believed that grandchildren came along just in time, just as the parent was beginning to miss something—an unusual position for a man to take in those days. Few men genuinely needed children in their lives as Frank did, and fewer still admitted it. He took to grandfathering with such thoroughness that his generic name slipped into Grandfather even faster than usual (a relief for Rosemary and me, who had been flinging up adult substitutes for Mummy and Daddy, none of which took). I suppose the same good timing that Frank talked about for the grandparents blesses the grown child as well. Because just as one has begun to wonder what to do with one's own parent, one can suddenly now send him off to the zoo.

The zoo is no idle metaphor in Frank's case. He adored zoos and the emptiness he felt as a parent of grown children may have been partly sheer zoo deprivation. Showing a child its first monkey and its first snake is, for better or worse, an incomparable experience. But it seemed that *anything* a child wanted to do was exactly what Frank wanted to do, from pantomimes to the Tower of London to playing on the swings. And if the kids didn't want to do anything, he either thought of something, as he had for us—the thing they *should* have wanted to do—or he agreed that doing nothing was very wise on this particular day, and joined in with gusto.

He wound up with seven grandchildren, and each of them had a special blue-plate Frank Sheed relationship with him, often cemented by one of his whirlwind trips with them to Paris or Sydney or wherever the spirit blew. His friends knew all the doings of the magnificent seven, and I was often surprised to find total strangers discussing my children in learned detail. Their pictures were whipped ragged from the haul and shove of his wallet and their faces were as familiar as public enemies'.

I emphasize this sticky-fingered, jam-around-the-face side of life because it came just in time in a sense Frank hadn't anticipated. For Maisie, the pleasure, as always, would come later when the children grew up and she could share her conspiratorial side with them too. But for Frank, the returns were immediate: he even got something out of baby photos. And this would come in handy, like my burst of sports the year before polio. Because in 1956, as I was engaging myself and Rosemary was thoroughly married, something happened to Frank that was to change his personal map of life and mind for a while, and it was God's blessing that a new family structure, a playground if you will, was about to be hammered up in both countries for him to repair to.

The King Lear Years
and the Flowering of Maisie

ON A WINDY FALL DAY IN 1956, FRANK STOOD AT HIS USUAL POST on the platform at Hyde Park Corner, presumably swaying slightly (he had a normal forward-and-back motion, for assertion and reflection) and clutching the platform crucifix for support. Accounts vary as to exactly what happened that day, but somehow the cross got broken and Frank lay on the ground still clutching it. According to legend he had been talking about the devil, so naturally Old Nick gave him a shove. Others thought they noticed something funny *before* the fall, a loss of control, perhaps a small stroke. With such a red face, Frank always looked as if he might be having a stroke, especially when he was strutting his stuff just above your head.

Whether it happened in the air or on the ground, the effect was devastating. Frank lay in coma for a dangerously long time, crying out occasionally in anguish of spirit. He had repressed his sorrows well, and witnesses were startled to hear this sunny man calling desperately for forgiveness. I believe some of the fun went out of him for good that night, leaving a lot behind, of course. The wildfire mirth became jollity, which was quite good enough for anyone who hadn't heard the real thing.

The first difference I noticed was that he didn't do crossword puzzles so well anymore. The lordly competence that had once permitted him to fill in the hardest of them with dots instead of letters to save the puzzle for others was replaced by more normal groping; his perfect handwriting had thickened slightly, like tired speech. Worst of all, his hearing was slightly off, and would get worse. In athletic terms he had lost a split second of timing, at the very moment a superfast game was starting—the theological jousting between the new theology and the old that led right into the conclave of Vatican Council II, like Errol Flynn pursuing Basil Rathbone.

If it was a stroke that sent my father flying, it was partly one of irony. Tension had been building in Frank for some time beneath the unflappable exterior (I once asked three of his New York staff at random if they considered him as relaxed as he said he was and they all said in effect "Hell, no"), and part of the cause of it was the same thing that had broken his father-in-law Wilfrid Ward forty-odd years before—Modernism, as it was called then, or "form criticism" of the Scriptures, as it was still called. Ward ran a magazine as Sheed ran a publishing house, open to all the voices. But here the stories diverge. Ward's heartbreak was largely personal: old friendships were sundered by the Modernist crisis, good men broke irrevocably with the Church, and his many voices fell silent.

Frank's worries were institutional. According to family legend, Ward died of cancer and melancholy shortly after the Modernists had lost; Frank, let us say, "snapped" slightly when they seemed to be winning. Wilfrid, a clubbable man, had friends among the Modernists and always accepted their sincerity. Frank was less inclined to do so. Feeling his age now for the first time, he saw the new critics as mainly a bunch of smart alecks nibbling like mice in a piano, to use a phrase of Ward's, at the very foundation of the Faith. If one began, like them, throwing out bits and pieces of the Gospels on scientific grounds, who was to say that some new and shinier research method wouldn't soon throw out the rest? One must draw the line at the first Gadarene swine, according to Frank's view (at least as I understood it: he wasn't under oath at the dining room table).

His anxiety was rooted deep in his lifework. Street-corner speaking necessarily stresses apologetics, that is, a good defense. And the thing to be defended at all costs had to be the New Testament itself, especially the difficult parts. So for a speaker to be told, after years in the front line, that we're abandoning all those outposts is a shuddering shock. The new critics were prepared to draw up all the Church's wagons around a bastion called the kerygma, namely, the hard core of the Christian faith, shorn of wonder stories and edifying later additions and—the word that made Frank especially bristle—"midrash."

Frank felt (I hope I do him at least rough justice) that thus stripped of its outworks, the kerygma itself mightn't look that impregnable in the next round of quarterlies. If the whole New Testament wasn't inspired by the Holy Ghost, then just hanging on to the more historically probable part was a losing game. And it was no use telling our grizzled veteran, as some new critics did, that the whole book was indeed inspired, but only "in a sense." He had no time for such mealy Protestant formulas. (I once asked a new critic if, in this same sense, one mightn't say that Homer was inspired by the Holy Ghost and he said, "Yes, I suppose one might.")

I had always felt that Frank's theology was tied much too fast to those apologetics. Although he was far too sophisticated to be a biblical fundamentalist, he had argued himself precious close to it with the New Testament. And he became rather desperately ingenious at explaining the book. His stroke, or whatever, could not have come at a worse time for this particular task. Because for a while, he slightly lost his balance intellectually too.

If a new critic made one mistake in his argument, Frank was on him with angry glee. "You see those beggars *don't know the Gospels.*" The old Frank had made it a point to judge a book or a cause by its pluses and throw away the minuses; but now he lived in a forest of minuses, and like one of his own hecklers, he lay in crafty wait for a foe to stumble, proceeding at that point to leap out brandishing logic-chopping devices he would once have scorned. "If you argue to win you're bound to wind up cheating," he used to say. But there were those who felt that he wasn't above cheating now himself.

"I believe that that fall from the platform was more serious than I'd realized," he said to me years later. I never doubted it. On the simplest level, I'd seen those crossword puzzles and knew that mental combat would be even more flustering. Also, and very strangely, he took to telling people how many nights in a row he had gone without sleeping pills (he got into four figures before quitting), as if he had

lost his sense of what interests other people. And this, too, had reper-
cussions in his private war with the new critics. For he took to poring
over minor texts of Scripture like Sherlock Holmes comparing ashes
in the carpet, while everyone else was looking, rightly or wrongly, for
larger forms and patterns.

At no time, even the worst, did this obsession dominate his
whole life. He was still wonderful company, though with an occasional tendency to tell stories in which he was the hero, as if to make
up for lost confidence. (He had once defended vanity to me as almost
a virtue, because it means you care about other people and what they
think, but he had seldom practiced it before.) Then as his brow cooled
he polished and daringly extended the private role of grandfather into
something like a work of art, and things returned gradually to more or
less normal. He still spilled over with kindness, and the tumorous
bulge of friends' addresses in his breast pocket grew alarmingly.

But something had permanently changed in the public Frank. In
some ways this was to be the most heroic period of his life. Anyone
can win easy victories (as he once scoffed at his friend Cicero's Roman
triumph over some small tribe called, I'll swear, the Catti); but here he
was, a general himself, being asked to hand over a hundred hard-won
arguments to the Protestant wishy-washies; to concede all the territory
he'd won, as a diplomat, over the roughnecks in the Domain (the
Hyde Park of Sydney), the smoothies of lunchtime Wall Street (his
favorite arena) and the empty air of London suburbs. If the new critics
had broken into his study and destroyed his lifework, they could have
done no more.

And it went far beyond personal loss. I have painted him to now
as a lighthearted man, because that's how he painted himself, but he
was always harrowingly serious about the Faith: and that stuff the new
critics had shredded *was* the Faith, as he had drilled himself and others
to understand it.

The others, his disciples, were perhaps the biggest problem of all.
Having his own world dismantled was bad enough, but what about all
the people he'd trained, personally and through books? Didn't he have
a duty to hold the line for them too?

In short, this avant-garde leader of the forties and fifties had led his troops so far, but he could in conscience lead them no farther. As a charismatic man, he could have pranced ahead indefinitely, or he could have started a countermarch. But as simply a loyal man with a bump on his head, he could only locate his guns and stick to them. Until now, anything that vaguely called itself Catholic was good enough for him. But suddenly he couldn't be sure. "I've had a good week," he would say. "I haven't heard a single major doctrine denied from the pulpit." Bitter.

For a publisher, this was particularly cruel, because some of the new heretics were marching straight through his own offices. His solution to this, born of wisdom or weariness, was increasingly to delegate the hairy editorial decisions to one Philip Scharper (U.S.) and his son-in-law, Neil Middleton (U.K.), and simply to block his ears. He knew that new things had to be said and he simply had to trust *somebody*. His natural openness and curiosity as a publisher warred with his stubborn, they-shall-not-pass attitude as a teacher, and there was friction in both offices as he vacillated between intervention and withdrawal in the nerve-racking sixties. But more of that in a moment.

The "they" who were not supposed to pass did, of course, pass: whole armies of his own disciples, priests who had first heard him talk in seminaries and were now wrestling with diapers, nuns in short skirts who were secularizing the very colleges which he had once ruled over like an emperor, lay people whose marriages he had long held together by main force, but who now needed something stronger than Frank Sheed. The mobs that swirled past him to the latest barricades were composed of friends. No wonder he dwelled on the stories where he still came out ahead.

"He showed me the way out of the jail," says Robert Hughes, the Australian art critic.* Hughes had been on the verge of joining the order of Christian Brothers, which is the very heart of the jail, when saved in the nick of time by Sheed and Ward books. But the jail proved bigger than the Christian Brothers, and Hughes and others like him just kept right on running all the way out of the Church.

---

* Robert Hughes is the art critic for *Time* magazine. He also wrote and narrated the TV series "The Shock of the New."

In elucidating this institution so thoroughly, Sheed and Ward had unwittingly revealed the escape plans for the whole compound. Without Frank Sheed in particular, many would never have known enough about the Church to leave it. "I hear they've put Gide on the Index [of forbidden books]" says one old nun to another, in a Sheed/Ward chestnut. "Well," says the other, "that'll teach those laymen to go teaching theology." Frank's apostolate to the intellect was always a dangerous game, and perhaps they did ban the wrong Gide at that.

However, here his native optimism, as battered but serviceable as his hat, came in handy. Again, he didn't count the minuses, but the gains. The ex-Catholics would, he hoped, wander back in God's own good time. Meanwhile, those who stayed had been toughened and smartened into better Catholics than ever. It was a working hypothesis.

He embraced Vatican Council II with a touching eagerness. His Church had spoken, and he loved the sound whatever it said. Vernacular Mass? But of course. In fact, he didn't have to stretch himself much to wrap himself around the whole agenda. In matters of practice and administration he had always been a liberal and nothing had changed about that. Accessibility to the sacraments, lay participation, power to the bishops—all this and more (he was also nuts about lay deacons) were old causes of his. The only thorn in his shoe, no bigger than a rosebush, was the authenticity of the Gospels, but this was not to the naked eye what the council was all about, so it was possible to see Vatican II as a ratification of his lifework, a Sheed and Ward agenda through and through.

The fact that many Catholics read the council to mean "anything goes" would soon bring on additional aches and pains. But that was not the council's fault. He could be disingenuous (the art of "auto-kiddery" as he called it) about things like that: all he could hear from Rome was the Holy Ghost (which was very Australian of him), while what many of us heard was simply some surprisingly bright and decent men negotiating over the previously nonnegotiable. It didn't matter how it came out. These were palpably human decisions, reversible by human vote. (I don't know what we'd expected: a bird to fly in through the window perhaps.) What finally weakened the old magic may have been simply the sheer sensibleness of it all: these were just the decisions we would have made ourselves. And no sane person can be impressed by a church of his own devising.

Sheed and Ward boomed briefly in both countries after the council, but Frank played a smaller part in it. He'd had his fun, as he might have said. "I never read anymore," he would announce blithely, perhaps because he sensed he wouldn't like what he read. He did approve of Karl Rahner* and some of Hans Küng. But speculative theology is always tinkering with the basics—the Eucharist, the divinity of Christ, the resurrected Body—and he felt, like many a simple pastor before him, that while this might be all very well for the clever fellows who could juggle earth-shaking concepts as if they belonged to somebody else, most believers had best hold tight to every scrap of faith they had. The average citizen probably didn't even know the basics to begin with, so his first word of them had better not be that they'd just been disproved in Holland.

Frank dug himself in. "The hungry sheep look up, and are not fed," he would quote—adding, "because the shepherds are all at the table talking to each other." Since the best of them were still talking under the auspices of Sheed and Ward, he could hardly say worse than that. But he admitted to me once, in a desolate moment, that he felt very old: the occasion was a conversation about a young priest who had disagreed openly with his bishop about something or other, and Frank swore that he would never in his life have done such a thing himself. "Are you sure?" I asked, and it was then that he felt old.

In this slightly worn-out, battered condition, he set out all over again to feed the postconciliar sheep himself. I admired him enormously for not backing off from his ground; if he had, all his teaching would have seemed retroactively empty. All the same, I wished he were younger now as he pursued his daunting mission. The deafness brought on by the devil's push grew steadily denser, and nothing makes a man seem so befuddled as deafness. I felt that in self-defense he was relying more on stock answers, in case he hadn't caught the question. His annoyance with the other shepherds also came perilously

* Karl Rahner. S.J., was at once the most probing and the most traditional of the New Breed. He ultimately reproached Hans Küng for giving up too much.

close to anti-intellectualism, as did his pose as a plain blunt man.* Yet it was in these years that he began preaching retreats to priests and even bishops. His itinerary stretched like a spider's web far beyond Middle America to take in the Philippines and India and the inevitable Australia.

When Maisie died, I could have started a stamp collection from their travels based on the condolence letters alone. If Frank had died that same year (1975), it would have been a *huge* stamp collection. In the early 1970s—just past his best, in my reluctant judgment—he was nevertheless enjoying his greatest glory, and not just for past achievements. He was still more than bright enough, with a wit like a whip, for any impromptu exchange he could manage to hear his way into. And many people, such as grandchildren, found it hard to believe he had ever been brighter.

He used every cell he had left with skill and speed, and with prodigious willpower. It had taken a towering intellect to land on such a high plateau. But instinctively—though he didn't admit it till later—he didn't trust his powers as much as he once had. He could now lapse into anger and stubbornness in ways his former self wouldn't have believed. But he wrung the most from these difficult years that could reasonably be wrung.

His lifelong affair with his wife had a lot to do with it. Until Rosemary and I had both grown up, Frank and Maisie never flew together for fear of making us orphans, so now they had this new pleasure. Wherever they went seemed a holiday, however much work it involved; in fact, the working holiday was their normal unit. And as Frank went into at least minor eclipse, Maisie seemed to come sailing out of the postwar clouds and shine mightily, to Frank's unqualified delight. As a publisher, he didn't mind whose light he glowed in, and as a husband, being Maisie's coach and trainer was quite possibly his proudest achievement: in fact, his joy in other people's good fortune, especially his family's, made up for almost anything else in his life. Vain he may have been at times, but never has a total lack of envy of others been so satisfyingly rewarded as now. "Did you hear about

* I use this phrase because he used it himself—with derision. Anyone who comes on as a plain blunt man will steal your socks, he advised.

Maisie's reception in Bangkok? Tell them, my dear"—an adoring, expectant smile—"she was really at the top of her form." "How do you do? I'm Wilfrid Sheed's father" (this dating back from when I was about twelve).

Maisie fumed about this and that in the new Church, but in very much her own way. She couldn't stand the new practice of chewing the Communion Host instead of letting it melt genteelly in the mouth: her feeling for the True Presence was powerful and primitive (she wouldn't have flinched from the term). She often told a story which had shocked her since childhood about a woman who'd spilled consecrated wine on her dress and been reassured right away by an Anglican minister, "Never mind, my dear, the new cleaning methods will get it out completely." Maisie's outrage was still fresh at each retelling. "Of course the woman became a Catholic immediately," she added.

I don't know if she ever noticed how, as the years went by, her audience responded less and less hotly to this anecdote. To her it remained the heart of the matter, council or no council. Although perfectly loyal, she felt no need for Frank's enthusiastic obedience. If she had an old devotion she liked or even a nonexistent saint, she simply hung on to it. She preferred a hundred private Masses at side altars to one concelebrated jamboree at the main one, because she had always liked it that way. Never mind the theology of it: the more Masses the merrier was her cheerful view. The council was splendid on the big issues, but the clever fellows should not be allowed to play with the tradition. Her faith was more basic and less a matter of choice and willpower.

She could also ride higher on theology because her other interests had started to bloom prodigiously. Unlike Frank, she was willing to admit she might have wasted too much time on the Guild, in a world full of things to do. If one had to sum up their temperamental differences simply in terms of Vatican II and its open windows: Maisie was probably more excited by the South American bishops and their cry from the Dark for social justice, while Frank was moved by the opening to the Eastern rite churches and the breach in institutional walls.

It was just a matter of emphasis, each shared the other's enthusiasms more than anyone else did, but Frank the lawyer thrilled to the settlement of ancient misunderstandings, while activist Maisie loved to see the Church in motion, "getting down to it," or on with it. I may have exaggerated her life-long aversion to fancy clothes—she bought enough nice ones for other people, and she kept a weather eye on clerical vestments—but she loved the electricity of a situation where they didn't matter, where priests or even bishops rolled up their sleeves and actually functioned. Next to a private Mass in a side chapel, there was nothing to beat a priest in khakis saying one in a moving Jeep.

In that same year of the fall, 1956, she had started something in London called the Catholic Housing Aid Society, the gist of which was this. Maisie and some friends agreed that if the Church was going to condemn birth control, it had better find a place to park the children. The housing shortage in England was so fierce in the 1950s for *everyone* that some of my contemporaries postponed even childless marriages, while Catholics wrestled grimly with the rhythm method of birth control and generally lost.

Maisie's group hit on the plan of buying up white elephants, big useless houses in London, and dividing them into apartments. Maisie and Frank, so close in everything that mattered, always had separate bank accounts, separate financial histories. Maisie's royalties and lecture fees swooped this way and that, pursuing her latest passion, and a lot must have gone into Catholic Housing. But emptying her pockets was just a detail with Maisie. The excitement was wading into the mess, which in this case meant everything from bearding town councillors about tiresome building regulations to mounting pulpits, where women were rarely seen, to shame the congregation into coughing up.

Maisie was not a natural judge of character, partly because the Wards were so unlike anyone else: few families can have taught one so little about human nature. But once again, as she had at Marycrest and in her farming ventures, Maisie found herself having to assess people anyway as the society tried to weed out unreliable tenants who could spoil the whole thing. An apparently pious and earnest couple might still have a little weakness in the matter of rent; and one good spouse seldom made up for a bad one.

All the old lessons came back, and Maisie, I believe, began to be more confident of herself from these sorties into practical life. Members of the society remember fondly her groans of "silly ass" and "the little fool"; Maisie's exasperation had a grand, period quality, a cry from some abandoned nursery. I can't imagine anyone being seriously scared of her, but she did make people jump. Her manner alone startled one into action. "Let's get on with it, then," or "Oh, dear, is this all we've done? It's rather disappointing, isn't it?" People wanted to please her because her pleasure was just as transparent and thoroughgoing as her peevishness. No one ever had to guess what Maisie was thinking.

The society grew and grew into a national organization, blessedly too big for Maisie to cope with, and she cheerfully passed it on to others. And so it still stands as a memorial to her astonishing energy and heart, and as living proof that her dedication to starting small, to helping the people next door, and then the ones next to that, was not outdated in a mass society.

Meanwhile, Maisie had begun fishing for something closer to her own size, and she found it in, of all bloated places, India: in the form of a village which, for just a few hundred pounds, could be turned from a slum into a garden spot. Again she hit the pulpits, harder than ever this time, and there were few Catholics in her ranging vicinity who didn't know the exact price of a new well in Kerala that year.

To my mind this was her most effective kind of speaking, even artistically, because it harnessed her passion to something that really needed it—as opposed, let us say, to Robert Browning. She no longer sounded the least bit stagy, and for what it's worth, I began to find her much more comfortable in private as well. We became, as we should have been years before, great friends and lunchers with a million things to talk about that hadn't been there before. The slow arc of her development became complete in her seventies.

As if to celebrate a coming of age on a lighter note, Maisie discovered the Dry Martini. It had taken forever to shame her out of the manhattan, the *vin du pays* at Schraffts, "A liquor for children," as Sam Johnson might say, but she now turned her back on it resolutely—and in no time came up with an invaluable tip. "Always," she advised me, "order the martini straight up, with rocks on the side. You will get about one-third more that way."

Maisie had always liked a drink, and once confessed to me that she thought she had come quite close to tipsiness on one distinct occasion. "I felt decidedly dizzy," she told me. Old teetotaling Frank looked after her liquid interests on the lecture circuit. "It's not like you to refuse a drink, Maisie," he said to one bunch of local prunes, who were withholding Maisie's prelecture booster shot. When nothing came of that, he said, "Maisie, if I were you, I'd *insist* on that drink." A bottle appeared.

One drink at mealtimes and perhaps a little execrable cheap wine (which she always found "remarkably good ... considering") was her limit. She hated to spend money on herself, while there were wells yet unsunk, and she drove a fierce bargain boozewise. My fondest memory was of our brown-bagging it in one of New York's last Automats ("surprisingly good food ... considering"). The plan was for me to scoop up glasses from the water cooler, and ice wherever I could find it, over which Maisie would pour a finger of premixed martini, followed by her truly lamentable red or rosé plonk. When a busboy came over to dispose of the brown bags, he said, "Hey, someone's been drinking around here." "Yeah," I told him, "a dirty old bum was sitting here a few minutes ago and he left this mess." "That showed great presence of mind, Wilfrid," Maisie said when the coast was clear.

The martini was to prove a small solace to Maisie in her last days, when business was finally done. But that seemed a million years away in her hectic seventies.

She received her earthly reward in India when she decided to drop in on her village, thus triggering off a three-day fiesta in her honor. "Welcome Mr. and Mrs. Sheed" said the signs. And one pictured a beaming, indestructibly English Maisie surrounded by Indian music, which probably sounded no stranger to her than most music, and by dancing which I know enchanted her. It was as if a grateful world, in microcosm, were thanking her for her life.

She also received her comeuppance from India, but of a kind she was getting used to. It seems that all the vigor in the village had been generated by one man, a Maltese priest who was her original contact. When he died, his successors proved averagely inept, but that wasn't what was so discouraging. It turned out that the villagers had meanwhile developed no self-reliance whatever: they were only as good as their leader, and one imagines them eventually drifting back to pretty much where they were before, with the addition of one superb well.

Maisie was saddened but not crushed. It had been worth doing at the time, it didn't have to last forever. And the same went for Sheed and Ward, which was also teetering toward its last days. (But that's more Frank's story.)

Chronology falls back helpless in the matter of Maisie: it all depends on which iron in the fire she was tending at that particular moment. Between activities, she wrote a memoir called *Unfinished Business* and she meant it. I suggested that she leave the family out of this book as much as possible, because I knew that she remembered every cute saying I'd ever uttered; but I'm sorry now I did this, because the result made her look less family-centered than she was. She could never have seemed like her bête noire, Dickens' Mrs. Jellyby, even in print, but the vast difference should have been stressed. A late memoir, *To and Fro upon the Earth*, summarizes better than I can the multiplicity (I seem to have left out about a hundred of them) and intensity of her social interests.

One last one of these does deserve mentioning, because it brought her into harness with her old friend and sparring partner Dorothy Day. Maisie was a vociferous dove during the Vietnam War—so much so that she forgot all the family rules about keeping out of American affairs and took the stump briefly (substituting for wife Abigail in California) for Eugene McCarthy in 1968. In fact, I believe we both spoke for McCarthy, at different times to be sure, on the same campus out there.

But her deeper instinct was to do something for *somebody*, some actual person. So she went with Dorothy to meet some of the draft resisters: not because she thought she could lift their spirits by her very presence—she never mistook herself for Eleanor Roosevelt—but because she wanted to convey their case to others, most specifically to those Catholics who harked back to the days when papists had to prove their patriotism again and again, and still could never prove it enough.

However, she may have been of some personal comfort to the draft resisters as well. One of the survivors, Tom Cornell of the Catholic Worker, showed me with pride a beautiful ring she had given him, no doubt on the spur of the moment. And that kind of ardent sympathy has to encourage someone.

But what *she* learned was the depth of discouragement prison reduces people to. Even the hardened Dorothy was shocked to witness the psychological unraveling of some of her disciples and, in her eyes even worse, their widespread loss of faith. She swore then and there that she would never again counsel people to do something she wasn't sure they could do.

It seems strange to say so, but I think that Maisie was slightly less surprised by all this than the street-smart Dorothy. It is a measure of how far she had come, and of how much *attention* she paid to people even as she helped them, that she knew human frailty so well, after her zero-base start.

She never wanted to know *all* about it. One day, on the steps of the Newark cathedral, she was knocked down by a bunch of roughnecks, who, in turn, were chased away before they could grab anything. Her face was smashed like a prizefighter's, and her tiny old frame ached all over, but she put it all down to "high-spirited play" and would never confirm the race of her assailants.

Sadder but wiser, what to do, what to do; and then blessedly quickly, the string began to run out for her. I remember once, when she was in her eighties, asking if I could accompany her across the street to the bus terminal (till the days they died, Frank and Maisie both took public transit almost exclusively), and her perky reply: "No thanks. I've just been around the world, you know. I fancy I can cross Eighth Avenue by myself."

In my memory, at least, it seemed no time at all between her being able to say things like that and a quite considerable helplessness. It must have seemed longer to Frank. "Maisie, take me home" had for years been his standard way of ending an evening. But now there was no joke about who was taking whom. "She's just like a child," he whispered to me once, in wonder and alarm.

They had moved to Newark in the sixties to be near the great Browning collection in the local library, and since then had moved on to Jersey City to be near nothing that I could make out, except possibly the subway line, which is not bad of its kind. (Once, when asked if Jersey City was hard to get to, Frank replied, "Well, of course, the native bearers desert halfway.") In many cases, I suppose it would have been depressing to find one's parents winding up their lives in utterly drab, lower-middle-class surroundings, but with Frank and Maisie the feeling didn't arise. They got on famously with the man at the desk and with a young local Jesuit, who in no time had introduced them to the cream of Jersey City's Catholic youth, which, in turn, formed a sort of group around them. What surroundings?

But as Maisie began to fade, the surroundings did sadden. Frank was a devoted house-husband, but his wings seemed clipped in that gray little place. Several of us suggested hotels (too expensive, or else even shabbier than what they had), regular nurses (Frank wouldn't have it—Maisie left alone with some stranger? Oh, no, no, no!) and finally a nursing home. Maisie was now mostly comatose, and it couldn't have meant much to her, but Frank still treasured their joint independence, however illusory. They should both be able to come and go as they pleased, and light out for anywhere.

There were several things wrong with Maisie, and she might have died of any of them. But the root of the matter seemed to be mortal weariness. For years she had perennially had something wrong with her—scar tissue on the lungs, or phlebitis, or some damn thing—but she had fought them all back with sheer vitality. Now when she reached for it, it just wasn't there.

One afternoon she raised her head sharply and said, "I still have enthusiasm." Her eyes glittered with challenge for a moment. Then the head plopped back. "But what use is enthusiasm without energy?"

Lots of old friends came round to help and, curiously, Frank at last allowed Maisie to be a bit of a burden on others in a way he would never allow himself to be. When his own time came later, he was perfectly willing to look into nursing homes or anywhere else where he wouldn't be a nuisance. But Maisie, he felt, deserved sacrifices; or perhaps he didn't think about it.

It was a hell of a place to find, that flat of theirs, and I blush to recall how often I had to ask directions. But among those who made the trudge frequently were the indomitable Dorothy Day and a friend they had in common, Eileen Egan, herself a champion in the world of Catholic Relief Services, but perfectly content to play second fiddle to the two aging titans.

Dorothy seldom did anything the easy way. It took two subways and a hike to get her from Staten Island and two more to get her back and she always seemed to be loaded down with shopping bags, and with nothing to hold her up but her old rayon stockings.

Nevertheless, she radiated vigor every time she burst in. Her face was stronger and handsomer than it had ever been, testifying strangely to a life in the slums, and she was always eager to talk. Unfortunately, Maisie was only eager to sleep most of the time, so the exchanges were somewhat one-sided.

"Maisie, do you remember that day on the BMT platform"— Dorothy always brought this one up—"when you gave me such a tongue lashing? 'Dorothy,' you said, 'you're just too damn precious about World War II.'"

If Maisie took this in, she may have thought that it wasn't worth repeating quite so often. It hadn't seemed so important to her: she was always saying things like that to people.

The scene shifts slightly to a dark room in St. Francis Hospital, Jersey City, but Dorothy is still there. "Maisie is carrying the cross for all of us now," says she. "She is doing our suffering for us today." It certainly looked so. Maisie, with her teeth removed, looked quite sunken and desolate. But I never knew how conscious she was. If she was awake right then, I'm afraid I can hear her thinking, Oh, Dorothy—come off it.

They were never quite fellow spirits, but they loved each other, and complemented each other in the Catholic Revival. "Humbug," Maisie might mutter, when Dorothy got carried away on wings of poesy. But Maisie never doubted her greatness or her goodness. We didn't bat the word saint around much, because it was such a cliché about Dorothy. But if pressed—of course she was.*

I asked my own doctor, Jeremiah Barondess, if he could somehow contrive to get Maisie out of Jersey City altogether. He persuaded her, through Frank, into his own bailiwick, New York Hospital, and there matters went into suspense. Maisie surely wasn't going to get better, except perhaps in Frank's eyes, but there was no telling how long she was going to hang on as she was.

I had to go west on Muhammad Ali business (I had been given exactly three months to write a picture book about the Great One) around then and it was there, in Maisie's beloved "Frisco," that I got the last word. Maisie had collapsed quietly on all fronts. I called Rosemary in London, and after a minute or so we were both joking and laughing and my hostess was looking at me with wild consternation. It was hard to explain to her that this was the first language we had all shared, the *lingua Franka,* as Frank rather grandly named it, or Sheedspeak, and it was as consoling now as anything we could think of.

On the hastily booked flight back, I was tormented by Noël Coward's song "The Party's Over Now." The world of Sheed/Ward was no more. It didn't help reminding myself that my mother was eightysix and due to go. I didn't give a damn how old she was. That force should not have been stilled, now or any time. My grief stunned me with surprise: we'd had so much time to prepare for this moment and resign ourselves to it, yet this period of grace was suddenly obliterated. She might as well have been hit by a truck.

Frank had called the New York chancery first thing to make sure that Maisie's funeral would take place in St. Patrick's, where it belonged, but he was given the bureaucratic runaround. "Maisie who? No, the cardinal can't be reached," and so on. He slammed down the phone and said, "To hell with them," and proceeded to arrange the funeral himself in a smaller and kinder church.

Frank's outer attitude was one of joy. Maisie is now with God. Inside, I think he felt "Then what the devil am I still doing here?" He

---

* The first time I met Dorothy, age (mine) sixteen, she whipped out a copy of Dickens' *Hard Times* that she'd bought for a nickel on Fourth Avenue. It was the perfect gift perfectly timed and I moved effortlessly under her spell.

insisted on an open coffin at the wake, as he had for his mother's, so we got a last look at Maisie, draped in a Dominican habit that an old friend had promised her, and serene in death. Frank's jubilation seemed to me to be slightly and touchingly overdone, as if he were still trying to teach us something. This was how a Christian *should* look at death, and not necessarily how one did. But at least it gave him something to do.

The funeral itself was rather stark, because Frank had asked for no music, and the ritual words seemed harsher in English than they used to in Latin. There seemed to be an awful lot of talk about the remission of Maisie's sins, which made me laugh. I couldn't think of a single one, unless perhaps she had omitted to say her morning prayers as a child. Anyway, it wasn't stark to Frank. "I can hear the trumpets," he told editor Alice Mayhew, at the back of the church. So *someone* heard music.

Cardinal Cooke had pulled his wits together and figured out who this was that had just died, and he appeared modestly at the altar—as an assistant. The celebrant was, at Frank's insistence, the young Jersey City Jesuit who had befriended them, and who now gave a fine little talk about Maisie that could only have been given by a friend, not a cardinal.

Afterward, Cardinal Cooke came up to Frank at the back of the church to express condolences. "Why, your Eminence," boomed Frank, "I didn't recognize you." My anticlerical friends grinned for pews around at what they took to be a calculated snub by the Great Layman. They didn't recognize the far greater insult—that Frank had meant it.

Maisie was driven back to Jersey City one last time, and buried in a plot dominated by a large anonymous apartment building of the kind she once used to fill with young Catholic couples. Frank lingered a moment. After all, he was looking at his own grave too, right next to Maisie's. I suspect that right then, and at other moments to come, he couldn't wait to get into it.

Leftover Life to Kill, as Dylan Thomas' widow, Caitlin, called her book. But Frank, being Frank, could never just kill time—waste it cheerfully perhaps, but not kill it. In fact, though he couldn't have guessed it that day, he walked out of the dingy cemetery into some pretty good years.

He would be on his own now, a solo, for the first time in fifty years (the golden anniversary had been just a breath away when Maisie died). He would have to travel even more lightly, which suited him fine. His lodgings seemed more than ever just the place he happened to be at the moment, identified only by the contents of his briefcase: the London papers, the scrawled-over legal pads. I never felt depressed visiting him in Jersey City, as I'd felt when he shared the dump with Maisie, partly because of his lordly transcendence of circumstance—and also because he was always just about to head off for somewhere else anyway. Now that Maisie was on her brief leave of absence, Frank had all the freedom that even an Australian could want, and he used it. He could still pay his way lecturing, anywhere he wanted to go, and where he wanted to go was where his friends were. Everywhere, that is. (Once when he and Maisie had just circled the globe one more time, someone asked them what hotels they'd stayed in. "Hotels?" said Frank in mock shock. *"Hotels?"*)

He was also lighter by one publishing house, and this was an unalloyed pleasure. A different sort of man might have found it heartbreaking to let S & W go: but Frank, who sometimes referred to himself as doing "my famous imitation of a businessman," was profoundly happy to pack up his swag bag and hit the road where he belonged.

However, to find out how Sheed and Ward had gone from being his heart's delight to a chain around his leg, we'll have to backtrack a bit, to the early sixties and the great Vatican II Concilium.

A Farcical Interlude

HERE MUST BE A CHINESE SAYING ABOUT THE PERILS OF HIRING one's relatives—something about sowing a serpent's tooth and inheriting a pain in the neck. Frank had a weakness for relatives, and if he'd had his way we would every one of us be working at Sheed and Ward to this day, grandchildren and all. As it was, he did manage to promote his son-in-law, Neil Middleton, to managing editor of Sheed and Ward, London, in the late fifties, at first harmoniously but later fractiously.

Neil was a brilliant publisher, as he was later to prove over many years at Penguin Books, but he was not a perfect fit for a small, somewhat rarefied Catholic house. As his own interests became more and more political, Sheed and Ward began to resemble a left-wing bookshop. But his differences with Frank overflowed from politics into the very way the business was being run, and were not helped by Frank's occasional post-fall tendency to muddle things and become proportionately dogmatic about them, or by Neil's rather drastic personality, and his cheerful tendency to take people like me to expensive lunches on the house.

If I were to print both men's versions of what happened between them, I would certainly wind up slandering one or the other, and possibly both. Fortunately, the details would only be of interest to another publisher, and fleetingly at that. Enough to say that Frank's visits to England were suddenly tenser for everybody, especially for Rosemary, who had to play piggy-in-the-middle, than ever before, although blessedly relieved by grandchildren and by Frank's spiritual daughter Erika Fallaux, a brilliant Austrian refugee, who had married a "splendid fella" (I quote) named Simon Young and produced yet another child, Amelia, for Frank to play with.

However, Frank wasn't quite ready to retire into baby-sitting. He was worried about London, and to a milder degree about New York, where Sheed and Ward also seemed to be drifting away from him. The question "Do we still need a Frank Sheed?" has recurred throughout the house's history, but there was some point to it now, because the latest lists, the actual books, no longer reflected his taste. He had virtually delegated himself out of the picture.

Perhaps to get a foot back in the door, Frank hit on the farcical expedient of asking me if I'd like to work there for a year. I didn't, in fact, like it at all, but since I was in Spain at the time, and dead broke, I gave him a grudging maybe, which in his eagerness he took for a hard yes, and before I knew it I was sitting at a regular desk like a normal person.

He could not have picked a more feckless representative. Let me explain why, in the form of a few notes about my career to date. Having written half a novel on Bishop Sheen's time (and at the expense of the foreign missions), I had that trick down cold. I could write novels anywhere, including a Volkswagen bus full of kids.

After Sheen, I worked at *Jubilee* magazine as film critic and odd jobs man, doing picture captions, turning news releases into on-the-spot reports (our editor Ed Rice was just as much a rogue as I), tapping out unsigned reviews and writing exposés of the funeral and church goods industries, which earned me the richest hate mail from these usually sanctimonious groups that I ever hope to see. All this took roughly two fun-filled days a week—the race is to the glib in such jobs—and I saw no need for *any* job to require more time than that.

It was all terrible training for Sheed and Ward, which greeted one with a chilling little time clock (though I wasn't actually asked to punch it) and where the staff wore suits and ties and worked in separate offices. At *Jubilee*, we strove to outslob each other in dress—if neckties were worn, it was around the waist—and my own particular makeshift office consisted of a drawing board in the middle of a clearing, from which I could hear every conversation in the joint. Rice had practically a real office, in which we tended to eat sandwiches, and Robert Lax had another next to the fire escape, so that he could duck onto it and crouch when he didn't feel like visitors.

Of which we had streams. Rice and Lax had been members of the old Thomas Merton gang at Columbia, which seemed to have generated friends beyond number. All the names in *The Seven Storey Mountain* checked in. The great painter Ad Reinhardt did some funny drawings for our ads. Even Jack Kerouac, of a younger generation of wild men, dropped in with his jug of muscat to contribute some religious poetry.

When the place wasn't crawling with middle-aged Bohemians and there was no one else about, we decided, like as not, to throw a party for each other: nothing fancy, just some wine and cheese and a chance to talk, which we did all day anyway. (I'm still not dead sure how we got out a magazine, but *Jubilee* won prizes every year.) I spent a lot of time with Bob Lax, allegedly editing copy but in fact writing funny stuff in other people's margins which had to be removed later. Lax's idea of a perfect editing job was to slash through the whole piece with a red pencil, until only one key word or, at most, sentence was left. He was generally right in his choices but we couldn't afford the blank space.

Lax was a great influence and a greater friend (like Caryll Houselander he "lived in the eye of God," while never ceasing to horse around), but the subject for now is how *Jubilee* undermined my already shaky character. Lax certainly did his bit, showing up at work when he good and felt like it, or else vanishing to places like Cleveland on his own mysterious imperatives. (He did this to me once over Christmas, finding at the last second that he couldn't face a family feast and settling for a bag of apples in a hotel room.)

He and I talked of writing a play about Thomas More, but got stuck after seven words. We also discussed a musical, but fell out over the royalty split before we'd written anything at all. Lax was an epic in feverish unproductiveness. His private journal was believed to fill at least a closet, and to be a potential spiritual classic. All it needed was a little straightening out. Some sweet girl (sweet girls were much drawn to the monastic Lax) volunteered to do just that, but when she was through, the Master contrived, like Samuel Beckett's character Murphy, to disarrange it back to its previous chaos within half an hour or so.

A deplorable role model for a guy about to enter the world of white-collar publishing. And to make matters worse, I had just sandwiched in a year in the South of Spain, writing and drinking and smuggling stuff from Gibraltar like everybody else and becoming more unemployable than ever.

Sheed and Ward for its part had become decidedly squarer since my father's heyday, as I found when I tried dropping in on people in the *Jubilee* style. I soon felt like a street Arab, wandering the corridors by myself, pestering honest working folk. It was partly a matter of layout: the previous Sheed and Ward had been an airy loft with haphazardous partitions, while this one seemed more like a minor government department. But it was also a matter of character. Sheed and Ward had gone and become a real business, which, like Henry V becoming king, had ineluctably induced a certain sobriety, with all the grim trappings and white collars of respectability.

Of course, you can't run a publishing house in maddened spurts as you can a magazine: the seasons are too remorseless. More to my point, I honestly didn't see how, diligently pursued, this profession could be combined with serious writing. Since the editor-in-chief at Sheed and Ward, the late Philip Scharper, was something of a one-man show anyway, there wasn't that much for me to do and, as you may gather, I didn't go looking for more. I did some copy editing, which I morbidly enjoy, especially when the authors are amateurs with something to say, but Philip never introduced me to the authors themselves, which may have been a kindness. If I wanted a publisher's lunch, I had to whistle for my own. (Fortunately Henry Robbins, my new man at Farrar Straus, was just up the street in Union Square, ever ready to oblige.)

If "Do we need a Frank Sheed?" was a good question, you can imagine what they asked about *me*. But it was time well spent. I learned a bit about publishing and I learned about Sheed and Ward, both of which were to come in handy in their ways.

The firm and I played out our parts with good-humored resignation, both sides seeing the joke, for about a year, by which time I had finished another novel and started a column for *Commonweal*, my next port of call, or flophouse, as you prefer.* I could have picked up the drift of Sheed and Ward's company politics without the inconvenience of going to work: all the principals were my friends already, and happy to talk. What I did do at Sheed and Ward was study the sales sheets every Friday and what I learned from these was not reassuring. The books just weren't selling that well, especially the up-to-the-minute books: the ecumenical, sociological, biff-bang New Churchy books. Frank's backlist was beginning to look better and better, and his own old-fashioned preconciliar theology remained one of our best stocks in trade.

Frank saw the figures too, and shook his head. He was a publisher and he knew the score. But he declined to interfere, either out of lack of confidence in his own currency, or because he'd given his complete trust to the new team. Meanwhile, management, dazzled by *overall* sales and not analyzing too closely, decided to expand. It invested in a computer, which might well have been called "Albatross II," and flirted with direct mailing and other businesslike things. It even signed up with an advertising agency, so that our stuff began to look like Harper and Row's, instead of our own homegrown corn. Hans Küng, our Vatican II meal ticket, pulled out, as hot theologians will, for more commercial pastures: never mind, there were plenty more where he came from. Other religious houses were bought up by the big seculars, only to be swallowed without a trace. Good—we had the field to ourselves.

What field? It was suddenly empty and we were welcome to it. Our traditional outlets withered to nothing in a few years. The super-

* *Commonweal* was a less Bohemian and more argumentative version of *Jubilee*. When we had no editorials or articles to argue about, we argued anyway. It was a Scotsman's paradise, and that side of me wallowed. Incidentally, I found I could run the book section and write the drama column in exactly two days.

duper seminaries were suddenly dust bowls, and the schools began vying with each other to see who could be less religious and get more funding. As I shambled up the greasy writing pole, I found myself being invited to lecture here and there—Yale, Columbia, and what-not—but never by the big Catholic colleges. It took years of rinsing out the old religion before Notre Dame and Fordham felt safe to take another bite. As for the few remaining Catholic bookstores, they began at first to dabble in church goods to cover costs, and then rosaries sank like a stone too, and the stores closed their lids. It would have taken one hell of a direct-mailing list to recoup such losses.

Nothing could have been done to save Sheed and Ward—it's no use shaking one's finger at a national trend. Management should undoubtedly have spotted the end five minutes earlier from those sales patterns, but the house would be just as dead today either way.

Now, as the old firm began to go down, the venerable backlist suddenly seemed the only thing about it worth selling. Belated overtures were made for a merger "with honor," but things were bad all over. Less than ten years after the council that we'd worked and prayed so hard for, the jig was up with Catholic publishing.

Comeback and Curtain

A T THIS POINT, 1970 OR SO, WHAT WAS LEFT OF SHEED AND WARD was only too happy to have Frank Sheed back to take over—if not to keep it afloat, at least to scuttle it with dignity and with no debts and pensions outstanding. The old man, whose day had, according to the new wave, passed ten years before, was the only one left who could understand both the business and editorial sides, on one salary, or less.

It wasn't too painful for anyone, considering. No one in the New York office had ever had anything personal against Frank. "Your father is a great, great man, but let's face it, as a publisher he's had it," said one young Turk, who has not gone on to greater things. It sounded plausible to me—Frank himself seemed to half agree. But now he was like Churchill returning to the Admiralty in World War II, which, if you recall, he compared to visiting the scene of a party the day after, with the streamers down and the guests departed.

I happen to know how well Frank handled his return from St. Helena because, in his incorrigibly hopeful way, he had asked me to sit on the board of directors both before and after his glorious hundred days or whatever. It was news for me to hear prosperous-looking citizens praying that the bank would grant them a loan, or extend them a loan, of amounts that each could have paid out of his own pocket. Was borrowing money the best thing that could happen now? Better not ask, sitting here in my gray suit, trying to blend in.

"All right. I'll talk to the bank," Frank would say, to everyone's visible relief. He understood money almost as much as he despised it, and I realized that he could have made a pretty good businessman himself—good enough to have built a publishing empire, instead of shuffling off a colony in his gray hairs. He was also curiously dispassionate about it. Sheed and Ward was not his monument. He balked at selling it to a John Birch prospect, or to Clement Stone of Chicago—one has certain standards. But otherwise his chief wish, if he *had* to dispose of the firm, seemed to be to get his and Maisie's name off it as fast as possible and give someone else a shot. It was like leaving his old school newspaper behind: it had been fun while it lasted.

No one else seemed to take the last days quite as lightly as he did. Sheed and Ward had been the Tiffany of Catholic publishing, and only Frank might think of saying things like, "All right, name me the Tiffanys of Ancient Rome. Or for that matter, name *two* publishers under the Pharaohs." He was not posing. He honestly didn't give a damn. Except for the people involved. He kept encouraging new talent both in-house and in the writing menagerie, even as the waves slammed over the deck. A new start—now that would be "sump'n" (where he got his colloquialisms, I'll never know, but "sump'n" was a regular, along with "atta boy"); but mere survival? No thanks.

He did sell Sheed and Ward at the eleventh hour to some people he liked and trusted, avoiding liquidation by a whisker—or to be precise, by one board meeting. But when the new owners asked if he would mind seeing the Ward removed from the title, he answered blandly, "Not at all, not at all." And when sometime later, they asked about the Sheed, he could hardly contain his glee. "Go *straight* ahead," he said. The story had ended cleanly. Nothing embarrassing would come out over his imprint again as long as he lived.*

The experience was enormously revivifying for him—but that's not quite what I mean by his comeback. He could have handled the Sheed and Ward crisis at any time: it was just good to see him back in

---

* The new firm of Andrews & McMeel did keep a small line of Sheed & Ward theological books, but theirs was the master imprint. Since then the *National Catholic Reporter* has acquired the name, and I wish them well with it. But Frank is home free.

action, and good for him to see himself there. It made a nice change from theology.

But the comeback I'm talking about was something deeper and on a level he took much more seriously than the professional. I wouldn't even now presume to talk about his soul: "I feel bathed in beatitude, my dear," he used to say to people who asked after his well-being, and that's good enough for me. What I'm thinking about is his own walks "to and fro on the earth," and the state of his friendships, his art, from the sale of Sheed and Ward through the ordeal of Maisie in 1975 to his own last days in 1982.

A man can be older at seventy than he is at eighty. Even before seventy, Frank had begun to curse an imaginary loss of memory. He swore he could not recall half the songs that had formed his private background music for so long, or those ever-ready yards of Byron and Tennyson. He was an old man now, and he fully expected to act like one.

By eighty, he was tired of all that: one can't sit around being old indefinitely. So the songs came back, and the zest to sing them.

Several elements conspired in this, and I'll begin with the least of them. After a lifetime of it, but especially after Maisie's death, Frank had mastered an art peculiar to himself: how to live a regular, even bourgeois life while constantly traveling. His ceremonial returns to Australia were now as ritualistic as putting out the cat, as he made orderly procession through his address book. "You don't know enough nobodies," he once said to Clare Luce, pointing unconsciously to his own strength; he knew enough nobodies to girdle the globe. And if possible, he tended to see them in the same order, from Sydney to Melbourne and back, following the generations and finding something to praise in each of them.

"Your [Australian] godson is a damned good painter." Or at worst, "I don't know what she thinks she's playing, but other people seem to like it." His unfathomable love of children was a sort of immortality because they grew up to become hosts and hostesses themselves and went into the good book of addresses which swelled like a passion fruit in his breast pocket. It was almost as if he were building a cult or community around himself, except that most of these people didn't even know each other and the community evaporated in his absence: he was the only thing it had in common.

On a recent trip of my own to Australia, I found a phrase recurring to me. Talking to the children he once loved who went on to have children he also loved, I found myself reminded of Churchill's phrase about FDR, that meeting him was like opening a bottle of champagne. Just to mention Frank's name now in their presence gives off a slight fizz. But these cork-poppings, these little baptisms, were every bit as refreshing for him as they were to them (which he made gallantly clear; condescension wasn't in him) and not just for reasons of morale. Because these graying children turned parents turned grandparents kept him in touch with the common life of Catholics, his fraying meal ticket.

Pious young parents, whose faith had once seemed as solid as the Maginot Line, began to find it alarmingly porous in the post–Vatican II melee—which may have helped fire up Frank's conservative crusading around then. But then suddenly the next generation didn't have any faith left to lose. One worried now about whom they brought home for the weekend and where they all slept; and one came to be relieved at any signs of order even in these arrangements, as the fear of drugs and berserkness swept through these once placid houses, where talk of Saint Thomas and the encyclicals still lingered.

Frank never ceased entirely to play the rock of Peter, something for his proxy children and children's children to return to safely when the winds of fashion died down. But he saw that for now you had to work with new materials and look for other qualities in people besides strictly Having the Faith or Living in a State of Grace. Religion in the heart, natural religion, something he had always viewed with suspicion, was better than no starting point at all.

As noted earlier, he had never, like many orthodox Catholics (notably the inevitable Ronald Knox), been really alarmed by Enthusiasm:* his Methodist boyhood and his ardent mother had both en-

* Knox wrote a book called *Enthusiasm*, pointing out its perils. Oddly enough he didn't ask Frank to publish it.

couraged him, in their different ways, to let oneself go in the love of God. So if Pentecostalism was where the Spirit was listing this year—well, it was no more embarrassing than witnessing on street corners. Like a classical critic faced with pop art, Frank would actually wind up telling the Pentecostalists what they were really up to and placing them willy-nilly in a tradition. In fact, his last project was to explain the Holy Ghost to these people who felt so violently moved by Him.

Among the many families that nudged Frank out into the open sea I suppose I would have to list my own, but this takes us back in time, to the days when Maisie was flourishing and Frank was not. In the late sixties, my wife and I decided to liquidate a fruitful,* but in the end impossibly turbulent marriage, and suddenly the plague was in his own house. The dreamy advice that was perfectly good enough for great-nephews-once-removed turned to cinders in his own heart.

A Sheed could do no wrong. So there must be something to this that he couldn't see. He turned to Rosemary—what did she think? Rosemary, living in and around the battlefield of modern marriage, said that separations were sometimes better than the alternative. Maisie, for her part, muttered her immortal line, "I'm at such a disadvantage when faced with reality." But faced with this most brutal of choices, she voted dejectedly for the happiness of her children over Church law. I felt monstrous putting them through all this and would have turned back a dozen times if I could have; yet in retrospect I suppose that somebody had to put them through it, if they were going to go on teaching anyone at all under fifty.

Frank's first reaction was flinty. "What about the kids' religion?" he snapped.

I wasn't in much of a position to dictate that, and hadn't been for some time. This was the sixties and the most tyrannical parents could no longer answer for their children's thoughts. Besides, my wife had given up on the Church herself and I was about to be severed from it smartly, unless I took a vow of celibacy. So—no answer to that one.

* Our three remarkable children, Liz, Frank and Marion, will have to wait for another book—or else write it themselves.

"You know this will break your mother's heart." I record this hesitantly as perhaps the only unworthy thing he ever said in a serious moment (I remember the other six; but they weren't serious). I rallied slightly against what I took to be emotional blackmail. Why not talk about his own heart for a change? Was he too grand to have one? Or was it only other people who suffered and needed help?

Actually, his heart, acknowledged or otherwise, was probably hurting worse than Maisie's. For his whole life he had reflexively sided with the woman in these matters; but now he didn't *know* enough to take sides. Perhaps he hadn't in other cases. His sense of justice, love of family, love of God must have been in terrible tension. Hence, his desperate remark. For her part, and after the first round of tears, Maisie's heart held up very well and she seemed quite pleased that I'd found another companion. In her still impenetrable innocence, she asked if I couldn't find a nice man to live with instead. Well, no, not in New York right now, I explained.

Remarriage, of course, was the sticking point. Couldn't I just live with a woman, and let it go at that? asked Maisie—casually proposing to me the kind of bohemianism that had caused lifelong ostracism in the world of her youth. She wouldn't have blinked over that. She had seen worlds undreamed of in the old family parsonage, and she never felt entitled to less distress in life than other people. She just thought I'd be happier in reach of the sacraments. "Do you still consider yourself a Catholic?" she asked me in a laboriously offhand way. "As long as they'll have me," I said, looking out an imaginary window. And we never directly addressed the question again.

Maisie proceeded to act as if nothing had happened and as if I were getting married for the first time. Frank felt he had to show a little disapproval at first (for my own good, no doubt). At a frosty luncheon for four, he inquisited my wife-to-be about the genealogy of her name, expressing amazement that she hadn't studied it in depth. It was purest piffle, and I have no idea what he hoped to accomplish, beyond sinking everyone in gloom. His duty done, he thawed in later meetings, and became once again the perfect guest.

But meanwhile, he had his own black sheep now and his own public to face, the people who looked to him and everything about him for reassurance in a mad world, and with them he resorted for a time to a species of cover-up, emphasizing the grandchildren more and more but keeping my divorce under his hat. He had always been obsessive about privacy and this was no time to stop. One does not show one's wounds in public.

But it's my strong guess that he began to notice around then how much people were keeping up appearances for *him:* couples pretending to go to Mass for his sake, or not mentioning an erring child or a rift between themselves. He had always turned a blind eye on such things, assuming basic goodness in his friends and expecting it to triumph over the day's folderol. But now the blind eye became a bland one.

He had never appeared to judge people, and had been privy to a million secrets in consequence. But somewhere in his seventies, and the century's, he really stopped judging them, and they must have sensed it. Because he began confiding the dark doings of old friends as if they were things that might happen to either of us: drugs, promiscuity, despair—things extremely unlikely to happen to him, but he had been brushed by them, had felt their breath. The old monsignor in him still might rise up over a silly sermon, but seldom again on a matter of personal morals. He knew that even the House of Sheed offered no sanctuary.

I sensed a certain relief in him. His policeman chores had never sat well, and the great fund of worldly wisdom he'd accumulated could now be brought into play without constant reference to the rule book. He didn't, of course, become a moral relativist, or spineless twit, but he did let out his hair shirt and ours a notch or two, and just in time, because Rosemary's marriage proceeded to hit the rocks not long after mine did and then suddenly the rocks were strewn with Catholic marriages. In my own crowd of journalists and deep thinkers, a few who had seemed to disapprove of my divorce at first were now in the same cracked boat. O pioneer! By chance, and a few minutes, I was the first of what we once called laughingly the Catholic Literary Establishment to lead us out into the barren land of alimony and child support.

Frank was braced for it now. He no longer asked about anyone's kids' religion: he saw that it was up to him to do something about it, if anyone was going to—and not to convert or reconvert them, but to keep lines open and listen. And this is where his second childhood came from, in the most benign sense. Like many entertainers he'd been gradually growing old with his material. Now he had a whole new room to work. Not that he addressed himself, like some old Pantaloon, or Danny Kaye, exclusively to children. But he had them in mind. And he knew that stale fights with Scripture scholars didn't quite make it with the *Jesus Christ Superstar* generation.

In his later work he took to exploring and celebrating the Bible rather than defending it (let it look after itself, if he could just get people to read it). With this in mind he took up Greek in his late seventies, at once buoyed and irritated by the fact that Cato had allegedly learned it at ninety. I was reminded of the new lease on life that Edmund Wilson had received from the Dead Sea Scrolls: a change is as good as a rest, as Minny Maloney used to say, even in intellectual pursuits. So Frank ceased spluttering over people with names like Bultmann and commenced to bubble over different shadings of the word "spirit." His fighting days were over.

In speaking as well as in writing, because his spreading deafness was making it harder to sort out the questions from the audience. He told me that he sometimes felt downright disoriented (he must have used a more pedigreed word than that) when the questioning began. His frayed nerve ends picked up all the babble, so there was no point in turning up the volume. Two people talking already sounded like a mob scene, and rock music was a torture. He experimented with various hearing aids, but they only plunged him further into bedlam.

Since he could only hear people one at a time, this became more and more his angle on life. In the last years, "I knew your father" became a much more precious phrase than "I heard your father speak." His private self was more nuanced and sophisticated than the old Orator. Shouting into a crowd, he could still resort to the old simplicities. Head to head, he spoke precisely to your interests. "Aren't you *really* saying such-and-such?" is usually a maddening locution, a crass attempt to change the other fellow's terms into yours. But when Frank said it, it had a diamond-cutter's precision. His concentration remained like a lawyer's in this respect: he was totally wrapped up in your words and responded on precisely your level of sophistication. People like to muddy their thoughts about religion, so that they can have it and not have it at the same time, and Frank could clear this up for you if you really wanted. But whereas he used to wind up this exercise with a glum reading of the prisoner's rights, he now added all the liberal good news he could think of: to wit, that all it now took to qualify for Holy Communion was a desire to have it.

This and other late developments he had gleaned from the same Continental theologians he might once have accused of making religion too easy. Likewise, when Rome began the avant-garde experiment of granting marriage nullities on purely psychological grounds, he leaped at the chance to get one for me. Never mind that the phrase was almost Protestant in its vagueness: perhaps religion *should* be made easier in this screamingly difficult world. At least his own flesh and blood should not be excommunicated; and if not his, whose? So he became full time his own better half, a purveyor of good tidings for anyone who still had the faith to want them. "Rule the obedient with a rod of iron," he used to say of old Church policy; but sometimes he had swung the rod himself. No more.

When he stood as witness, alongside his lifelong person-Friday, the astonishing Marigold Hunt, at our Catholic remarriage, I felt myself standing in the middle of a historical footnote: not just to family history, but to Church history. If Frank Sheed the rock, the hard-headed Scots lawyer and Irish True Believer, could come so far, then this was where the new line should be drawn. However, just to remind me that I wasn't getting away with anything, he muttered, "Now make your Easter duty, you lazy beggar."

There seemed to be one exception to his new tolerance, and that was in the matter of married priests. I say "seemed" because I never heard him talk about it: but when a particular name came up, I would usually sense a complete loss of respect for that particular man. He didn't despise them all, but at best he thought they were silly fellows, lightweights—especially those who continued to tell people how to live. If they couldn't keep *that* vow, that trust, it didn't matter what they thought about anything else.

On a light, cruising level, he was sorry for the ones who had expected marriage to be easy, and naughtily pleased to find that quite a few of them proved impotent; but in the deep dark well of his soul, he felt a betrayal so grievous that it could only be forgiven in a silly man.

Otherwise, Frank's sunniness was only broken by things like angina attacks and a prostate operation. ("I find spiritual fortitude much easier than physical fortitude," he said after screaming his way through the latter: his lack of stoicism surprised and interested him. But I took it for a welcome crack in his mighty defenses. He didn't *care* if people heard him scream.)

Between these events, he complained more of his good health, claiming that it would take at least a bus to kill him. Since he systematically looked the wrong way in both right- and left-hand-drive countries, I thought his chances of this were fair. But what I feared more was a fall downstairs, similar to the one that had killed his father years before in Sydney. (Frank never told me the details of that and it's possible that he didn't know, but I learned just recently that John Sheed stumbled to his death while relieving himself of his millionth or so glass of beer.) Once I saw Frank totter on some subway steps as his hat blew off, and I thought, My God it's the fall from the platform all over again: he'll hit his head and damage his mind, just when it's come back so far. But he righted himself, clamped his hat down defiantly and trudged on.

With Maisie gone, Frank was manifestly eager to get going himself, though much too polite to mention it to us. He took to rationing his visits into shorter and shorter bursts, so that he wouldn't be a nuisance and perhaps, it occurs to me now, so that his hosts wouldn't be either. And when he was around he was the essence of light-footed tact, slippering off quietly to Mass—only to lock himself out on the porch; and making his own breakfast—only to blow up the coffeepot. "These hands are *useless*," he would say despairingly, but they were perfectly good hands. They just needed a less absentminded owner.

"I see I can take a ferry to Shelter Island, and then another to the North Fork, and from there a third one to Connecticut, which is practically a stone's throw from Fisher's Island," he'd announce on the second or third day.

"Okay, if you must, you must. I know we've got a schedule some-place."

"No need. The Connecticut ferry leaves at three-thirty, and I should be in Fisher's Island by six or so," he'd say, all the while pulling out scraps of paper relating to obscure ferry lines. Where he got them I don't know. But I remember his cherubic happiness as he peered at the little fellows. Timetables were a sort of scripture to him; they told him that he could keep traveling, and how. Small wonder that our wandering Australian had actually written a book called *The Map of Life*.

In his honor, I decided before finishing this story to stir in my own torpor, which is near-total, and revisit Australia. The place turned out to feel even more like home than I remembered and after a few weeks it was all that my torpor could do to turn me around and get me back.

I expected to find all our tribal bones and campfires in Sydney: Frank was so urban that he had never understood my own move to the country. Yet it was in the Outback that I remembered Frank most vividly. The smell and the ghostly look of the eucalyptus trees, the strange olive browns of the soil, the loneliness—and the sheer delight at meeting somebody: these are what an Australian packs when he travels. Or at least this particular Australian, Frank Sheed. I was surprised to learn that as a boy the old city slicker had spent a lot of time hiking by himself in the Blue Mountains outside of Sydney; and it came back to me as I drove over all the dry creeks with the funny names how he loved to recite poems about the Murray and the Darling rivers and the road to Gundagai, and the Mickety Mulgar quarterback ("who was commonly known as Bandy Jack"), and to reel off the names on the Sydney North Shore railway line ending with the majestic Woroonga and Warrawee. Perhaps he disdained the country elsewhere simply because it wasn't Australian. Anyway, he'd fed his spirit on it as a boy. After that there was work to be done in the city.

On his last trip home, aged eighty-three, he made a recording of the old songs and there he was and is, warbling, in excellent voice, a chant to an ancient rival: "And now God bless our land/Give the Varsity Council prudence/And bless its noblest work on Earth/The Melbourne Varsity students/*Toujours, toujours, pour Bacchus* and *les amours.*" Melbourne might be a Second City, but that was only because Sydney was incomparable. In any other country, Melbourne would do.

That was his last trip home, and he came back through England, where he rose at dawn to watch a test match, and complained of chest pains twelve or so interminable hours later when he returned to Rosemary's. He shook them off, but slowly.

The next time I saw him, he was singing again. I know the world does not remember him primarily in this role and I should emphasize that he could be silent for considerable stretches. But this evening I egged him on; egged him halfway through *The Mikado*, in fact. It was a dinner party and he was incandescent. Let me transpose a line of conversation from another session of the same period to catch his flavor: Guest: "What do you *do* in Australia when you're not throwing the boomerang?" Frank: "Oh, nothing, nothing at all. The boomerang ruins you for everything else. [Pause] Of course—everything else ruins you for the boomerang."

He was in that sort of mood, the mad lunchtime mood of Torresdale, and he wound up singing our anthem from the Horley bus stop, "Oh by jingo, oompah, oompah, oompah." He stayed up beyond his bedtime, but shimmered off around twelve-thirty, looking seraphic. When I asked him the next morning what had happened to the second verse of "Jingo," he said, "I decided to spare the company. So I sang it to myself in my room."

The end was coming, according to all earthly signals, but we had ten golden days together at my place talking about his boyhood in Sydney, and just like that I began to write this book, out of his mood. I felt I was getting back a boy in place of an old man, and would always have him so, along with young Mary Maloney, sailing to Australia at fourteen and perhaps singing one of her specialties, "Impudent Barney, none of your blarney, impudent Barney O' Hea," and even old

John Sheed, the saturnine founder of the feast. "Don't you think he loved you a little bit?" I had once asked Frank. "If so, he proved it with many a belt and strap," he answered icily. But now he said, with slightly strained enthusiasm, that he looked forward to seeing his father in the next world, "the old devil." The last barrier between him and peace seemed to be down at last.*

Frank toughed it out in Jersey City for a few more weeks—the old man that is, all solid gray flesh, and not the boy that I was blithely conjuring—but one morning in November 1981 I got an early call from him. "I seem to have had a small stroke." It seemed that he had managed, stroke and all, to wiggle his way on a three-legged stool all the way from his bed to the phone to make the call: a short distance, maybe ten or fifteen feet, but a nightmare, all the same, that must have lasted several hours, to judge from medical estimates, as he blacked out and pushed on and struggled for his normal voice before dialing.

When I saw him in the hospital, he was composed but bone-weary, like Maisie. As John XXIII said on his last day, "My bags are packed, I am eager to depart." Frank talked that day, with a faith which passes belief, of seeing Maisie soon and his mother—his last jubilant arrival somewhere would be in heaven itself. (I half-expected him to produce a timetable out of his pajamas.) There was a yellow legal pad next to his bed, on which he'd scribbled his notes on what to tell the Pentecostalists about the Holy Ghost. He had also written, "Hope to finish my book at Wilfrid's."

Alas (a word he would never allow me to write, incidentally; it was almost as bad as "albeit"), he didn't quite make it. He became comatose, but scrupulously so: always a kind word for the nurse or doctor, before closing the eyes in sleep. The last time I saw him, the night before he died, he heaved about slightly, in his hospital gown, but was

---

* On my postmortem trip to Australia a friend confirmed something he told me during those last days. It seems that when Frank began to speak outdoors for the Catholic faith in the Sydney Domain, old Marxist John always turned up to listen—with what? respect? pride? At any rate, he never heckled. What I find deeply sad about this is that Frank knew about it all right but never thought it worth telling me until the end.

otherwise out of it. Yet he managed, through sheer willpower, to sustain a sort of conversation. When the nurse brought in what was, I guess, his last meal—a flabby piece of fish and sundries—he lit up briefly until he'd had a good look at it. Then he pushed it around with his fork, and said in a weak voice, "I fancy I'll let it live."

His last words, as far as I know, and perfectly in style. After my wife and I left, I imagine he slipped quietly and gratefully to sleep. If we'd stayed, he'd probably be talking still, out of politeness.

Early next morning, we got the fumbling word from the doctor, and half an hour after that Bill Buckley called excitedly to say that he'd succeeded in getting Frank into the Mary Manning Walsh home—a retirement paradise, mostly for well-heeled contributors: once again Frank would have been a scholarship boy.

It wouldn't have suited him. The irony stung about as long as a dab of iodine, and then I thought of Frank without his tickets and his timetables, and decided that God had chosen the right time.

Not that it helped right now. A flood tide of grief opened in and around me, in everybody I talked to. My children were desolated, as if the worst thing that possibly could have happened had just done so. That presence, however helpless and doddering it might have become, was simply irreplaceable. "Of whom does Dr. Johnson put you in mind? He puts you in mind of nobody." So it was with Frank.

In the hysteria of the day I managed to obtain for Frank what he had failed to get for Maisie, a full-blown funeral at St. Patrick's. I didn't quite say to Terence Cardinal Cooke, "My father did more for the Church than you'll ever do," but that was only because I couldn't reach the cardinal. Frank, I reflected, had given some fourteen thousand outdoor speeches without once passing the hat, and that wasn't even his principal work for the Church. Yes, I thought he deserved a decent funeral.

I risked his posthumous disapproval by ordering music as close to Gregorian as possible. He had ordered no music for Maisie, which was defensible for that most unmusical of creatures, but he had no business ordering it for himself. It was unthinkable that Frank should leave this planet in silence.

To make it up to him, I also asked for a priest who didn't use metaphors, and the chancery said they had just the man for me. He was a Franciscan who had served a stint in the Evidence Guild and was an old friend of Frank's. He chose to treat the funeral as a celebration, in which jokes were not strictly forbidden, and for a few minutes this witty unadorned man made it seem like Easter morning, as Frank hurried off at last to join his bride Maisie in everlasting bliss. That day, at least, I believed every word of it.

More prosaically, he joined Maisie in that humpty-dump Jersey City cemetery in the lee of the nondescript apartment building: as anonymous a spot as any street corner. In this I was definitely following orders. Consecrated ground is consecrated ground wherever it is, and both parents had wanted specifically to be buried in the communities where they happened to be at the time. Still, it seemed like a strange place for the two pilgrims to wind up.

The day that Frank died, I was certain of at least one thing and that was that I wouldn't be able to write about him anymore for a long, long time. But after telling enough obituary writers how to spell "Sheed," and jousting with the chancery and sharing my children's sorrow and my wife's, I realized I could only find some equilibrium by returning at day's end to the young man in Sydney who was still on the threshold of all this, with the adventure all in front of him. The ending of my first chapter is thus not a special effect: it's exactly the way it happened.

Still, I'm glad the young man in Sydney lived to be old, if only for selfish reasons. If he had died earlier, especially at the time of my divorce, there would have been something unresolved between us, some canker in my feelings about him. But now we'd had our talk out—not specifically about our differences (we were a reticent pair who just happened to talk a lot), but in such a way that the differences dwindled to nothing. Touchingly, he sometimes seemed almost to defer to me as if I, being in the thick of life, was now the person to consult. But above all there was a great sweetness felt by everyone he met, now that the battles were well and truly over, and a serene, uncluttered, uncritical love of his myriad friends and his family.

"On the one hand," said a young relative of mine with, I believe, Marxist leanings, "you have the horrors of the Catholic Church," which he proceeded to list with bloodcurdling thoroughness. "And then," he said, after pausing for breath, "on the other hand, you have Grandfather." Quite.

Adieu

N AUTOPSY SHOWED THE TRACES OF A SLIGHT STROKE WHICH might have occurred around the time of Frank's fall off the platform. So that question was settled. There definitely was a part 1 and part 2 to his life. The proximate causes of death were technical and I don't think he'd consider them worth publishing. Like Maisie, he just died of death.

My mind returns to his funeral day as to a tryst. The turnout in St. Patrick's was big enough to justify the use of that venerable barn, and was more than duplicated at a memorial service in London, where people had a little more warning. I received two visitations at St. Pat's—one in the form of a light tap on the shoulder, like a kiss of peace: Clare Luce, in severest mufti, whispered in my ear, "You're a big boy now!" This was nice to hear, because I certainly didn't feel like one. But Clare was gone before I could say anything at all.

The other was from Terence Cardinal Cooke and I was sorry I'd ever thought anything bad about him, because he was now manifestly sick himself and looking somehow unadorned like the small-town priest I think he really was. He beckoned me outside for a few words and a blessing, and I had to cut through a wall of friends, including some old Sheed and Warders who were laughing it up in the back, telling the old stories. I dearly wanted to join them, but by the time I returned they had been asked to leave on account of uproarious behavior: another Mass was due, the life of the Church must go on.

To be bounced from St. Patrick's was a very suitable Sheed and

Ward ending. Meanwhile, across the street, an immemorial religion hater was railing against the cathedral in general, and I could almost see Frank's dreamy smile: "Now *that* fella could make a meeting go." Then once again, the gloomy trip to Jersey and an earthly end to Sheed & Ward, ampersand and all, although the firm still lingers on in London. Otherwise the old place floats blessedly free at last, like the Holy House of Loreto, as a memory and a reverberant inspiration. Camelot would be an awfully dull place by now, if some damn fool had kept it around, and no songs would be sung there. Sheed and Ward lived just long enough.

And here I must leave them, not, God knows, in New Jersey, but with Frank wandering out of this book eternally talking and Maisie, alive with excitement, simply being herself. Since, maddeningly, I can only remember bits and scraps of what Frank said, what follows is more a mood than a conversation.

Mooching around the English countryside, Frank says apropos of nothing, or maybe of some cow he doesn't like the look of, "Of course, conscience is simply the moral judgment of the intellect."

Of course. Just what I was about to say. Actually the thought is important to him. Frank is forever so busy putting down mumbo jumbo, like a brushfire that won't stay out, that he can't allow any "small voices" (the popular notion of conscience) into the soul. Conscience is an activity, not a thing.

"Ah but in that case," pipe I (oh, maybe ten years later on Forty-second Street), "why do you put so much stress on the distinction between intellect and will? Aren't they also just activities of the soul and not separate things?"

He allowed that this was so, but that he still found the distinction useful. "And I shall go on using it, dammit." Although he believed totally in the unitary soul, indestructible because it has no parts, his imagination was always merrily splitting it anyway. For instance, "The writer and the man are of course quite different people," he said (in the South of Spain this time). Life had sent him enough cranky little men who wrote like angels and large slow nuns with minds like razors to justify the superstition. But just to keep things going, I said, "That's like saying that the man at breakfast is different from the man playing poker" or whatever. You can't divide your precious subatom by giving it a typewriter or a full house.

He gave me a wait-till-you're-older smile (I was only about thirty by now). He knew that writers were monsters quite unlike any other, and he was dashed if he was going to subject this certainty to scholastic hairsplitting about being and essence. In getting Frank's proportions right, it is crucial to remember how often the theologian in him took the day off, allowing his cheerful partner to skylark. The theologian and the man are *not* the same thing.

In fact, what kept all our strands of conversation going from roughly my twelfth year to the end of his life was his playfulness as we chased each other's sticks around the yard. I could tell if he was having a bad day when he *refused* to play. One time I told him that I secretly expected God, at the Last Judgment, to say, "To begin with, I want to apologize to all of you for this particularly cruel and pointless joke I've just played on you." "So," said Frank, beetling, "you imagine God stepping out of eviternity to say that?" He was serious—not about my little blasphemy, but about the theology of divine communication. Too much for me, sir.

He always considered himself a simple man whose psyche had not changed materially since his first memory. But I found him most agreeably divided. Despite our above argument (and we had a hundred like it), I could accept such concepts as Man the Croquet Player, not to say Man the Father and the Son, more easily than he could, with his essentialist metaphysics, and I was glad to have as many of him as possible.

The thing to do when Police Constable Sheed the theologian was on duty was to turn the subject quickly to cricket, about which we would gratefully gabble, to a point where my mother, in the divisive way of women, once said, "I don't know which of you is humoring the other, but I know *one* of you is." Hot protests from the males of course, but also a nasty little seed of doubt: perhaps the *other* one is humoring me. A good moment's work for Maisie.

This *particular* cricket conversation took place, so help me, in Rome. We always seemed to be either walking or on vacation as we talked, because that way one received the full blast of Frank's attention. In restaurants and hotel lobbies, he was okay, but he tended to hear things. "I looked at him kinda cool," says a voice at the next table. "Not mean, not cold, just bland." (The original adjectives were better but I've lost them.) Or again, this time on a bus, "He's pseudo, he's bogus, he's false. I sometimes wonder if he's real." Nobody's eavesdropping ever gathered stranger fruit than Frank's.

Later, as he grew deaf, the opposite problem wheeled up: he couldn't hear anything if more than one person was talking, and I dreaded our occasional lunches at Luchow's where, to surmount the Bavarian roar, I bellowed out family secrets and assorted gossip. So again, walks or foreign places, where one could talk quietly into his good ear, were best. But through thick and thin and frayed ear nerves, the conversation went on. Unfortunately, I was no Boswell, and a million great lines have gone to rest.

Here at least are his verdicts on the three-and-a-half countries that had made him what he was. Of the Irish, he liked to say, "They have wit but no humor," chiefly because of the gratifying (and confirming) howl this always provoked in Dublin. Of the Scots, he said, there were two vitally important things to remember, "One, that they love philosophy, and two, that they're no good at it," a remark I was often tempted to throw back at him when he had me in a corner. As for England, "The unmixed English are horrors." And finally, of Irish-America, his half country, "The Irish are just no good at being rich." (Concerning Australia, he could find nothing even faintly critical to say. There had to be a perfect country somewhere—else where would the concept have come from? "I'm sure Saint Anselm would bear me out on this.")

Well, these were just *some* of his verdicts. His best stuff was more free-floating than that, pure humor in fact, but I find these specimens interesting because they sound cynical, but aren't: they're too buoyant. His mighty heritage of sarcasm had been distilled into this lighter affair, a sort of tap dance between asperity and charity that delighted me all my days, not to mention several hundred other people's.

Not that he was always dancing. But unlike so many people who can't shift from funny to serious and back without a mighty grinding and stripping of gears, Frank made the change almost imperceptibly. Here are just a couple of his reasonably serious "fatherisms" plucked from memory: One of us is worried about somebody else's good opinion. F: "Would you ask that person's advice about anything truly important to you?" [A splutter of "no's."] "Then why do you give a damn what she thinks about *you*?" Another time one of us complains that the people at a party seemed empty and superficial. F: "Do you mean that they wouldn't pay attention to you?" [Damn right.] But always, and especially for me after I took to reviewing, his favorite Latin motto: "Eagles do not kill flies." If we weren't exactly eagles, at least we could act like ones. *He* always did.

One other thing. Just last week I found myself muttering in all seriousness, "Where's Frank?" A piece of song had drifted into my head, and I was sure nobody else in the world knew the rest. "*Amo, amas*, I love a Lass, like a [something] tall and slender. Sweet cowslip's grace is her genitive case, and she's of the feminine gender" followed by a chorus of rollicking dog Latin. It took me a full moment to realize that I'd just have to live without it.*

My thoughts of Maisie are altogether different. She was a speaker, not a conversationalist, and when she wanted to say something quotable, she simply quoted someone—Newman, Chesterton, Austen, one of her old reliables. I think of her more characteristically in situations, with her Polish beekeeper and her strange farmers and the whole wild menagerie that such a life recruits. I remember her also on the platform, looking so fragile and vulnerable until somebody crossed her, at which point she turned, just like that, into Churchill. Her mind when aroused was incredibly swift and sharp, and I was every bit as cautious about arguing with her as I was with Frank—if the argument was serious. Frank had no peer at the Silly Argument.

Maisie's favorite form of recreation, when she wasn't planting things and watching them grow, was reading detective stories, of which she could easily wolf down three a day. During Lent each year she would grimly give them up, but would continue to stockpile them in the closet for the big Holy Saturday bang. "Oh, dash it, I've

* Thank God, I don't. Rosemary, over here on a visit, just filled me in on the rest. When we're gone, God knows what there'll be left to sing.

already read this one," she would sigh as she got to the last page (up to then, she hadn't recognized a word).

She went through the things like a box of chocolates—or perhaps instead of a box of chocolates. For she also possessed a mighty sweet tooth, and one of those maddening figures which won't declare itself: which never quite gets fat, but won't stay thin either. Whenever thinness seemed to be winning, she would discover an irresistible new blend of ice cream, a black raspberry-pecan or a rum-pistachio, no combination was too bizarre for her curiosity. And she would succumb ruefully. On the other hand, "Chocolate, vanilla, strawberry"—I can still hear her tolling the words glumly to waiter after waiter when her exotics *weren't* available. "It's *always* the same isn't it?" The sheer misery in her voice was enough to make a waiter cry: you'd suppose she was talking about the food at San Quentin.

Cozy memories. For all her dartings about the globe, and her doubts of herself as a mother, I associate Maisie after all with hearth and home, Frank with the road. It was Maisie who put the stamp on a place, made it officially ours. Whereas Frank's possessions could have been heaped into one suitcase, and the whole thing thrown away without loss, Maisie bought things and kept things which established our household gods for us wherever we went—a necessary thing when you're raising gypsies. To Frank, all the world was a hotel room; to Maisie it was just one little home after another.

Toward the end, she gallantly even tried to tackle cooking. Till then she was mostly distinguished for burning the soles of fried eggs, and for glad cries of "I know what! Let's have some nice cold cuts." But now, in her eighties, she actually bought a book and went at it in earnest. "I fancy I have rather a knack for it," she beamed proudly, and by george, she did turn out a passable casserole or two. She had been raised, and had raised herself, to believe there were so many things she couldn't do. But all bets were off in her eighties.

Mothers are, of course, supposed to cook, at least in America, and in the New Class which the Edwardians had viewed with such trepidation—a class totally *without servants*. (Even liberal Edwardians thought that *educated* people should have servants—or how was civilization to continue?) Maisie never ceased to marvel over even the most lackluster housewives ("How on *earth* does she do it?") who managed to get through the day without nervous collapse.

Maisie admired enormously the gifts she didn't have, and with nothing to show for herself in the house-crafts line but her shapeless knitting and her "leave-it-to-grandmother" sewing, she must have felt like a funny kind of mother for the twentieth century. Even at things she was good at, she was given to little bursts of trepidation. "Was I any good at all?" she'd ask after a lecture. Or sometimes, glowing, "I thought I was *damn* good [timid pause], *wasn't* I?"

As to this motherhood business, I can only say that other people's conventional twentieth-century mothers seemed awfully dull by comparison. Maisie's readings aloud around the fire were worth any number of apple pies when we were young. Later on, her steady care for me during the polio years (which left me, to be sure, incapable of even calling the dentist for myself) made a potentially bad time jubilant and easy. For instance, she went to great lengths to get me a Ping-Pong table and plenty of places to swim (she knew every indoor pool in New York). She even allowed me to bash a rubber ball against my bedroom wall with a cricket bat until the wall ran red with stains.

When Maisie was absentminded, she was awesomely absentminded. She would walk into empty rooms talking, or full ones reading, and proceed to eat her lunch reading and leave again reading—pausing only to howl, "That *ass* Ullathorne?" or "What on *earth* did Froude think he was doing?" Blessedly, Frank always knew what she was talking about and would drop whatever he was doing to cluck over the asinine Ullathorne or the pig-headed Froude.

But Maisie was not an absentminded mother. No one ever concentrated more on the details, the galoshes and indeed dental appointments of life. If Rosemary or I stayed out all night, she worried mightily—not about our morals, which were cast-iron by definition, but our safety. She also had a theory that no one in the world got enough sleep: a situation she tried to remedy single-handed by dropping off at nine, and napping in the afternoon. (To be sure, she also rose at four most days, took a long hot bath, her indispensable luxury, and worked in the stillness of dawn.)

Of course fussiness without love usually only makes things worse with mothers. Maisie, contrariwise, fairly brimmed with love. If she hadn't seen you for a while, she would give a little bob to her head as if she wanted it to convey more pleasure than was humanly possible. "It's wonderful to have you all together," she would exclaim in the middle of lunch, her face giddy with happiness. Her love was as naked as the rest of her mind and she counted it a miracle that she'd found a man who could return it. They would both go on about each other's excellences at what seemed wearisome length when we were young; but this mutual star-struck quality was the dynamo that made the whole thing work, family, publishing house and all.

"Your mother is a very great woman." "Your father is a remarkable man." In this book, I have only hinted at their achievements and scarcely mentioned their books, which I leave to some better scholar than they were able to produce themselves. But I would like to mention just one title, Frank Sheed's *The Instructed Heart*, one of the last things he wrote. It is a sort of spiritual meditation on Maisie, and its title celebrates the highest human attainment he could conceive of. It's a private, somewhat inaccessible essay, based on his latest linguistic adventures: the sense of the word "heart" in the Scriptures, and their languages. This is Frank, in his eighties, presenting his latest gift to his bride. Then, after waiting around patiently, fruitfully, he goes with absolute certainty to join her. *Consummatum est.*

ABOUT THE AUTHOR

Wilfrid Sheed, distinguished novelist and essayist, is the author of eight novels, including *Transatlantic Blues, Office Politics* and *People Will Always Be Kind*, as well as *Clare Boothe Luce*, a profile. Twice nominated for the National Book Award in fiction, Mr. Sheed was drama critic for *Commonweal* and has written a television column for *Sports Illustrated*. He has reviewed movies, plays and novels for, among other journals, *The Atlantic, The New York Review, The New York Times, The New Yorker* and *Esquire*. Mr. Sheed writes regularly for *Gentlemen's Quarterly*.

Printed in the United States
By Bookmasters